Creative Arts In Worship

Creative Arts In Worship

written by
Dennis Doyle

edited by
Michelle Beaumont

Published by
"Hands up for God" ministries

Copyright © Dennis Leonard Doyle 2000

The right of Dennis Doyle to be identified as author of this work
has been asserted by him in accordance with the Copyright, Designs
and Patents Act 1988. Published 2000. All rights reserved.

No part of this publication may be reproduced or transmitted in any form
or by any means, electronic or mechanical, including photocopy, recording
or any information or retrieval system, without permission in writing
from the publisher. The only exception being the scripts, sketches and object
lessons, which may be photocopied and enlarged solely for use in church
services and acts of worship, without permission. They may not be reproduced
in other publications without express permission from the publisher.

Text design and page make-up by Bookwork
Stroud, Gloucestershire

Cover design and reproduction by Tempus Publishing Group
Stroud, Gloucestershire

Cover illustration by Piers Bois, Jersey

Chapter heading illustrations by Ed Sumner of Pocklington

Photographs by Dennis Doyle, Louise Doyle, Graham Webb & Pam Webb
(except balloons by Allen R. Cook)

Printed by T.J.International Ltd
Trecarus Industrial Estate, Padstow, Cornwall, PL28 8RW

Text printed on Fineblade Extra 130gsm
supplied and manufactured by Smurfit Townsend Hook, Snodland, Kent

Scripture references are taken from the Holy Bible, New International Version
Copyright (1973, 1978, 1984 International Bible Society.
Used by kind permission of Zondervan Bible Publishers.

Clip art by kind permission of Serif. Inc. Nashua, USA

ISBN 0-9538829-0-X

Published by "Hands up for God" ministries
34, Holbourne Close, Barrow-upon-Soar, Leicestershire, England, LE12 8NE
e.mail: dennis@dldoyle.freeserve.co.uk
www.dldoyle.freeserve.co.uk

Dedicated to Suzanne,
for her love, patience, support and encouragement.

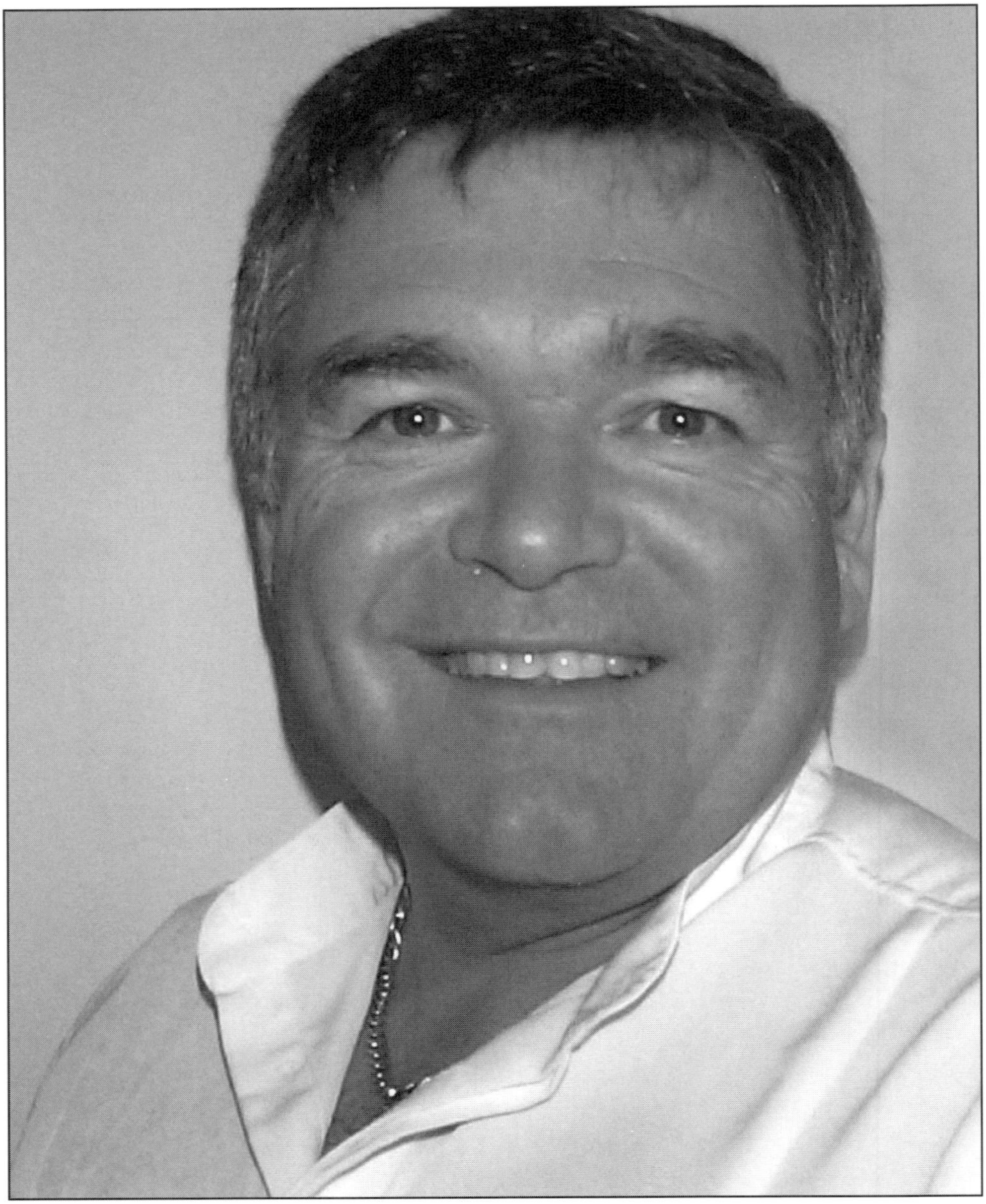

Biography

Dennis Doyle was born in October 1949 and grew up in the village of Netley Abbey in Hampshire. He has a 'proper job' as a salesman with paper merchants, Denmaur Papers plc, and lives in Barrow-upon-Soar, Leicestershire with his wife Suzanne, and daughters Louise and Andrea.

Dennis became a Christian over twenty years ago and has worked as a Shell and youth club leader at Droitwich and Barrow Methodist churches. He is a local preacher in the Loughborough Circuit and particularly enjoys leading all age worship. Dennis and Suzanne formed the "Hands up for God" puppet team in 1995 and continue to lead worship with the team at festivals, churches and other venues throughout the UK, including a successful tour of Jersey schools in 1999.

Dennis learnt the techniques required to perform 'magic' at Leicester Magic Circle and the Fellowship of Christian Magicians Europe. He presents "Gospel Truth Through Illusion" cabaret at a variety of venues including churches, schools and prison. He enjoys sharing his gifts and encourages other Christians to develop their creative skills in worship by presenting lectures and workshops.

The Rev. Dr Rob Frost has been an inspiration to Dennis and the "Hands up for God" ministry, which was formed after a Share Jesus team worked with the Barrow-upon-Soar church. The team have been privileged to be able to play a small part in fulfilling Rob's vision for equipping the modern Church, by leading worship for several years at Easter People, and on Share Jesus Missions.

Acknowledgements

This book has been enriched by the hard work, dedication and support given by Michelle Beaumont, a very dear friend who wielded her editor's red pen with great skill and sensitivity.

Our thanks go to churches all over the UK, who gave us the opportunity to minister to them in a unique way. We were privileged to lead worship several years running at Easter People and Share Jesus Mission. This provided a shop window to a wider audience and we are so grateful to Rob Frost and Marian Arthur, and all the hardworking Rob Frost Team at Raynes Park for giving us that chance.

Sue and I have received support and encouragement for 'Hands up for God' from so many people and it would be an impossible task to name them all. They know who they are, and we offer them all our heartfelt gratitude. Special thanks must go to all our friends at Barrow-upon-Soar Methodist Church, and of course Don and Barbara Mitchell, John and Joan Thursby, Jill Flinders, Christine Beaumont and the wonderful young people who put their hands up for God in our ministry team. Without their love and commitment, it would have been impossible to fulfil the dream, and difficult to respond to God's call in the way that we wanted to.

I pray that this book will help others to fulfil their dreams, and that it may go some way toward thanking God for all he has done for the 'Hands up for God' ministry team.

Contents

Introduction to Worship	xiii
Creative arts – the basics	1
Music and song	19
Drama and scriptwriting	39
Mime	67
Dance, movement, flags and streamers	89
Puppets, and ventriloquism	113
Gospel magic	149
Clowns, balloons, and storytelling	171
Visual aids, sketch board and object lessons	193
Resources, equipment and the Internet	219

'Hands up for God'

I pray that some of the ideas expressed in this book will help lead others to find new and imaginative ways of showing their love for God, and through that expression, draw nearer to Him. May we do so with humility, in the knowledge that the skills we use are a gift from God.

INTRODUCTION

The driving force and principal reasons for writing this book are to provide resources, teaching tools, motivation and inspiration for those Christians who are keen to effectively use creative arts in order to worship the God of the Old and New Testament and wish to enable others to hear the Good News of our Lord and Saviour, Jesus Christ, the Son of God. It is hoped that those of you who read it, will find in its pages, words of great encouragement, together with advice and a wealth of ideas that will enhance worship within your own communities. Whether we use the ideas at special one-off occasions, on a regular basis at Sunday school or weekly worship, or as part of ongoing ministry in schools, institutions or on the streets, I pray that we do so with humility and in the knowledge that the skills and talents that we use, are a gift from God. That all that we do will honour God and assist those who strive to glorify Him and learn more of His love.

Who do we worship?

I personally and unequivocally proclaim that Jesus Christ is Lord of all, Lord of my life and my personal Saviour. Jesus Christ came to earth two thousand years ago, ministered to God's people, performed miracles, was crucified and died. Like us, He was separated from God, until by a supernatural act of God, He was resurrected from the dead. He showed Himself to many people and ascended into heaven. He lives with us now through His Holy Spirit. Jesus Christ is the only way that humankind can gain access to, and be part of, the Kingdom of God.

The reader may be forgiven for thinking that the above is more like an introduction to a creed than a work on creative arts, but I do believe that before we even begin to examine the creative arts, their relevance in worship and how we can use them, we need to be clear as to whom it is that we worship; what we mean by worship; and how and why we worship. Unless we are absolutely sure that we know the answers to these questions and keep focused on our objectives, then any ministry that we may wish to develop is bound to fail.

Why do we worship God?

I hope it is clear from the personal statement above, who it is that I worship. I trust that all that follows will honour and glorify Him and provide a means for others to do likewise. It is God, the Creator of all things that we worship. It is the God who created the universe and everything in it, who is the object of worship in this book.

John 3:16-17 (NIV) states 'For God so loved the world that he gave his one and only Son, that whoever believes in him shall not perish but have eternal life. For God did not send his Son into the world to condemn the world, but to save the world through him.'

Our God came to earth in order that we might be saved from our sin. Because we were not able to reconcile ourselves with our Creator God because of our continued

> 'For God so loved the world that he gave his one and only Son, that whoever believes in him shall not perish but have eternal life. For God did not send his Son into the world to condemn the world, but to save the world through him'
>
> **John 3:16-17 NIV**

disobedience, God sent His Son, Jesus Christ to die for us. Jesus took upon Himself, through His death on the Cross, all our sin, together with the accompanying guilt and shame. Through His Resurrection and the anointing of the Holy Spirit we are able to be changed and gain new life in Christ.

How do we worship?

It is because of all this that we wish to worship God. So what do we mean by worship? Pope John 11 said 'We are an Easter people and Hallelujah is our song,' defining the Church as a people of joy praising God as a thankful and adoring response.

Perhaps one of the clearest definitions of worship was written by William Temple in his 'Readings from St John's Gospel.' In it he said that 'Worship is the submission of our nature to God. It is the quickening of conscience by His holiness, the nourishment of minds with His truth, the purifying of imagination by His beauty, the opening of the heart to His love and the surrender of the will to His purpose"

Although access to God is achieved only through Christ, worship enables us to experience God and provides us with the means by which we can express our feelings towards Him. Thus, corporate worship, or more simply, God's people worshipping together, is a combination of many elements. These include praise, song, prayer, meditation, hearing God's Word, the sacraments and spiritual gifts etc.

There are many forms of worship practised and enjoyed by Christians all over the world. I support the view that the most effective forms of worship are those where worship leaders follow a properly designed structure that incorporates the essential elements of worship. I am mindful that there are also some who feel very comfortable in unstructured worship times where spontaneity is a key factor. I would not wish to hinder or appear to be inhibiting those who prefer this form of worship, or in any way be perceived as denying the work of the Holy Spirit. However, there is a very strong case for arguing in favour of those who hold that, in order that a congregation is to be fed properly, the whole meal has to be fulfilling and satisfying and all the ingredients must be used in the right proportions so that the food is wholesome and nourishing and the menu is complete.

> 'Worship is the submission of our nature to God. It is the quickening of conscience by His holiness, the nourishment of minds with His truth, the purifying of imagination by His beauty, the opening of the heart to His love and the surrender of the will to His purpose'

That is not to say that the same structure must be followed in the same order for every act of worship. Worship leaders should recognise that our function is to assist the congregation to worship in the most effective and fulfilling way that is relevant to that particular audience. Whether the act of worship is a traditional Methodist Sunday morning service, family worship, an example of Evensong liturgy, or a much more adventurous service using creative arts, the corporate act of worship should include the following elements in one form or other:

A call to worship, adoration praise, penitence, forgiveness and an acceptance of that forgiveness, Good News from the Word of God, thanksgiving for His blessings, intercession and petition for others and ourselves and the dedication of our lives for His service. Quite simply, we need to prepare ourselves in worship to approach our God, hear the ministry of His Word and then respond in love to His message.

Our God created us in His image and provided us with a wonderful world in which to live. He blessed us with many gifts, both physical and spiritual. I believe that we should respond to God's love for us with all our body, mind and spirit. We should use all His gifts to us to worship Him in humility, but in a creative way, expressing our love for Him and giving Him all the glory. I pray that some of the ideas expressed in this book will help lead others to find new and imaginative ways of showing their love for God and through that expression, draw nearer to Him.

There is no intention here to push aside the rich traditions of our Church, but more a reasoned appeal to the senses which attempts to enrich and expand our horizons when planning worship. Modern congregations expect worship leaders to push back boundaries.

Chapter One
Creative arts – the basics

Why creative arts in worship?

This book addresses ways in which we can use different creative arts to enhance our worship by harnessing our emotions and spiritual awareness, yet still retaining the framework and essential components of the corporate worship model described in the introduction. There is no intention here to push aside the rich traditions of our Church, but more a reasoned appeal to the senses which attempts to enrich and expand our horizons when planning worship. Worship leaders are encouraged to be more inclusive and more responsive to the needs and aspirations of the existing modern congregation, and to the needs and expectations of our wider potential congregation.

The Church is often said to be in decline in the Western world and certainly the numbers of churches closing in the UK is outstripping the number of new churches being founded. (a net loss of around 900 churches in 1999). The established denominations appear to be less able to attract new membership than the so-called free Churches such as Pentecostal and house churches. We need to examine why this is so. Perhaps our congregations are telling us that worship leaders need to offer a more personal message, a more dynamic approach or a more exciting experience.

After travelling to lead worship at different churches and venues throughout the UK, it has become apparent to me and those who so generously give their time and talents to the 'Hands up for God' ministry team, that whatever the reasons for the decline in numbers attending regular acts of corporate worship, all of us who have the privilege of leading that worship need to take a close look at our own ministry. We need to examine the needs and aspirations of those whom we lead and provide that community with the means of fulfilling their spiritual hopes and dreams by offering them a rich tapestry of Gospel based worship that is relevant to them. That worship should compel them to continue to actively explore their personal faith and spirituality in a meaningful way.

Moreover, the worship leader must be aware of the secular diversions which continually compete for the attention of God's people. Sunday shopping, sporting commitments, enhanced leisure activity opportunities, family commitments and apathy are just some of the elements which serve to compete for attention on a Sunday, the day traditionally set aside for worship. The modern worship leader is bound to provide an act of worship which will attract people to listen to the Word of God. No matter how good our message, unless we can first of all attract people to listen to us, then we will not be effective worship leaders because we simply will not have a congregation to minister to. This means that it might not be enough to provide superb worship opportunities just in our church buildings. In order to reach more people we may have to take our message to where those people are. This may require some of us to preach on the streets, in the shopping malls, village greens, holiday beaches and even individual houses.

'The worship leader must be aware of the secular diversions which continually compete for the attention of God's people'

Essentially, this means that we need the courage, vision and foresight to adjust our minds to the fact that the Church must change the way that it presents itself and its message. I am not advocating that we change the message. Far from it; I firmly believe that God's Word is enduring and that His values have not been altered by the passage of time. The same Good News of the Gospel of Christ needs to be preached, but in a simple and effective way that our audience can relate to and understand. We need to re-establish God's Church as the people of Christ who live our lives in the way that God intended us to. We desperately need to communicate the fact that Christ provides us with the means to be free of the guilt, shame and sin that binds so many of us to a life of misery and despair. We have a duty to ensure that all can know and embrace the gift of forgiveness and love that is offered freely and unconditionally by God.

The message is still very much the same but it needs a bright new package or it will be lost to millions who will not hear it because we refuse to embrace the wind of change that is desperately needed in some of our often draughty, colourless and fading churches. As one worship leader said, 'Is the organ part of the message or part of the packaging?'

If a particular artefact or packaging is a hindrance to people hearing and responding to God's Word, then for God's sake let's have the courage to get rid of it and replace it with something that appeals to the modern worshipper's senses and enriches the worship experience for all. If we are to take the Word of God to the lost then changes in the packaging are essential. The creative arts are one of the ways in which we can introduce a new dimension that incorporates modern thinking, creative ideas, individual and corporate expression and a new spirituality that lifts the senses to a new plane. This will bear fruit in a new awareness of the nature of our God and His love for His Creation.

Assuming that we worship with a purpose, the service should flow and take the worshipper on a journey, from an approach to God, through an understanding of His Word leading to a personal response to that message. We can use creative and performing arts to enhance this experience and introduce creativity to all the elements of worship so that song, meditation, praise, prayer, offering, teaching and intercession can all be enriched both on a personal, individual level and in a corporate way. The creative arts element can be a small part of worship or can be the main

> 'Is the organ part of the message or part of the packaging?'

ingredient, providing the end result is the same. That objective is to honour and glorify God and to enrich the overall act of worship for those present.

This book assumes for the most part that readers are seeking resources for corporate acts of worship in the setting of a church or such venues as schools, youth clubs, homes for the elderly or children etc. That is not to exclude worship outdoors or preaching on the streets, as it is hoped that many of the ideas found here can be used in a variety of different settings.

'Creative worship' in this book is the collective term used to describe any individual or corporate act which uses creative skills, processes or initiative to enhance an act of worship and can take many forms. The creative skills discussed in this book include the following disciplines:

> Music
> Dance
> Drama
> Mime
> Storytelling
> Puppets and Ventriloquism
> Signing
> Gospel 'Magic'
> Flag, Streamers & fabrics
> Clowning
> Street work
> Sketch board
> Visual aids
> Multi-media

No single creative skill is given prominence over any other and all can be used to good effect depending upon the circumstances and the skills available within any given congregation or worship leadership. Each of the disciplines will be discussed separately and ideas and resources provided for each. There are certain elements, problems and pitfalls that are common to all these disciplines and we have to be aware of these before we start. So the following pages are designed to be a template to be super-imposed over each chapter in order that common problems are not endlessly repeated. We shall address issues such as safety, finance, team building, child safeguards, training and publicity to name but a few of the factors which must be considered by those who lead worship.

USING CREATIVE ARTS – COMMON PROBLEMS AND PITFALLS

Whilst most worship leaders have a vision of the way in which their acts of worship should be conducted and the elements they would like to use, we are all subject to various restrictions of available time, resources, space and skills, and need to be mindful and aware of our limitations lest we get carried away and attempt to bite off more than we can chew. We should aim to present the best we can within the restraints of our resources and abilities and not take either our congregation or those who lead them, beyond their accepted limits. I am not suggesting that we do not attempt to stretch horizons, but merely remind ourselves that we know our own limitations, those of our audience and the scope of the tools that we use.

In this way we will provide a challenging opportunity for people to worship in a vibrant and dynamic way, taking them forward on their spiritual journey, rather than threatening them with material that is inappropriate and serves only to diminish their experience and awareness of God's presence in their lives.

We have already discussed who we are worshipping and why, but we must also be very mindful of the make up of our audience or congregation. The nature, size, character, age and cultural background will all have a bearing on the way in which that particular congregation will want to worship and how they will respond to the leader's prompting. The effective leader will therefore take pains to know the make up and character of their congregation. This will determine the approach, for whilst a stack of Marshall amplifiers and speakers thundering out a Christian rap from bands such as the World Wide Message Tribe or Christian rock from Delirious or other contemporary bands will perhaps be appropriate for a large teenage gathering in a theatre or festival, it would probably not be appreciated at a meeting of senior citizens at the local 'Golden Age' or 'Evergreen' club in a rural village. Not that our senior citizens are not open to some good music! Far from it, but you get the picture!

The question of modern music as opposed to traditional hymns, has sadly become a persistent bone of contention in the Church. This issue has probably been the root cause of much of the dissent in the Church today. Forget the problem of the Sea of Faith movement, women ministers, sexual orientation and gifts of the Spirit, one of the most contentious issues which holds back today's Church is 'whether we sing the real songs that Wesley wrote or whether we have to endure that modern rubbish by that Noel Richards and the like!' to quote an elderly member of one church that we visited.

During our travels with our ministry, I have seen or heard no other subject so dominate discussion about worship. More of this later; for now it should suffice to say that surely it is a question of balance and common sense. Unfortunately these divisions in music have spilt over into much more important issues and there now appears to be a perception that all-age worship need only contain a couple of Graham Kendrick or Ishmael action songs and that will suffice to shut up the revisionists who are perceived by some traditionalists to be infiltrating the Church. This attitude simply will not do and worship leaders must grasp the fact that effective and meaningful 'all-age' worship is one of the keys to revival. Despite the misguided efforts of some authorities, the family still remains vitally important in today's society and worship leaders ignore corporate family all-age worship at their peril.

The Church really does need to organise its resources so that funding is made available to properly train our worship leaders to be able to take up the challenge of all-age worship and reflect the real needs of the Church family. All-age worship at its best is an enriching experience which blesses those who take part and brings an awareness of God to all. Make no mistake, drama, puppets, dance and flags need not be the threatening beast perceived by many. Our puppet team regularly rejoice in seeing and hearing the delight of both the very young and very old after they experience one of our puppet praise services, which include many different creative elements. These things simply need to be presented with thoughtfulness and a sensitivity which includes everyone in the service. Sadly, not every preacher is willing or capable of doing this. This sad state of affairs serves merely to remind us of our shortcomings and ensure that we must act right now to equip our ministers, preachers and worship leaders to respond to the challenges and opportunities that the 21st century brings.

It is therefore important for all those involved in worship to keep an open mind and to keep abreast of the resources that are available. The Internet for example, is a fantastic tool and there are hundreds of web sites which offer an ever growing store of advice, ideas and resources

> 'The real issue is whether we sing the real songs that Wesley wrote or whether we have to endure that modern rubbish by that Noel Richards and the like! said one elderly member'

for worship. We will discuss those resources later, but at this stage we need to be aware that there is more to service planning than the lectionary.

The layout of the venue where we are to present worship is instrumental in determining how we approach the act itself. Some churches offer the facility to worship 'in the round' whilst others have fixed pews offering little in the way of flexibility and precious little comfort. Some buildings are blessed with superb acoustics whilst some have little to offer in this respect and no worthwhile sound system. A full scale dance routine is difficult to perform in the cramped worship area dominated by a nineteenth century raised pulpit found in many older churches. Conversely, it would be difficult to present certain Gospel 'magic' illusions in a central worship area of a church set out in the round, as lines of sight may be far too revealing for the aspiring illusionist! Clearly layout is important and it pays to check with church stewards before arriving at an unfamiliar venue to ensure that available equipment and space are adequate for your requirements and those of your team.

Many churches and organisations are keen to participate and learn new ways of approaching worship. The hands-on workshop is a popular means of experiencing and acquiring new skills. When leading workshops it is essential to have an idea of the skill level of the participants, and also to have some control over numbers. It is disappointing and frustrating for both leaders and participants to find that the material chosen is either way below or far above the abilities and aspirations of those present in the workshop. It is equally frustrating to have prepared an intimate studio drama workshop only to find that two hundred aspiring thespians have been invited to join in. Of course, we cannot absolutely control these events or we lose our flexibility but it is important to know the make up of your workshop group when preparing events and ensure close communication with your venue contacts and organisers so that no major misunderstandings occur to spoil what should be an exciting and challenging experience.

Often, age determines ability, but do not be put off by being confronted with a large proportion of younger people or children. Our experience is that they are often less inhibited and much more imaginative and creative than older members of the church fellowship. You may have to work hard at the beginning to break the ice with some teenagers, but once won over they will be extraordinarily receptive to your ideas and will readily contribute their own.

Sometimes it is the leaders own fear of introducing new ideas that inhibits a workshop or worship time, but we have found that many of those in a particular group whom we perceive to be staid and unwilling because of age, culture or background, often turn out to be amongst the more innovative. Participants have continually surprised us with their enthusiasm and imagination. We always need to keep an open mind and not underestimate the resourcefulness of those whom we seek to lead in workshops. Be bold and go for it!

GO FOR IT – BUT BE PROFESSIONAL!

Whilst we should be aiming to assist and bring out the best in congregations and enable them to reach their full potential, it is important to remember that worship leaders are there to provide a lead. It is vital that everyone in the congregation and the leadership team is fully aware of what they are supposed to do and when they should be doing it. It may seem an obvious point to many, but how many times have you been present as a member of a congregation and been left guessing whether you should be sitting or standing, responding or just listening or even be in a different place! Be clear and leave your congregation in no doubt as to what may be expected of them but be sensitive when you do it. Sometimes, people just want to watch and listen, so don't be too pushy!

Another vital point which hopefully is second nature for most, is to be professional. We are after all, serving God and His people and therefore everything that we do should be done in an efficient and as polished a fashion as possible, using all the best resources available to us. Being professional doesn't just mean using sophisticated new technology, but doing things properly and in a courteous manner. Simple measures such as turning up in good time, dressing appropriately, being fully rehearsed and offering a polished and confident performance are just a few of the elements which distinguish the seasoned presenter from the sloppy amateur. Good preparation and planning leads to a smooth running act of worship. We would do well to remember that those organisations that offer the competing secular diversions that we referred to earlier, have already learned that professionalism is important.

The worship leader who does not heed this advice will soon find that congregations will quickly tire of any unprofessional conduct and will vote with their feet.

Practice makes perfect

Whether you work alone or with a team, time spent training and rehearsing will repay itself tenfold, and any performance will be enhanced by time spent refining and rehearsing routines. There are several international sportsmen who have had their exploits belittled by those who say that they have been lucky to win so many times. I think it was Gary Player, the champion golfer, who said it was strange that the harder he practised, the luckier he got! There are ample training resources available for most creative arts, either in book or video form and in many instances workshops organised by local theatres and leisure centres. They probably won't show you how to present worship, but they will in the most part prepare you to use your particular creative skill in a more polished manner.

Of course all performers must practice their skills, whether working alone or as part of a team. Rehearsals are particularly important for groups, as each member must be aware of not only what they are doing but how and when they fit in with other team members activities. For teams in ministry the rehearsal time can be a time of hard work, but also a rewarding time of fellowship and fun. Our own puppet team rehearses every Friday and the evening includes a time of relaxing and playing table tennis, table football and pool, followed by an intense time of rehearsal, choreography and creative input, finishing with a time of open prayer. Of course each team must find what form of rehearsal suits them, but our team has found that being able to relax and pray together, enables us to work together better as a ministry team.

Listening to others

Working on your own enables you to work exactly as you wish without the need to refer to others, unless of course you are just one element in an act of worship. This has the distinct advantage of allowing total freedom of expression, but has the disadvantage of not allowing for immediate and instant constructive criticism during rehearsal, so it can be useful to spend

> *'I think it was Gary Player, the champion golfer, who said it was strange that the harder he practised, the luckier he got!'*

some rehearsal time in front of a friendly audience who have been commissioned to observe and advise on performance faults, no matter how small. It can also prove very useful to make use of video from time to time to check on your performance.

I have spent many hours in front of audiences performing Gospel 'magic' and preaching in front of large and small congregations and feel that I usually present myself and the message fairly competently, but I still make silly mistakes sometimes and I really do benefit from constructive criticism and analysis. No matter how long we have been leading worship, and no matter how well we feel we are versed in stage craft, we all make mistakes and even the best of us can become complacent, perhaps because of the familiarity of our routines. Do listen and take on board the feedback from your colleagues and from your congregations.

Video provides an uncompromising demonstration of our fallibility and I recommend that you regularly video your presentations both in rehearsal and 'live' performances. It is a practice that will pay rich dividends.

TEAM BUILDING

I have been so blessed by the commitment and enthusiasm of the members of our 'Hands up for God' ministry team and I pray that those of you who seek to build a ministry team will be blessed and rewarded in the same way. But it must be appreciated that a successful team is not built overnight. You can bring together a group of people and provide them with a shared vision, but a team is only built over the course of time. Before a team can operate as a cohesive machine that thinks with one mind and acts in a co-ordinated manner, the team members will probably have to overcome growing pains. They will need to learn to rely upon one another. This confidence will develop as they become more comfortable in each other's company.

I have had the privilege of leading an exceptional team of young people, mostly teenagers, and I am constantly reminded that this gifted bunch of people are also a group of highly charged bundles of hormones, capable of all the violent mood swings and temperament changes normally associated with the average teenager. Maturity and experience are not an automatic passport to success and people aren't perfect just because they become part of a ministry team. Whilst building a team is fun, there will be times when people become frustrated, angry, tired and just plain belligerent. It's all part of the process and we need to be patient and to prayerfully work our way through it. It's not always easy, but hard work and a sensitive approach will help us all through the pain and bring rich rewards.

A team has to develop and learn to rely upon one another and a good leader will act as the catalyst that enables this process and provide the bits of glue that binds the team together. There is no complete blueprint for success in this process, as every team is different and team members need to learn about one another as the team develops and matures. There is little doubt that the problems that emerge as the team explores its strengths and weaknesses, will fade away and leave a team that has learnt to love one another as it ministers together.

Developing a ministry team is a matter of balance and the astute leader must seek to encourage progress and to sensitively criticise weaknesses and failures. There must be a recognition that each team member will probably be keen to develop his or her own personal talents, yet at the same time they must be encouraged to contribute to the team effort. Inevitably some will display more talent than others, but we must be careful to avoid any special favouritism or elitism, yet at the same time we should not be too slow to praise outstanding individual contributions. I believe that it sometimes pays to praise in public, but you should keep criticism of individuals as a private matter.

All too often, ministry team leaders, particularly those who lead children and teenagers, forget that these lovely people offer their time willingly, but voluntarily. We do well to remember that they don't have to be there! Whilst our ministry work is ultimately designed to enhance worship and to honour God, it surely has to be enjoyed by those who present it. After all, worship should be fun, shouldn't it?

Above all, the members of any team need to be committed to their objectives and it pays to lay out those objectives and a statement of intent, so that all are aware of the shared vision of what the team is striving to achieve.

I firmly believe that teams need to be aware of their own statement of faith, and to be encouraged to build upon that foundation. It may not be absolutely essential for each member of a team to be a longstanding Christian, as the team ministry can support and build up individuals on their own personal journeys of faith. All members of our 'Hands up for God' team have gained a deeper understanding of Christ as a direct result of being part of that ministry. However, I find it difficult to envisage a situation where any member of a Christian ministry team is not already committed to a simple belief in a Creator God and is not actively seeking a deeper knowledge of Jesus and what their response to His teaching should be. Any less commitment than this will lead to confusion in the team and to those to whom they are ministering. After all, Christian ministry teams are teaching Biblical Truth and seeking to spread the Gospel. They are much more than just a social club!

This work demands commitment and any team must have its ministry work at its core, the work of spreading the Gospel of Christ. No matter how wonderful the social side of the team turns out to be, the team has been formed to do God's work and teams who do not keep God at their centre and this vital work as its focus, will ultimately fail!

Safety and safeguards

As worship leaders we have an awesome responsibility and this responsibility not only involves providing a rich worship experience, but also to provide a safe place in which worshippers hear our message. This safety aspect can take various forms and we must ensure that the worship area, and indeed all areas where people are rehearsing, performing, worshipping or simply relaxing, are completely safe and do not present any obstacles to enjoyment.

Modern communication technology in many cases inevitably leads to endless plugs, cables and staging, and it always pays dividends to make someone responsible for ensuring safe cabling and electrics and a neat and tidy environment for all to enjoy without fear of injury.

This is especially true where the elderly, infirm, young people or children are concerned. Some folk find it difficult to step over loose cables and some may not even be able to see them! Toddlers are naturally inquisitive and will make a bee-line for that loose wire or unsteady lighting rig. It really is worth the effort to tape down cables and make sure tripods that carry OHP screens, lighting rigs and speakers are well secured and in no danger of toppling even when subjected to the attentions of persistent children.

If you use sophisticated equipment whilst performing, you may wish to give someone the sole responsibility of ensuring that people do not encroach into potentially dangerous areas. Mark out no-go zones and point them out to your congregation before you start. Be safe! Be careful and double check everything, and after all that, be insured! Most larger insurance companies will have insurance policies designed to protect you and your congregations. Make sure that the venue you are working at is properly insured and that you have your own personal third party insurance and legal liability insurance.

It is absolutely vital to ensure the well-being of all those in our temporary care and to safeguard their interests. This is most important of course in the case of children. All too often we hear of instances of child abuse in one form or another. Sadly, the abuse of children by those charged with their care is a problem that is unlikely to be completely eradicated in any organisation. Most established traditions in the Church try very hard to ensure that all is being done to provide suitable people to work with children. Those of us who lead teams of co-workers must play our part in screening these prospective helpers. Those who seek to work with children should not object to a searching screening process, secure in the knowledge that we are only seeking to provide the safest possible environment for those in our care.

All worship leaders should acquaint themselves with the guidelines for appropriate behaviour for those who work with children and young people. There are procedures laid down by most denominations. If you do not have access to these, you should obtain guidance from local authorities and social workers' offices. These guiding principles not only protect those in our care, but are also designed to prevent well meaning but naïve leaders placing themselves in compromising and difficult situations through ignorance.

SUPPORT FROM YOUR HOME CHURCH – IT'S VITAL!

In order for any ministry to thrive, it must be supported by prayer! This is worth saying again. All ministries must be supported by and soaked in prayer! Our own team has its own open group prayer times and these are richly rewarding, enabling us to grow spiritually and to learn to trust one another. It is also supported by prayer groups within our own Methodist church at Barrow-upon-Soar and in other churches that we have visited around the

'In order for any ministry to thrive, it must be supported by prayer!'

country. At the beginning of every service we ask for that host church to pray for us on a regular basis and we value the warm response that we always receive to that request.

The support of one's own local church is a vital ingredient for any successful ministry as it is usually at one's home church that we are fed with the spiritual nutrients that feed the teaching of our ministry. Part of the work of any church fellowship is to build up, encourage and nurture its members and I can testify to the warmth and love that one can find at the home church. My wife, Suzanne and I have found great strength in the support of our home church and delight in seeing familiar friendly faces encouraging us at local puppet team events.

No matter how experienced we are, and how far along the road we are perceived to be, none of us can be so self sufficient that we do not need regular feeding in the Spirit and the Word of God. I believe that it is vital to take time out from ministry to receive, in order that we are able to give again in outreach. This is why our own ministry team do not take to the road on a weekly basis, and why we have a break from the work in summer and at Christmas time. We all need time to be ourselves, to spend time with family and friends and not always be 'the worship leaders'.

Props and equipment

Some of the disciplines that we shall discuss require little in the way of props and equipment, whilst others are well served by good lighting, sound systems and other sophisticated equipment and I would urge you to use and buy the best quality that you and your resources allow. I have always been a sucker for new technology and just love to play with a new toy.

I am mindful however that the message of the Gospel is central to ministry and not the communication system that carries it, or indeed the performers who present it. However we are examining the use of the performing arts, and there is no doubt that performances can be greatly enhanced by good props and quality sound and lighting systems. We shall explore the most suitable systems for each discipline in the appropriate chapter. For the moment it is enough to note that we must endeavour to use the best and most appropriate props and equipment available to us and to ensure that it is secure and safe from damage whilst in transit. You must also consider the bulk and weight of all your equipment, as you will probably not be

> *I have always been a sucker for new technology and just love to play with a new toy*

blessed with unlimited space within your car, van or trailer whilst transporting to your venue.

COPYRIGHT

The creative arts are a wonderful expression of our own individuality and often we bring much of ourselves to a particular piece of work. Sadly not all of us are blessed with either the time or talent to write all of our own material and it is important to establish whether a particular script, song, poem, dance or drama etc that we may wish to use, is available to us from the public domain, or whether permission or a licence to perform it must be obtained from someone else who owns the copyright.

Much church music is available in the public domain and many churches have a CCL licence which enables copyright music to be used in worship. Drama groups are able to use many scripts in books designed for corporate worship, but we must be sure that we are being fair to the originator of any piece of work. If in any doubt, check with the publisher or author and obtain written permission before you use the material.

Many Christian artists will be only too pleased for you to use their work for non-profit making exercises

> *If in any doubt, check with the publisher or author and obtain written permission before you use the material*

in worship. We must be careful to understand that often the author no longer owns the copyright. It is usually a fairly easy matter to establish ownership and to obtain permission.

FEES AND BOOKINGS - FOR THOSE WHO TRAVEL

Having established and trained your ministry team and equipped it with the latest technology and costume, you will be keen to load up your intercontinental trailer and take to the road to convert the world's lost souls, but first you will need to sort out finance, booking arrangements and publicity. Fees for those who minister in the church is a complex subject and it must be left to individuals to charge a fee that they deem to be appropriate. Full time professionals needs to provide for themselves and their families. It is therefore reasonable for host churches or other organisations to expect to pay a fee for those services.

The part time or voluntary ministry team will have differing needs and I can only advise you to seek to recover those costs which you feel are appropriate to your own circumstances. Our own 'Hands up for God' ministry offers its services free of charge except for travelling expenses. We then advise our hosts that we would be pleased to receive a love gift in addition to those costs if the host church felt it appropriate. We have found that most churches are very fair and willingly respond. You must assess your own resources and needs and charge or not charge as you see fit. We have found that funds will always be provided when they are needed! Go forward in faith, but plan according to your available resources.

If working with a host church for a weekend you will need overnight accommodation for you and your team. Apart from one glorious week of luxury whilst on mission in Jersey, the 'Hands up for God' team is all too familiar with the kibbutz style of hospitality afforded by sleeping on camp beds in church halls. Whether you opt for the same flagellant lifestyle or you crave the luxury of real beds, or even hotels, the basic necessities such as security, food, warmth and shelter need to be considered beforehand so that everyone knows what to expect and what to provide.

Publicity

Having set a date and agreed your fees, you will almost certainly want to advertise your ministry worship event. You may advertise your ministry using church newspapers, magazines, newsletters and local radio. Once you have been booked, you will probably need to enlist the help of your hosts and will need to rely on them to publicise your particular event. You must ensure that they are fully informed of exactly what you will be doing, where you will be doing it and when it will be done. It may be that you can produce posters on computer for distribution, or leaflets for schools and homes etc. Whatever your ministry, if you are to reach out to the community, you must organise effective publicity.

The personal touch is often well rewarded and I will always remember a trip to a wonderful Assembly of God church in Kent. After our journey from Leicestershire the team were invited by the pastor to tour the village housing estates on a door to door basis. Wearing our puppets on our arms, we issued a personal invitation to families on the estate to come to the puppet praise service at the church the next day. The result was astonishing and the church was packed to the gunwales thanks to simple but effective advertising and God's blessing. I am not suggesting that each church takes to the streets for every event, but you can see that effective publicity is paramount if you want to persuade people to come to see and hear the Word preached.

> 'Whatever your ministry, if you are to reach out to the community, you must organise effective publicity'

Leave it to God

We can all work tremendously hard at 'our' ministry and feel at the end of a service, a praise weekend, or even a week-long festival, that we have done alright. We can argue that we could have performed better or that the congregation could have been more charitable or forgiving! In any event, if we have soaked the ministry in prayer, prepared ourselves and our congregation well and presented ourselves and God's message to the best of our ability, then we can safely leave the rest to God in the sure knowledge that He will have initiated, carried through and finished His work through you His servant, by His Grace. Be glad that you have been blessed with the gift of creativity and pray that by the action of the Holy Spirit, your creative ministry will be anointed by God.

CREATIVE ARTS IN WORSHIP

Music is used in most forms of worship, and there are issues which challenge every worship leader as we choose songs, lead workshops, compose songs, or try to get the best out of musicians to enhance worship. These type of problems are addressed here.

CHAPTER TWO
MUSIC IN WORSHIP

MUSIC – AN INTEGRAL PART OF WORSHIP

Music in the context of worship has a tremendously long history and the earliest reference in the Bible is that of Jubal, a descendant of Cain, who is described as 'the father of all who play the harp and flute.' Genesis 4:21 (NIV) After the Flood, the first mention of music in the Bible is in Genesis 31:27, where Laban speaks to Jacob; and the first example of singing praises, that of the Israelites after their deliverance from Egypt. (Exodus 15:1) There followed a rich period in Jewish musical history, in the time of David, Samuel and Solomon and that prolific vein of creativity is reflected in contemporary worship songs.

The techniques employed for music composition, song writing, singing, playing and the use of music in worship have developed in many different ways since those early days. This chapter explores some of the ways in which up to date techniques can be applied to these skills and disciplines in order that they may be effectively used in contemporary worship.

There are many aspects to music in the context of worship and it is not my intention to provide a technical course on how to play particular instruments or to teach music notation. There are skilled musicians who can tackle that task far more competently than I. However, music is used in most forms of worship, and there are issues and questions which challenge every worship leader who is choosing music, leading workshops, composing songs, or trying to get the best out of musicians to enhance worship. It is these type of problems which we will address here.

MUSIC WITH A PURPOSE

Just consider some of the tasks that music accomplishes and you quickly get a feel for the complex problems that may arise when we try to use music creatively. Correctly and sensitively chosen, skilfully played music can help us to praise, celebrate, meditate, relax, focus, raise our spirits, remind us of the past, move, dance, challenge and teach. Through music we can express our worship, sing and pray in tongues, set a mood, enhance drama, stories and poetry, stimulate thought processes and hopefully, it will bring us to a greater understanding of Scripture. It is important to appreciate that music and song which is ill chosen for the occasion, ineptly played, or simply introduced at the wrong time in the service, will serve to have a negative effect and will hinder the pursuit of these stated objectives.

It follows then, that we have to be clear on what our goals are and how we achieve them. So perhaps it is appropriate to record now, that whilst music is regarded as a very important part of worship, it is only one element in the equation. St. Paul wrote 'What then shall we say, brothers? When you come together, everyone has a hymn, or a word of instruction, a revelation, a tongue or an interpretation. All of these must be done for the

> 'Let the word of Christ dwell in you richly as you teach and admonish one another with all wisdom, and as you sing psalms, hymns and spiritual songs with gratitude in your hearts to God'

COLOSSIANS 3:16 NIV

strengthening of the church.' 1 Cor 14:26 (NIV).

Encouraging and building up the congregation's faith is a vital part of the worship leader's brief and it is clear that music has a very important part to play in this process. The words, the music and manner of presentation all play their part, and all these structural elements must relate to the rest of the act of worship. It is equally important that the music enables worshippers to offer themselves to God and be aware of His presence. The music should aspire to be worship in its own right, not simply a means of enhancing worship. Thus, music is not simply a means to make the service more attractive, although well chosen songs can have this effect. We must also avoid the trap of using contemporary music simply to appear trendy to young people. Use contemporary music by all means, but use it with a purpose, and in the context of the overall service.

In 1993, the General Synod of the Church of England produced a very worthwhile report on music in worship called *In Tune With Heaven* which urged worship leaders to be mindful of what each piece of music is saying to us and how it speaks to a congregation. This will create some conflict in so far as we need to strike a balance between satisfying the musical expectations of the people with the need to reach and teach congregations about God. Whilst we should certainly enjoy the music offered, we should always strive to provide songs that unite the congregation and mostly reflect the teaching needs of that particular body of people; not the individual taste of the worship leader.

> 'Use contemporary music by all means, but use it with a purpose, and in the context of the overall service'

THE NITTY GRITTY – CHOOSING THE SONGS

I never cease to be amazed whenever I look around a music department, secular or Christian, and see the rich variety of music that is on offer. In most stores, music of every style, in a wide range of languages, using every conceivable instrument is on offer. It sometimes makes me wonder how I would respond if I were ever invited to take part in Desert Island Discs and have to choose the ten pieces of music that I would take with me to that fictional desert island.

In one sense, that is the dilemma facing worship leaders every time we choose songs and music for worship. There is such a variety of music to choose from and so many different expectations from congregations that we have a very difficult balancing act to perform.

Whether we are choosing songs for family worship, street evangelism or a children's praise party, we need to focus on the needs of our congregation. This will be determined by many factors, not least of which is the theme of the service. There are lectionaries available to the established Church traditions which offer readings and themes throughout the Christian year. These usually provide a ready made source of relevant hymns and songs which will fit the day's theme. The Christian calendar often determines the type of songs required such as Christmas, Easter and Harvest, and these festivals demand some traditional songs and carols. However, there is no reason why leaders should not be creatively minded in these areas. Indeed, these occasions lend themselves to innovation and the experienced worship leader can put together a good blend of traditional and contemporary material that may well be inspirational.

Most congregations feel comfortable with familiar songs and there is an often quoted maxim that one should not introduce more than one new song at a service. Whilst I understand the reasons why this should be advocated, I do believe that most congregations are willing and capable of learning more than this and indeed welcome the challenge, provided they are given sufficient time to learn the song properly. It can be effective to introduce new songs or tunes before the service, using them to prepare the congregation for worship. Try playing new worship songs from CD or tape, or by the worship band if you have one, and if people like the song, ask them to sing it at a future service.

However, the limitations and worship experience of the congregation should be reflected in the choice of song. At a simple level, consider songs to be chosen for a praise party designed for two contrasting young people's groups. Those leading worship at an established boys/girls brigade or Christian Union would feel able to choose songs that contained pointed and obvious Christian references and language. Conversely, the leader of a praise party designed for un-churched youngsters would be better served by using simple action songs or music which set a mood and atmosphere that led to a different style of reaching and teaching. The astute worship leader will always be aware of the nature of their congregation and will consult those with local knowledge, working together with them to achieve goals.

> 'The limitations and worship experience of the congregation should be reflected in the choice of song'

Different congregations display differing characteristics and there will be many different tastes within each congregation. We should be mindful that, unless songs are designed to be used by a soloist or choir, they should promote congregational singing as a group experience and the lyrics should be chosen with as much care and thought as the melody. They should both complement one another and should provide a range of tempo, styles and poetic forms in order that a variety of music is offered.

It is impossible for any third party to identify the ideal songs for services that you will lead, other than to suggest sources, as there are thousands of songs available in many different styles. Whether we use Psalms, traditional hymns, chants from Taize, meditative Celtic or Ionian anthems or modern worship songs and choruses, the words and music must be appropriate for your congregation.

Leading worship songs

One of the most important choices to be made, is how the songs will be led. In other words, will the accompanying music be played on the organ, by a worship band, music group or even audio tape, CD or from MIDI files? Will a choir lead, a singing group, or a worship leader; and with or without accompaniment?

Singing which is weak or lacking in confidence is very distracting and is a real hindrance to focusing upon God as we worship. The feeling that the song isn't going well is infectious and the meaning and significance of the song words will quickly be lost under these circumstances. Therefore, whichever method of leadership is employed, it is vital that a confident and competent individual or group of people lead singing in worship, so that the congregation are provided with a clear and strong focus.

The organ is the traditional instrumental lead in most churches, closely followed by the piano and the guitar. The richness of tone and depth of these instruments can easily be lost if playing is inept or hesitant. Sadly, some 'resident' church musicians who have given years of valuable service, outstay their welcome and are very reluctant to take a rest from these duties, for a while at least, in order to give someone else the opportunity to use their gifts. Instead, they sometimes stubbornly cling to office despite the fact that their performing gifts and skills may have been diminished by age or infirmity. Worship leaders who are forced to rely upon such willing souls, must try to persuade the relevant church leadership to have the courage to take appropriate action in such situations, albeit with much sensitivity. The needs of the congregation and the work of the Church must surely take precedence over the needs of such individuals, although it is understood that the decision to relieve that person of his or her duties will be a painful process.

It may well be that there is no competent musician available to a church, or even someone who is competent but unwilling to play the type of music required. It is then that we need to employ the services of available musicians from other churches or rely upon tapes, CD's or MIDI files, or even a combination of both so that the congregation has the opportunity to experience a wider range of musical styles. Any of these media can be used successfully. Our puppet team is often responsible for leading a family service or praise weekend, and whilst there are competent musicians in our team, we use CD's at virtually every service. We use a combination of all age action songs such as those produced by Ishmael, Alan Price, Doug Horley and Dave Cooke, as well as traditional hymns and contemporary songs taken from collections such as Mission Praise, Sing Hallelujah and Stoneleigh Worship. We firmly believed that congregations would respond to this combination of music, and as we did not have the means to present the songs live, we decided to use them karaoke style, which has been tremendously successful. It is still important to provide the congregation with a proper focal point when adopting this method. Our own team presents the songs with three or four strong singers, using good quality microphones to provide this necessary focus.

Modern music equipment and MIDI files often allow for split track recording and backing tracks can be used by competent lead singers as musical accompaniment, provided your sound system allows for good balance and mixing. A good mixer will also enable you to handle and balance microphone, CD, tape or MIDI inputs and there are more and more resources emerging in this area. 'DM Music for Churches' is a Christian company specialising in sound and music resources for worship. This company has hundreds of traditional hymns and contemporary worship songs on MIDI file, CDs and discs.

USING MUSIC IN CHURCH

A wide variety of hymns, anthems, Psalms and worship songs are frequently used in most services to enhance worship. We are fortunate in our own church that Joan Thursby, our regular organist and keyboard player at the time of writing, is a forward thinking, qualified worship leader with a vision and heart for innovative worship. Sadly, not all those responsible for music in our churches share that same vision, and there is a need to educate musical directors to the fact that there are many different ways of using music, other than just providing an accompaniment to singing.

Music is of course allied to dance. Dance and movement will be dealt with in a separate chapter, but it is worthwhile recording here that creative movement can increase the impact of worship songs, enlivening and enhancing their meaning. This is achieved by offering our congregations the opportunity to experiment with simple action songs, rap or dance music, or even by adding more sophisticated and co-ordinated choreography to familiar, established worship songs. Using our bodies in this way enables us to be more expressive. Through dance the music can become a vehicle for physical communication, besides its value in purely auditory terms. Perhaps one of the best known examples of this is Doug Horley's *We Want To See Jesus Lifted High* which is usually instantly recognised by most of the congregations that we lead in worship. The

> 'There is a need to educate musical directors to the fact that there are many different ways of using music, other than just providing an accompaniment to singing'

song has the ability to stir most to spontaneously carry out the same universally accepted actions and movement. Familiarity enables the congregation to be less inhibited and more expressive, resulting in a rich and fulfilling experience. This is the mark of an inspired worship song. It is worth noting that the use of overhead projection or data projection is very useful in these circumstances as holding a song sheet or hymn book does not lend itself easily to movement or animated physical expression. Whilst many of us find overhead projection helpful, some people do still appreciate song books being made available, particularly those folk who may be visually impaired.

Some powerful and dramatic songs, such as those performed by Ray Boltz or Carman, lend themselves to mime enactment. These can be a tremendous aid to storytelling, adding 'punch' and dramatic effect to even the simplest of stories. Rodd and Marco are a full time Christian writing and performing team who produce very creative and humorous material which combines music and drama. This is available in complete form, or as backing tracks with scripts for the more adventurous.

A raising of spiritual awareness can be achieved by using music as a background to 'voice-overs' accompanying prose, or even prayer. This is especially useful when we need to bring a meditative atmosphere to a prayer time. For example, during prayers of intercession, quiet background music can enable worshippers to focus and meditate. In much the same way, some musicians play quiet, reflective and meditative pieces whilst the Sacrament of Communion is being shared or an offering is taken. Appropriate music from the *Methodist Worship Book*, Taize, Iona or Celtic worship can be particularly helpful in this respect. It should be remembered at this point that silence is sometimes more appropriate and we should welcome moments of quiet in a service.

MUSIC FOR YOUNG PEOPLE AND ALL-AGE WORSHIP

Multi-media is an important part of today's culture. Presentations using video walls and light shows are especially familiar to the young. Video clips can be used very effectively to create a reflective atmosphere and can initiate a very intense emotional response to worship. There are several songs that may be enhanced by appropriate video clips that are cued to suit the lyrics. These need not be restricted to Christian songs as there are also well known secular songs that can be used in this way to good effect. An example of this is Bryan Adam's *Everything I Do, I Do It For You*. When cued with video of the Passion sequences from various Gospel films, such as Zefferelli's *Jesus of Nazareth*, the combination of song and video provides an exceptionally powerful preparation for preaching and teaching.

A similar result can be achieved with parody music, which is very popular in the USA. Musicians such as Mark Bradford, and bands such as Apologetix, produce a large number of songs that parody established secular songs, substituting Christian lyrics over a sound track which imitates the original. Very familiar songs from such artists as the Beach Boys, the Beatles and Queen have been used very effectively in this way. Our own team has used several of these to great effect in creative arts weekends. One song worthy of mention is the song *My Heart Will Go On* sung by Celine Dion in the film *Titanic*. We use a very effective Christian parody version of this song, entitled *His Love Will Go On* which we combine with a video clip of Jesus appearing to various people after His Resurrection. Meanwhile, a human arm puppet sings the song and a team member signs the lyrics. Congregations have been greatly moved by the whole audio-visual experience.

Times of worship which are designed around a particular musical theme can be inspirational. Many churches have enjoyed a successful *Songs of Praise* evening where members of the congregation choose their favourite songs and a give a brief reason for its selection. Equally successful services have been arranged around the *Desert Island Discs* format. A well planned service where a member of the congregation or guest speaker is invited to offer a number of favourite worship songs, and to provide reasons for choosing them, can be a great time of testimony and witness. This can be very effective as a church service or as a house fellowship evening, combined with a meal perhaps. The more adventurous may wish to introduce a series of special guests from the Bible, such as Moses, Elijah, Jonah, Samson, Paul or some of the disciples to choose a song and give their testimony. This approach opens up tremendous opportunities for creative and innovative preaching, as well as providing for a rich variety of songs for all ages. Combined with drama, mime and stories about the guests' experiences and the impact of God upon their lives, the event has the capability of becoming a service to be remembered.

Music in Sunday school and children's groups

There are numerous traditional musical games such as Musical Bumps and Musical Chairs. Whilst not very appropriate for worship, they have served children's workers very well as warm up games for musical workshops for instance. Well chosen action songs are always welcome and these can be used to great effect. Whilst it is recognised that some songs are very popular and that familiarity can be a strength, it is important to remember that both young people and adults will appreciate efforts made to source, introduce and teach new and fresh songs. There is a constant stream of new Christian song-writing talent emerging and worship leaders will reap rich rewards by carefully and prayerfully researching music publishers, Christian music shops and the Internet for new material.

Modern technology has inspired innovation, such as the interactive CD-Rom, *Ready To Go* produced by Alan Price, a very talented children's evangelist and songwriter with The Teknon Trust in Derby. This collection of songs for all-ages worship can be enjoyed when played on a standard CD player. However, when played on a computer's CD-Rom drive, the interactive features are brought into play. The album incorporates video clips of Captain Alan and some of his crew demonstrating suggested actions for the songs. This is a great resource for CD player, home computer or data projector. Doug Horley is producing a similar interactive CD at the time of writing, but there are only a few collections produced in this exciting format. Hopefully other Christian musicians will offer their work in this way in the future.

Quizzes are an interesting way of teaching and musical quizzes can be devised to encourage young people to explore Christian music. Quizzes designed around the *Name That Tune* format help to develop discussion around the themes found within familiar songs, whilst new songs can be introduced, listened to and then a memory quiz organised to develop a questioning response. This non-threatening quiz format may then lead to a deeper discussion about certain basic beliefs, theology or Christology

Many young people enjoy singing or playing musical instruments and Church worship bands and music groups often feature gifted young people who possess the musical talent to sing, or play a musical instrument. It is rewarding to put together a worship band within a young people's group and enthusiasm will carry the group part of the way. However, a confident and competent musician who possesses organisational and leadership skills is an essential attribute when considering putting a band together.

It is important to remember that it is not only the truly gifted who can offer music in worship, as a worthwhile worshipful sound can be generated with a variety of percussion and wind instruments when in the hands of enthusiastic youngsters. It is vital that we nurture youthful enthusiasm and encourage, rather than discourage participation in worship. It may be that you wish to limit the amount of time devoted to listening to this often challenging form of worship, but I am convinced that several of our contemporary talented young musicians were first encouraged to make a joyful noise with a home made shaker or kazoo by an enthusiastic and patient children's worker. We have taken part in one or two hilarious workshops where young people have made drums, kazoos, shakers, tambourines and milk bottle xylophones, using them to praise God in an exciting and innovative way. Not for the faint hearted, but good stimulating worship. Be bold and give it a try.

Dame Thora Hird, at 90 years old, summed it up when she said, 'If we're going to worship the Lord, let's get on with it!'

Musicals and festivals

Several musicians/songwriters such as Roger Jones and Paul Field, have produced superb musicals written to be performed by choirs and churches. These can serve as entertainment, worship, a chance to express emotions and use a range of creative skills to provide a great opportunity for outreach into the community and within churches. Resources are usually made available in the form of a music score for live performing, backing tracks or split track recordings for accompaniment, and full production albums for listening pleasure. Many musicals provide the opportunity for gifted musicians and singers to lead and encourage others to develop their skills in public performances and serving God in mission. The musical *Hopes and Dreams* produced by the Rob Frost Team and written by Paul Field, Stephen Deal and others, is a celebration of Christ's millennium in the year 2000. This is a good example of a Christian musical which combines drama, music, dance and puppetry, encouraging churches to unite in a project that harnesses the skills and gifts of a variety of people, bonding those communities with a common objective of witnessing to God's love.

Great Christian festivals such as Christmas, Easter and Harvest, provide good opportunities for musical productions for both adults and young people. These are occasions that should be planned well in advance of the festival date. All too often, Christmas or Easter approaches and worship leaders bemoan the fact that they now don't have time to prepare and rehearse special projects found just a few months ago in magazines or Christian bookshops. This kind of ill-prepared compromise often results in a sub-standard production of the Nativity or Passion that will more often than not, waste an opportunity of effectively reaching out to congregations that include an unusual number of un-churched people.

There are some superb festival resources available, but they really do need rehearsing and polishing. The foresight and hard work is well worth the effort. Our puppet team prepared and rehearsed material for presenting four services each year at the Easter People festival, one evening a week for six months of each year. It is only by applying this sort

> 'Thora Hird summed it up when she said,' If we're going to worship the Lord, let's get on with it!'

of effort that a polished and 'professional' presentation can be achieved. Commitment and forward planning are vital if we are to make full use of the wealth of resources available to us.

Workshops

Workshops are superb ways of exploring music in worship. These can take the form of making basic percussion instruments, learning to play simple instruments such as hand bells or bell plates, developing established playing skills in a master class, putting together a mini-musical or concert or exploring new ways of singing and song writing. Most churches have members with musical skills who can be persuaded to provide good quality teaching. Those churches that do not have such talented musicians can attend events designed for teaching and developing the skills required to lead music in worship, such as those organised by Kingsway Publishers. Thousands of Christians have gratefully seized the opportunity to learn new skills and develop established ones at these well organised events.

On a smaller scale, I fondly remember a creative arts weekend organised by the Methodist church in Droitwich Spa, where my wife Suzanne and I were members when we lived in the West Midlands. The weekend was led by Bill Denning, a visiting Methodist minister in other appointments from Bristol who specialised in creative arts in worship. Bill was instrumental in inspiring Suzanne and I to respond to God's call to develop this style of ministry. He was careful to encourage people to try different skills and fooled them into volunteering for groups that they would probably not have normally joined. Bill asked all those who played a musical instrument or read music to put their hands up and promptly placed those who responded in the clay-modelling group! This proved to be a very effective method of actively re-distributing talents.

Whether or not you agree with his methods of forming the workshop groups, they were all remarkably successful. Most of the clay modellers produced superb works of art, which perhaps not totally technically correct and perfectly proportioned, were nevertheless very expressive and gave great pleasure to both creator and viewer. Moreover, those who professed to be proficient in painting and drawing, (and were subsequently placed in a song writing group!) produced a superb worship song that consisted of three beautiful verses and a very catchy chorus. This song was used to great effect in the act of worship that was the climax of the weekend. I am not suggesting for one moment that we should abandon professionally produced music, or discard the trained musicians in our midst. I simply make the point that we need not be afraid of exploring new skills and that we do not need to have had formal training to be able to produce a worthwhile piece of music for an act of worship. I am quite sure that God will appreciate the effort!

Making music

It is fair to say that virtually any instrument may be used in Christian worship to good effect. However, there are certain instruments that are more important than others, in the sense that they are more accessible to budding musicians through frequent teaching in schools. Most churches can call on musicians who play, sing or lead on a regular or weekly basis as well as those who play occasionally. There can be few who are not moved by a young child nervously taking the first steps in leading worship by singing a solo, playing a recorder or even hitting a few wrong notes on their first public offering on piano, violin, flute or clarinet in Church. I believe that it is vital to give such enthusiasts the opportunity to play, in order for them to gain the valuable experience which is so necessary in helping to develop their musicianship. They should not be asked to lead congregational singing until they are competent, sufficiently confident, or indeed willing to do so. There is no reason why they should not be given opportunities to play before the service, as the congregation leaves at the end, during coffee time after the service, or in a spot in the main service itself, perhaps specifically reserved for emerging talent. When this opportunity is provided in the context of family worship, it also serves as a tremendously effective witness to other young people and the rest of the congregation.

The organ, piano and keyboard are perhaps the most commonly played instruments in church, closely followed by the guitar, both acoustic and electric. The remainder are less common, but there are more and more violins, flutes, clarinets and saxophones being played in church, and this is adding to our rich musical heritage.

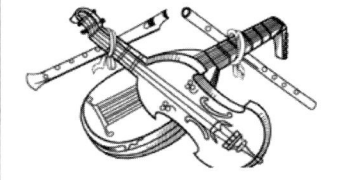

The worship band or music group can be a tremendous asset in worship, but different instruments played together can bring problems. For example, using transposing instruments which play in a different key, such as clarinet or saxophone. Unless the musicians can transpose as they play, manuscripts will require advance writing in the correct key for the instrument concerned. It is possible to get around this problem by using a transpose button on keyboards which have that facility. This allows the tune to be played in a key which allows the player of the transposing instrument to read directly from the music book. There are resources which offer arrangements for worship music for B flat and E flat instruments, and these can be really helpful.

Acoustic pianos are very widely used and are extremely versatile instruments when played by skilled hands. Unfortunately, many churches do not properly use microphone technology to effectively amplify their instruments and the piano is very often neglected in this respect. A richer and more powerful sound can be achieved by channelling the sound through a pre-amp equaliser and subsequently through a mixer/amp. When skilfully used, this type of equipment will compliment and enhance the natural sound and tone of the instrument.

Many churches these days opt for a digital keyboard. This modern instrument offers terrific opportunities to develop new sounds through the introduction of MIDI files and preset digital sounds and voices. Digital keyboards incorporate ever increasing and innovative technology and at the time of writing, Yamaha offer a 61 key, touch sensitive keyboard with host port and MIDI sockets, which can connect to a computer and other external devices. Over a hundred memory banks and registration memories allow the user to create and store song combinations, tempo, rhythm and styles for instant recall which can be easily copied to floppy disc. Vocal harmony slots enable the user to sing along to pre-recorded MIDI files, or to use as self accompaniment. It can also magically convert your voice into four part harmony!

Most guitarists will have their own instrument, albeit acoustic, electric lead or bass. It is useful for a church to have guitars as stock instruments as the very presence of these may well encourage some to explore an emerging gift. Remember though, that bass guitars need specialist heavy amplification. Electric guitars for lead and rhythm will normally be personalised by players and churches should not invest large amounts of money in these instruments for stock. A reasonable instrument and amp can be purchased quite cheaply and a good keyboard amp will normally serve as an adequate multi-purpose amp for churches on a tight budget.

A permanent set of drums is a must for the worship band, if only to prevent endless setting up and dismantling. Buy a good set and let a good drummer choose the equipment. One does not wish to discourage aspiring musicians, but it is a mistake to allow people to play with, rather than play the instruments.

One set of instruments that demands special attention, are hand bells, or the more economic, but excellent bell-plate chimes. These are tremendous instruments, which can be used by almost anybody, providing one is prepared to practice for a few hours. Joan, our church music leader, taught a group of adults and youngsters to play two pieces of music from scratch during an afternoon's workshop at a Methodist church in Haslemere. With imperfect timing and harmony that would have benefited from more practice, a passable performance was coaxed from people that she had never met before. With minimal coaching, people can satisfyingly create pleasing music very quickly that people will enjoy listening to. This is very rewarding for all concerned. Most churches order three octave sets that can be handled effectively by around ten to a dozen campanologists. Music can be arranged in order to use these instruments for stand alone pieces, or as an accompaniment to choir. Chimes are available in notation form, coloured symbols or simply with letter notes. Provided a leader is available with musical knowledge, almost any piece of music can be arranged for hand bells.

Using quality rhythm instruments and microphones to support a music group, will put a strain on many sound systems. It is a pity to spoil a well rehearsed worship song by failing to provide the singer or musician with adequate microphones and to offer a sound system with insufficient range, power and inputs. It is vital to achieve a clean and feedback free sound and whilst this may be a fairly expensive business, it is better to go for quality at an affordable cost. Monitor the sound, service the equipment properly, insure it and protect it with sturdy flight casing if you travel.

SONG-WRITING

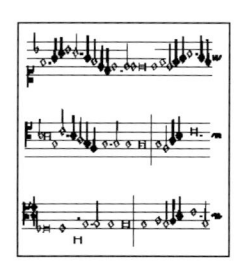

It is probably the case that many talented individuals could write a worship song or two, but that few are called to do so on a regular basis. There is a particular skill to writing and structuring a song, and the muses are not the only elements involved in the creative process.

There are no strict rules to writing songs, but a pattern or framework does emerge when we break the process down. The inspiration for the song can come from a special time of worship or personal devotion. It is often likely to emanate from one's own experience of receiving a particular spiritual blessing from God. This blessing will inevitably be reflected in the song theme and thus most songs adore, offer thanks or praise God in one way or other. This is not always the case. Some worship songs reflect on the human condition, whilst others are more meditative in theme and character.

Whatever the theme, a worship song designed for corporate worship should first of all be one which most congregations are capable of singing. The key range should be easily within the vocal scope of the singers, and the dynamics, tempo and rhythm should be kept fairly constant. Where these elements are variable and tempo is changed during the song, the changes should flow and give more impetus to the song rather than make the song appear to falter or stutter, thus impeding continuity of words and melody.

A song which focuses on God will challenge a congregation to do likewise, with a passion and a heart for all that He has done for us, or may do for us in the future. It is vital that the lyrics reflect words of Scripture honestly and with integrity. Any inaccuracy is confusing and misleading. No poetic licence is granted to musicians to change the basis of truth in Scripture. We must not bend the truth to fit the tune!

Lyrics will often be more effectively delivered if the words are familiar to the singers. Some theological terms may be precise and convey clear ideas and themes to the Biblical scholar, but the sheer intensity and complexity of some words may cloud the issue for an individual, when used in worship. We have seen earlier that familiarity provides a comfort zone in which many feel safe, and this is often a real asset in a worship song. If we feel comfortable, we are usually more relaxed and thus are more ready and willing to be expressive, releasing any tension or stresses which may inhibit us from approaching and praising God. It is therefore important to keep words and music simple, ensuring that the worship song may be easily learnt, thus enabling worship to quickly and seamlessly become whole-hearted and God centred.

The worship song that proclaims accurate Scripture

will reach and teach. It may well reveal a particular piece of Scripture in a new and vibrant way, enabling the singer to perceive or experience God's presence, viewing Him in a different, more revealing light. This will normally have the benefit of eliciting or inspiring a response and possibly even shaping the reaction into something that would have been inexpressible earlier. This expression of worship may be understood generally, or may even motivate a prophetic response in the Spirit, which may even be in tongues. When we listen, play or sing music, we are dealing with another form of language, so we should not be surprised if the response it inspires, is itself in another language.

My own limited experience of writing worship songs is that a few of the lines seem to be truly inspired and flow off of the pen, seemingly capable of enabling the listener or singer to reach new heights. Then, writers block sets in and I mistakenly struggle to search for filler lines to round off the verse or chorus. This is a major error. There should be no filler lines, as every word of every line should add to the importance and relevance of the overall aim of the song. Moreover, the whole song should speak to the Church, or at least the local community, ensuring that worshippers can relate to the themes within the song, hopefully finding something relevant either to their own condition, or a friend's situation.

Individuals who are more accomplished in these matters should be encouraged to tackle the technique of song writing. Songs should be memorable, inspire congregations to want to sing them, and contain elements which contrast between sections to create and maintain interest. Many songs that bear singing more than once display a verse, chorus and bridge arrangement which builds tension in the song, often leading to a release of energy and emotions which lift the spirit and increase awareness of the Holy Spirit's presence.

A song which illustrates a theme, has a clearly defined beginning, flows and develops to a clear conclusion, will be more likely to initiate a positive response in the singer or listener. It is recognised that some chants and choruses will sometimes rely more on shape, rhythm and expression than a precise Scriptural theme. It really depends on what objective the writer has in mind and how God wants to use that particular song in worship. Having our minds open to the prompting of the Holy Spirit to inspire and motivate us is vital. We should also be aware that He may wish to intervene in the creative process even when it appears to us that we are on the right track. His ways are

> 'No poetic licence is granted to musicians to change the basis of truth in Scripture. We must not bend the truth to fit the tune'

not our ways and perhaps we should be more mindful of those valuable words of wisdom when writing our songs.

Music as therapy

There is a particularly enlightened branch of the medical profession that relies upon skilled musicians to provide music as a form of therapy, mostly with young children. We would do well to recognise and adopt the healing and pastoral properties of our music in worship.

At its most simple level, a song sung at a wedding, baptism or funeral, will often invoke memories of that previous experience when heard or sung at a later date. The piece of music may then serve to strengthen a relationship, bind a person more closely to baptismal promises or help to ease the healing process of grieving. This leads me to conclude that we would do well to bear in mind the power of music in aiding the caring work of the Church. Perhaps we should be more aware of the nature and use of sound, tone, rhythm and lyrics when selecting appropriate music, in order to meet directly or indirectly, the needs of a particular congregation or act of worship.

Pinpointing specific songs which have these qualities is in itself a difficult task. Modern songwriters should be aware of their responsibilities to provide music which reflects the particular pastoral needs of modern congregations. Thomas Troeger, professor of Preaching and Communications at Iliff School of Theology in Denver captured the essence and importance of this responsibility when he wrote: 'Part of the importance of new hymnody is that it represents opportunities for providing pastoral care of the peculiar needs of our own age. New hymns alone are not sufficient because one function of worship is to connect the present to the great cloud of witnesses from the past. But new hymns belong in any healing understanding of liturgy.'

Providing we can learn from, and effectively make use of the rich traditions of our musical heritage, always striving to combine this with innovative technology and contemporary songs, we shall maintain and enrich the store of jewels that enhance the worship of today's and tomorrow's worshipping people in Christian fellowship.

> 'Part of the importance of new hymnody is that it represents opportunities for providing pastoral care of the peculiar needs of our own age. New hymns alone are not sufficient because one function of worship is to connect the present to the great cloud of witnesses from the past. But new hymns belong in any healing understanding of liturgy'

CREATIVE ARTS IN WORSHIP

One of the advantages of drama is that it can be used in worship as more than an introduction to sermon topics, but also to raise awareness through using dialogue and visual aids, enabling congregations to relate to the topic or scripture being discussed.

Chapter Three
Drama in worship

A rich drama heritage?

Drama has had a chequered history in the context of worship. There are records of drama having been used by the Roman Catholic Church during services celebrating Mass in the tenth century. Examples of mystery and miracle plays in the Middle Ages were performed both in Church and at open air markets and fairs. Unfortunately, those who presented and enjoyed watching drama, quickly came to be perceived and portrayed as depraved. Subsequently, many plays were held up as indecent by the Church authorities. The flavour of some drama at that time was indeed 'earthy' and certainly satirical. The Church, being anxious to retain control over Biblical thinking actively discouraged drama as it brought a new understanding to Scripture, leading to unwelcome questions from the masses.

The Puritans crushed most theatrical activity in the seventeenth century and consequently the Age of Reason in the eighteenth century, with its emphasis upon science and philosophy, led to a fortress mentality within the Church. All things spiritual were jealously defended. This resulted in a rejection of anything considered to be secular. The Bible, prayer and worship were thought of as sacrosanct in every respect, and drama was not considered to have any role to play in the Church.

It is astonishing to think that it is only in the past twenty years or so, that drama has begun to be re-established in the Church as an aid in worship. It is still widely perceived as something for youth to do, rather than recognised for it's potential as a broadly based teaching tool. Drama is one of the most effective communication media used on earth. A casual glance at the role of television, cinema and theatre will confirm this fact. It is surprising that more churches have yet to grasp the opportunities offered by drama, to reach people in a vibrant and dynamic way.

> 'Drama is one of the most effective communication media used on earth'

WHY DRAMA?

Forms of drama such as role play, monologue, storytelling, Bible re-enactments, sketches and workshops all lend themselves to be used in the worship environment by all age groups. There are those who believe that drama is more a form of entertainment than a means to enhance worship. There is no doubt that entertainment for its own sake will find little support in Church, and rightly so. One of the attractive features of drama is that it is entertaining. So is music, but there are few who would advocate not using it in Church as a result. The fact that drama is often entertaining is one of its inherent strengths, as when it is appropriately used, congregations are more likely to listen intently to interesting and entertaining dialogue. If this is the case, then surely we should be making more use of tools in worship that capture the attention of our congregation, preparing them for the next stage in the worship process, albeit teaching, prayer, meditation or reflection. When that tool has the capacity to teach, instruct and inspire us, as well as presenting the Good News as a stand alone medium, then we surely have to sit up and take notice, actively encouraging, nurturing and supporting those who are gifted in using their dramatic skills in the worship environment.

Drama is great fun for all concerned and as a result, barriers that sometimes prevent effective communication can be broken down. This leads to several ways in which drama can be used and these will be explored later. For now, it is sufficient to note that one of the advantages of drama is that it can be used in worship not just as an introduction to sermon topics, but also to raise awareness through using dialogue and visual aids, enabling congregations to relate to the topic or scripture being discussed.

Drama provides an opportunity for people to offer their gifts to God and to His Church and as such is an ideal way to bring a lot of people into ministry. That is not to say that all church members have a gift for acting. They don't! This is worth highlighting, as it is a major mistake to allow every individual to join a drama ministry in an acting capacity simply because they believe that they are called to do so. I am sometimes asked by individuals if they can join our puppet team as a puppeteer. Careful consideration of personal qualities sometimes points to the fact that they would not be suited to that ministry. I am sometimes reminded of an article that suggested that if you can't play a musical instrument you wouldn't be allowed to play in a worship band. So why do we accept everyone who asks to act in a drama ministry. There are plenty of other areas of drama that require many different skills. Prop building, painting, script writing, costume design, sewing and special effects, all provide opportunities for ministry. If you feel that someone is not suited to participate in an acting capacity, be sensitive to that person's calling and suggest tasks that would assist that individual to be able to contribute in some other useful way to the drama ministry.

Drama is a group ministry and like all group activities, can lead to uniting members of all ages within a church in all sorts of ways. Our own puppet ministry team has benefited in this respect. I continually see other examples of people coming together and relating to one another positively in many different ministry activities.

Finally, we must recognise the power of drama to reach so many different people in all sorts of situations and its ability to grab their attention. It is possible for well presented drama to encourage an audience to think more about the theme which it is portraying, simply because of the visual impression that it can make upon our senses. For example, there can be few who fail to stop and watch street theatre, if only for a few minutes. In that short time, the evangelistic drama ministry must make its impact on an individual, planting ideas that could motivate a thought process which leads to a first encounter with the message of Christ.

Who are we acting for?

Firstly we should not be presenting drama to simply satisfy a creative urge. All performances of creative arts in worship must have a clear objective and raison d'etre. This is particularly the case in drama, due to the vast variety of themes and methods of presentation available. Reasons for staging a sketch could be to illustrate a Gospel theme or Bible story, to challenge and provoke a response in the audience, or to invite and encourage a congregation to view a particular situation in a different light, or from a different perspective. This will of course have a great bearing on how we approach the selection of a sketch.

Not all sketches will be suitable for every audience, as Biblical knowledge, worship experience and cultural background will all have a bearing on selecting material, as well as the location or venue. Usually, the piece of drama will be a part of the overall act of worship, rather than a stand alone presentation. It is vital that everybody is aware of the content of the sketch, who it will involve, and how it will relate to the rest of worship. No matter how good a sketch or how talented the acting, direction and staging, drama is not a substitute for Biblical truth or sound teaching. It is a vehicle for teaching certainly, but should be used principally as preparation for preaching and teaching, based on Scripture.

First steps

Ambitious drama enthusiasts seek to build an energetic and committed team who will meet regularly for rehearsal and training, who then take to the road to spread the Good News at other churches, schools and on the streets. There are superb established drama teams that do this

> 'We should not be presenting drama to simply satisfy a creative urge'

successfully, such as the Riding Lights group, and also very successful and effective ministries which present and teach drama on a grand scale, such as that led by Steve Pederson at the Willow Creek Community Church in Illinois, USA. However, for most of us, drama ministry means presenting the occasional sketch at our home church. More ambitious teams may travel to other local churches and organisations, leading workshops at youth clubs and creative arts weekends. This vital ministry requires much hard work, rehearsal and inspiration in order to be effective. Once you are clear on your objectives, you will need to gather together a team of people with appropriate skills and begin to meet on a regular basis, ensuring that you will develop as a unit.

Even if you are to only present drama in worship on a single occasion, it is important to meet together a few times to get to know the script and adapt it where necessary. You may need to arrange for props and lighting, and of course, will need to rehearse. If you are intending to build a team that will present drama more frequently, then regular team meetings are vital to the development of the group, and in establishing and maintaining variety and credibility with those who will become your regular audience.

Sensitive, but strong leadership is required to develop any group activity. Those who lead drama groups need to be aware that a good sketch will be appreciated, but some congregations will be slow to respond. On the other hand, a bad sketch is likely to attract a lot of comment and can have a damaging effect upon the worship experience. It is for this reason that a leader must ensure that the team are well chosen for the sketch and have rehearsed it thoroughly. Simply assembling a group of your friends and giving them scripts to learn in the hope that they will make a passable attempt to get it right, will simply not do. Sadly, this is the case in many churches, and a piece of drama that could have been effective, is often performed enthusiastically, but ineptly. This impacts upon the congregation in a negative way as they quickly lose interest in badly performed drama. Children should be encouraged to take part in drama, but unless they are unusually gifted performers, they will usually be more effective presenting short and simple sketches.

Training and rehearsals

Some church drama teams will be fortunate enough to include actors who have been formally trained and no doubt those members will pass on the benefit of that training to others. In all probability, they will have inspired the team to begin its ministry in the first place. Most teams consist of enthusiasts who want to participate in ministry and enjoy acting. Whilst we should rejoice that people are willing to come forward in ministry, we must be careful to provide plenty of rehearsal and drama training exercises to ensure that each recruit becomes an effective member of the team.

In order for rehearsals to be successful, it is essential that they become much more than just times of hard work for the group. They should be occasions when team members can relax together and have some fun. It is important to recognise that everyone will appreciate an opportunity to share their own ideas and to bring a personal touch to their roles and to contribute to the overall project. Rehearsals should be enjoyed and the key to this is good advance planning. If challenging sketches are properly adapted to suit the venue, parts allocated to the appropriate actors, and staging and presentation well thought out, then the rehearsal is likely to run smoothly. The rehearsal time should be well planned, clearly structured and all team members kept fully informed of how and when they are to perform. Add to this heady combination, a few drama games and fun exercises to relax and lighten any tension, and the result will be a formula for really effective and worthwhile rehearsal. It is important to be aware of the clock at these times, as team members will not appreciate rehearsals that extend far beyond reasonable concentration spans.

Teams will find a format that is appropriate to them. The following is a suggested framework for rehearsal that fulfils the needs of most drama groups.

> **Opening prayer**
> **Relaxing warm up exercises**
> **Warm up theatre type game**
> **Rehearse sketches**
> **Feedback and discussion**
> **Refreshments and closing prayer**

Rehearsals will naturally help to bind the team together. Working towards a shared objective in an informal social setting often has that effect. However, rehearsals are also a time of creativity. There will be times when disagreements emerge based upon different artistic viewpoints. These are times that test team spirit and the man-management skills of the leader. It is important to give people space in these situations, both mentally and physically, working towards, and focusing upon common ground. A sensitive leader can defuse a potentially damaging situation, helping those involved to channel their thoughts in a positive manner towards a compromise. The problem may not disappear totally, but tension will evaporate, thus enabling the leader to steer the group towards solving the issue at a more appropriate time. Prayer both before and after rehearsals is a powerful ally in preventing tensions and aiding the healing process.

REHEARSAL WARM UP EXERCISES

It is worth spending time to warm-up with relaxation exercises. There are several variations on this theme. A useful starter is to encourage everyone to lie on their backs on the floor. Participants should begin by concentrating on their toes and focus on relaxing them. The idea is to gradually shift the focus up the body until every limb and muscle is relaxed. Many use this method to relax before going to sleep, but we don't want to go that far! A few minutes performing this exercise should relax the whole body and when followed by stretching and shaking exercises, will bring life into the muscles, gently toning them. It can be useful to accompany this toning with long 'oohs' and 'aahs' to loosen the vocal chords. It is important to maintain sufficient breath in your lungs to facilitate these vocals so that the sounds are not forced.

Mirror exercises are a great way of bonding the team and encouraging them to work together. Split the group into pairs and ask one partner to carry out a series of random movements that should be copied by their partner. First of all, a series of slow movements should be tried, progressing to pairs concentrating on a few simple actions, gradually increasing the tempo until this can be achieved at high speed. A little imagination will lead to several variations on these exercises. Try to use games that encourage participants to express a series of emotions or to portray characters from written instructions. The aim is to have a bit of fun whilst reducing tension, to relax and tone the muscles, and also to heighten concentration in order for the team to progress towards more demanding work.

Having warmed up your bodies you will need to tone the parts of you that are specifically needed for acting. Jim Custer and Bob Hoose of Jeremiah People, an American

> 'Prayer both before and after rehearsals is a powerful ally in preventing tensions and aiding the healing process'

drama ministry, described these as acting muscles, listing them as observation, memory, imagination and concentration. Drama games which develop these 'muscles' are invaluable as teaching tools for the group. For example, someone could be asked to present a sequence of actions or dialogue in the role of a child. Each successive group member memorises the movements and repeats them, each taking the role of a successively older character. There are variations on this theme such as taking the character of different animals or professions.

Story games stimulate the creative juices. One game familiar to many, is similar to the game of consequences. One person starts off with a sentence such as, 'the taxi driver was worried because he thought he glimpsed a gun under his passenger's jacket …..' The rest of the group take it in turns to continue the story, possibly adding appropriate movement or expression. It doesn't matter if the story becomes very confused or even nonsensical, provided the responses and links are imaginative and begin to involve drama skills.

I have personal experience of a beneficial game called 'scene changers.' This is a role-play game that relies upon inspiration, improvisation and spontaneity. A group of two or three, act out a short scene as gangsters. After a few lines of dialogue, one of the group has to find a credible way of leaving the scene. Immediately after that happens, another actor joins the scene and introduces a line of dialogue, changing the setting entirely. To a space station, for example, or a board room. You may wish to reverse this process and have a team member join the group to change the scene, prompting another to find a way of leaving. This is a challenging game and needs to be fully explained beforehand, giving a little time to the participants to think through the possibilities.

Newspaper and magazine articles provide dozens of opportunities for encouraging creative role play. I have used this technique successfully with young people drawing on topical news items. One group acts out the story whilst others work together to discover what the news item is about.

Once the team is thoroughly warmed up and in the right frame of mind, rehearsal of the drama sketch to be used can take place. Time should be spent reading and discussing the dialogue, agreeing entrances and exits, use of props, effects and scenery, pace and blocking. After working through rehearsals, the group leader should ask for feedback from the team in order that ideas can be shared and any misunderstandings cleared up. A short prayer time would be appropriate, possibly followed by a refreshments time, giving everyone time to wind down together.

Ways to communicate using drama

There are many forms of drama, including monologues, sketches, Bible stories and parable re-enactments, story narrations, song interpretations, or even complete productions of plays or musicals.

The monologue is a very powerful tool, but one of the hardest to do well. I have often marvelled at the acting skills of Thora Hird when she presents a monologue. I would recommend anyone who wishes to use this form of drama, to watch video footage of this superb actress, noting her delivery style. The monologue is of course a single actor affair, and as such does not involve the need to organise group rehearsals. However, you are well advised to ask another team member to watch you, as they will probably be able to offer constructive criticism. Video is a very useful tool for self analysis in this respect.

Sketches that reflect contemporary living are a very popular way of presenting Scriptural themes and discipleship. Presenting snapshots of the challenges and problems that confront us, through drama, is a way of involving the congregation. Many will be able to identify with the real life situations they see portrayed, which they may have personally had to face in the past, or can envisage facing in the future. Most contemporary sketches will discuss these challenges and pose questions. Some will even suggest the answer, but principally it is the role of the actors to prepare the congregation for the teaching that follows the sketch. The ensuing sketch illustrates the point.

I developed an old story into the following sketch, which reflects the frustration and anger that Christians sometimes feel when their lives take a dramatic turn for the worse after a long time spent serving the Lord. It is at these times that some feel cheated and hurt, because they have given unselfishly, and then appear to have been dealt a harsh unwarranted blow. The sketch gives the audience the opportunity to identify with the characters, the situation, and delivers the Good News at the end. The way is then prepared for the preacher to develop the themes of heaven and God's promise to His people.

You are invited to use the sketch freely in your own ministry if you feel it would be appropriate. It is written for two main characters and a minister. John and Madge have just returned to Britain after a life spent in mission overseas. Madge is terminally ill. The setting is a scruffy boarding house near to an international airport. The only props required are two telephones and perhaps a couple of chairs.

IT'S NOT FAIR

JOHN: It just isn't fair! Look at this place. I wouldn't house a dog in here. Bloomin' scruffy hotel.

MADGE: Oh John. You are depressed aren't you. You've been moaning ever since we got on the 'plane in Bonga Bonga. What is the matter with you?

JOHN: I'm sorry I sound so miserable Madge, but I just don't think I can take much more. Just look at us and how we've ended up.

MADGE: Oh John. It's not so bad is it? The Lord has done great things at the mission. We've left it in good hands and soon we'll be back in Leicestershire among friends.

JOHN: I really don't know how you are always able to see the good in everything. I'm afraid that my cup always seems half empty, whilst yours always seems half full. How do you do it?

MADGE: Oh. It's easy. I just look around me and I can see all of God's creation everywhere that I look. Just think of all that He has blessed us with over the years.

JOHN: Well, yes. There have been good times of course, but just look at us now. We have just spent 30 years at the mission, in appalling conditions most of the time, and arrived here with no-one to meet us at the airport. No home to go to, no job and no pension. What do you say to that?

MADGE: I say 'Yes, that's true but God will look after us. He always has done.'

JOHN: Sometimes He seems to look after the wrong people. Take that footballer who was on our 'plane for example. There was an army of fans waiting, a brass band and dozens of TV people waiting to greet him and he's only been away for a few days on holiday. What has he done to deserve that homecoming?

MADGE: You're out of touch John. He's a gifted international footballer who's going to sign for Leicester City for £30,000 a week. Why, as well as kicking lumps out of anybody who comes within ten yards of him, he can do joined up writing… and even do up his own boot laces as well.

JOHN: Huh! Just compare old 'Golden Boots' achievements with what we have done. With God's help, we've built two schools, a church and a hospital, and have nothing to show for it except malaria and a few grateful villagers… Not to mention the fact that you picked up this dreadful leukaemia illness thing. It's just not fair Madge. Where's God in all that?

MADGE: I'm sure there's a purpose to it. We don't always know why God does what He does. And you have to remember that often, God is not responsible for what happens. He's not responsible for the choices that we make, is He?

JOHN: Well, no, but I just don't think that it's right that we have nothing after all these years and that footballer gets a welcome like that, not to mention his £30,000 a week for the next three years.

MADGE: You've got to get things in perspective John. I think you'd better take time out to speak to God about this. I'm sure that He'll sort it out for you.

JOHN: OK. Maybe you're right. I'm sorry Madge, I shouldn't be moaning at you. We haven't got that much time left together have we? I'll spend a few minutes on my own to pray about it and see if I can get a few things straight in my head.

MADGE: Right. You go ahead. I have a 'phone call to make.

Exit John.

Enter Minister side stage

Madge picks up the telephone and dials a number.

Minister hears ring and picks up the telephone.

MINISTER: Hello. Reverend Rogers here…………..Hello Madge….. How lovely to hear from you. You said that you'd call as soon as you got back ……. Sorry to hear about   ………you know …….the illness and all.

MADGE: There's no need to worry about that. I've had a good life, but I need to make some arrangements about the funeral and thought I would ring you whilst John's out of the way. He gets upset about these things you know.

MINISTER: Well yes, I can understand that. How can I help?

MADGE: I want to be buried with my Bible in one hand and a fork in the other, and I want you to explain to the folk at the funeral why I wanted that done.

MINISTER: Why, of course Madge, anything you ask, but I'm not sure that I understand. I can see why you would want your Bible, but the fork? Why on earth would you want a fork?

MADGE: Well, you see, before we went on mission, we went to lots of fundraising teas and social events at different churches and I was always so pleased when one of the ladies collected our dinner plates and said, 'Keep your fork, dear, you'll need it later'

MINISTER: Why was that then?

MADGE: Oh, that's simple. You only needed to keep your fork if the pudding was going to be really special. Not just jelly or fruit cake, but something really special like a chocolate gateaux……….It meant that the best thing was yet to come.

MINISTER: Ah! I see, yes… The best is yet to come. And that's how you see your future then Madge?

MADGE: Yes. That's how I see the future for all Christians. The best is yet to come for all of us, and I want you to explain that to the folk that come to the funeral.

MINISTER: Thank you for calling me, Madge. I'll be pleased to do that for you and I look forward to seeing you soon. 'Bye!

MADGE: Goodbye Reverend.

Reverend puts down 'phone and exits.

Madge puts down 'phone.

John enters front stage again.

MADGE: Well! You look a lot happier. Did you sort it out with God in your prayer time?

JOHN: Yes, but more like God sorted it out for me.

MADGE: How's that then?

JOHN: Well, He explained that the footballer has had his homecoming party, but probably won't have a lot more to look forward to when his playing days are over, and the fans don't worship him anymore.

MADGE: OK, but how does that help you?

JOHN: God also said that we're not home yet......For us, the best is yet to come.

Both exit.

Sketches that use just two or three characters are suited to most churches, as many only have a handful of people willing and able to perform drama. Fortunately, there are plenty of sketches available for small drama groups to try, and of course rehearsal is easier with fewer actors to consider. That is not to say that more elaborate productions shouldn't be tackled. Far from it. Churches that have larger numbers of talented actors are able to produce more complicated and sometimes full length plays and musicals. These are sometimes more effective in reaching out to many in the local community, simply because a full length production is often perceived to be more of an attraction. Larger productions sometimes stretch the resources of a single congregation, which then leads to a cooperative effort. The core drama group then works together with others, both inside and outside of the Church. This was the objective of Rob Frost's *Hopes and Dreams* Millennium project which inspired hundreds of communities all over the United Kingdom, to work together to produce the multi-media musical during the year 2000.

BIBLE STORIES AND PARABLES

The narrated Bible story enacted by a small Sunday School group or youth group, is a regular feature in many churches and has much to commend it. For example, a story which is narrated without dialogue enables children and adults to act without having to learn lines. One of the problems is that many group leaders seem to believe that these productions will miraculously be alright on the night even though the actors have only rehearsed for ten minutes before the service. Rehearsal for this relatively simple task is still vital.

The Bible has a rich store of dramatic material, as many of the books of both the Old and New Testament contain exciting and thought provoking situations. All too many youth group and Sunday school leaders regularly push two or three reluctant six year olds onto centre stage with crumpled scripts in their hands and towels on their heads. This may seem endearing for a short time, but it is not dynamic drama. Congregations quickly tire of this sort of effort, (as do the children involved) no matter how well meaning. Any message or relevance will be quickly lost if Wayne or Sharon crumble into tears when they forget their lines, or leave the stage to go to the toilet! I strongly believe that we should encourage everyone to use the gifts with which they have been blessed. However, we must remember that we are discussing using these gifts to enhance corporate worship. Therefore, we should be offering to God, and to the congregation who have entrusted us with the task of preparing drama for worship, our very best efforts. Bible stories and parables are superb vehicles for drama, but please, please, produce them properly. Allow sufficient time to prepare the actors and those who lead worship and intend preaching on the theme. This will ensure a professional production with

'Many group leaders seem to believe that these productions will miraculously be alright on the night even though the actors have only rehearsed for ten minutes before the service'

good continuity. It is good practice to ensure that the preacher has sight of any drama scripts that will be used, so that they can readily pick up on key points in the dialogue.

There are some excellent resources available to those of us who wish to use Bible stories in drama. As well as the many Biblical drama books to be found in Christian book shops, there are other good tools such as the Dramatised Bible produced by The Bible Society. This presents most of the situations and events in Scripture as sketches, breaking them up into narration and dialogue. There are also good quality audio tapes and CD's of Bibles that contain dramatic narration and dialogue, as well as excellent sound effects and music. Congregations should be familiar with most Bible stories. Many can be brought to life by drama and made more interesting, bringing relevance and dynamism to the Bible in a very visual way.

Besides the traditional forms of drama, there are some other very creative ways of using drama skills, such as song interpretation and dramatising rhymes or poetry from different cultures and traditions, including rap. These may at first glance appear quite simple. There are fewer lines to learn unless the actor decides to recite the rhyme or sing the rap, rather than acting the role whilst the piece is narrated by another. However, poems, rhymes and raps all require precise timing and as such need a lot of rehearsal. The extra work involved is well worth the effort, as rap and rhyme are popular and should be well received by an audience. This type of drama should provide a stimulating challenge to any group.

DIRECTION – PUTTING IT ALL TOGETHER

Someone in the group needs to exercise overall control over the production, assuming the role of director. This person needs to provide structure and guidance in achieving the team's objectives, encouraging the team to pull together in order to produce an effective piece of drama - and to have a bit of fun whilst doing so. Steve Pederson of Willow Creek Drama Group, rightly said that the real power of drama lies in a simple story with believable characters. Whilst we must rely mostly upon our choice of sketch and writing style to ensure this, the director and actors have the responsibility of bringing the sketch to life. We can do this is in several ways, but basically there are two approaches.

> The real power of drama lies in a simple story with believable characters

The first approach to enlivening a sketch involves building sets and props, using full sound, lighting and special effects. There can be few churches that are blessed with the space, resources, talent and will to produce regular dramatic offerings on a large scale. Therefore, the permanent theatre stage environment is a luxury few can experience. If you are fortunate enough to enjoy these facilities, then it will pay to bring in professional help in order to set up an effective and appropriate creative sound and lighting environment.

The second approach is much more simple. It is commonly used in our churches, involving minimum props and costumes, no special effects and just adequate sound and lighting. This approach leaves much to be achieved by the actors, so it is worth investing in a few basic tools such as microphones and lights.

Props and effects should be used to enhance drama and to convey mood or meaning. Some larger productions tend to over use special effects, thus detracting from the central core of the drama. Quality acting can enable you to dispense with props altogether, however it is helpful to employ some simple effects which assist in the understanding of the setting. For example, a few chairs arranged in various ways can give the impression of airline seats, the back seat of a car or a row of seats in a boat. A lamp upon a table can indicate a lounge. Replace the lamp with a couple of washing powder containers or cereal packets and the set has instantly been transformed to suggest a kitchen. The congregation will readily use their imagination, and drama groups need to recognise this fact when putting a sketch together.

A common mistake when presenting drama is trying to say too much, too often and too quickly. This heavy handed approach, where playwrights attempt to preach in the play, is usually inappropriate. The most effective drama is that which draws the audience into the situation, providing them with a hook with which they can identify. Different responses and reactions within the sketch will initiate thought processes in the minds of the audience. This has a liberating effect on the actors and writers, allowing them to fully develop the characters and the plot, usually resulting in a more credible, life like situation. It is the worship leader who then has the task of developing the theme by drawing upon the life situations in the play. Identified reactions and responses of characters can be compared, and teaching introduced which the congregation can consider and reflect upon. The message is re-enforced by the drama, serving to provide a visual memory tag to the preaching. Thus, the drama and the preaching work in tandem. The drama illustrates the life situation and the preacher provides teaching and Scripture interpretation.

A drama group must seek to present these life situations in a credible manner. Sketches should not take on the characteristics of pantomime or melodrama unless they are specifically intended to do so. This is ensured by developing the characters during the sketch, and is achieved through sensitive, skilful writing. A good script needs to be complimented by effective direction and competent dialogue delivery. It is worth noting at this point that sketches should depict a range of life situations, including both the negative and the positive challenges that we encounter in daily life. Whilst it is recognised that there are many broken people with a great deal of problems to solve, one of the tasks of the worship leader is to provide an uplifting experience for the congregation. It is vital that the Good News is preached in our churches in every act of worship. Certainly, all congregation members have their problems. Our preachers and drama groups should address these, though ensuring a balance.

BLOCKING

Blocking is the technical term attached to the process of organising the movement and position of the actors during the sketch. The director should know the script well and read it through a few times before making the first adjustments to the dialogue. Most teams will adapt scripts to suit their own style and this is a legitimate exercise. It is good practice to mark up the script with what you perceive to be the required blocking, positions and movement. These may be adapted following subsequent rehearsal. These initial notes should only be used for guidance as it is best to allow rehearsals to develop, giving the actors the opportunity to interpret the movement and positioning. The director has the advantage of viewing from a different angle and perspective, and should use this in order to adapt and improve the production. Rehearsals should ensure correct and uninterrupted lines of sight, with dramatic emphasis through movement. Ultimately, the piece should visually draw the audience into the heart of the action.

Lines of sight are vital, and actors masking one another is a common fault. A brilliantly delivered speech by the actor playing David, will not be appreciated if he is completely hidden from view by the actor playing Goliath. Blocking is not just about lines of sight, but also how actors use their bodies and movement for expression. A test of good blocking would be to act out the sketch without dialogue, relying totally upon expression and movement in order to sense the meaning of the sketch. Certain conventions have developed in theatre, such as never turn your back on an audience, and always make hand gestures with your upstage arm. (away from the audience) These guidelines are for the most part, good practice. However, it is important to be aware that they are not the only way to approach stage direction. On some occasions, it may be better to face away from the audience or to make gestures with opposite hands. This depends on whether the required action is a natural one or not. There are times when an upstage stance should be employed, although ensuring audible dialogue.

The most important factor in deciding upon movement on stage is whether a particular action is necessary; in other words, studying what motivates the movement. For example, a knock at the door will usually initiate the turning of heads towards the sound, and movement from one of the actors to open the door. This is because the movement is automatic, obvious and correct. Most of the time, actions are not automatic. Therefore, it is up to the actors and the director to arrive at a position whereby the movement fits the scene, through clearly defined motivation. For example, consider a very strong character with bold dialogue, arguing with another much weaker character. It would be visually inappropriate for the stronger character to be submissive in pose, with the weaker one delivering his lines aggressively, staring his opposite number in the face.

Nervous fidgeting can often ruin a good sketch. Any movement, whether necessary or not, draws the audience to it, focusing their attention on the one who is moving, and thus away from the speaker. This is a common problem with novices and children. The distraction does not have to be a major one. An actor who inappropriately scratches their head at one side of the stage, draws the audience away from an important piece of acting at the other side, especially when there is a pause in the dialogue.

Most movement in dramatic productions tends to be parallel to the front of the stage. The director can make movement much more interesting by employing diagonal movement. This is particularly useful to consider when

> *'A brilliantly delivered speech by the actor playing David, will not be appreciated if he is completely hidden from view by the actor playing Goliath'*

attempting to give depth to a set. Diagonal movement can be used to imply more space, and also to emphasise dialogue when one actor crosses the line of sight to another actor, to whom their dialogue is directed. The following few short lines demonstrate the point. Imagine an anxious parent greeting a teenager who has returned late from a party.

PARENT: There you are. I was worried about you. What kept you?

TEENAGER: What do you care?

PARENT: That's unfair. I've been worried sick, especially after that awful night when your brother was injured in that car crash.

TEENAGER: I'm sorry Mum, I didn't think … I'm sorry.

This short cameo could be presented with both actors static and facing one another, but this would result in a rather sterile and shallow scene. The emotions would be demonstrated more effectively if the opening line were to be delivered from a seated position, with the response given by the teenager as he moves across and away from the parent in a disinterested manner. The parent then stands up, raising her voice as she shouts out 'That's unfair,' angered by the lack of concern. She then moves half way towards the teenager, lowering her voice as she speaks the line about the crash. The teenager realises the mistake, turns and goes back to the parent to apologise, perhaps re-enforcing the contrition with a gentle touch. The scene has now been enhanced by the movement and is given depth.

Too much movement or rigidity can be a hindrance, and it is important to strike a balance. Experienced actors will have an awareness of, and a feeling for the appropriate amount of movement. In the absence of experienced team members, it is up to the director to eliminate any unnecessary action. A leader who is familiar with the script and has prepared an outline of how the sketch should be staged, will be able to offer advice when called upon, thus instilling confidence into the acting team.

Often, a sketch can stand or fall on significant moments, especially when storylines are well known to the audience. The timing and pace of a sketch will have a significant effect on the overall impact. Some sketches call for punchy and fast moving action, whilst others require a more studied and careful approach. It will not take too much variation from the required pace to dramatically reduce the impact of the sketch. More often than not, a sketch will be performed too slowly. This is partly due to an inherent expectation of the audience, based on television and cinematic productions. These tend to tear along at a cracking pace. Not surprisingly, we are easily distracted when faced with a slower moving piece of drama. It is important to remember that lines should be delivered succinctly and precisely. However, a piece of drama should be as true to life as possible, and life is rarely leisurely these days.

Correct pace is important, but with the dynamic nature of drama, variation in pace will often be beneficial. It is a mistake to allow a piece to fall into a rhythm which dulls the senses. Adequate rehearsal should determine appropriate action and movement, providing time to refine the performance, as each cameo in the sketch is worked upon. Eventually, the final run through will be performed, and after some adjustment, will be ready for the stage.

Sets, sound and lighting

For most drama groups, the stage will be any open area directly in front of the pews or chairs, preferably raised for better viewing and hopefully not too cluttered. Many sketches will only form part of an act of worship, therefore actors may have to work around a communion table, communion rail, pulpit, lecterns, musical instruments and all manner of other equipment associated with a church building. It is certainly useful to clear some of the easily moved tables and chairs. However, it is important to be mindful of people's sensitivities in this area. Drama groups must be careful to be respect the views of those who feel uncomfortable with the sanctuary being used for creative arts. It is better to gradually introduce a hesitant church to a different way of utilising resources.

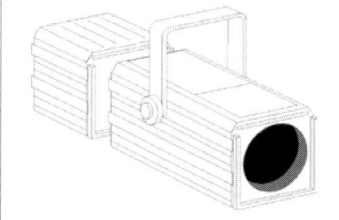

All groups must learn to adapt, whether working in a purpose built theatre or a cramped worship area. Groups must be flexible and aim to achieve the best worship possible, with whatever resources they have. It is not too expensive or too difficult to purchase and use some simple lighting and sound equipment. A pair of strategically placed spotlights or par 56 cans on T-bars, will enable groups to add mood, atmosphere, focus and emphasis to a piece of drama. The very act of switching on lights at the beginning, and switching off at the end of a sketch, immediately focuses a congregation's attention to the action, providing a clear start and finish. Using one or two coloured lighting gels will create a setting of evening, sunrise or twilight. A more sophisticated set-up with a lighting controller will allow for dimming and spotlighting. This is especially effective in adding impact and focus to a fairly static two handed sketch, which may take place at a table for example.

In order to ensure that a message is received, you have to be heard, so it is important to coach actors to project their voices. In larger rooms it may well be necessary to amplify actors' voices, employing the use of lapel radio microphones or free-standing equipment designed for the stage, such as a wide angle condensers or conference plate microphones. These should be as unobtrusive as possible. A discreetly placed microphone can make a world of difference to the effectiveness of a sketch. Note that microphones are not selective and can pick up unwanted sounds from on and off the set – so be careful!

Simple backdrops such as plain or painted fabric, sturdy wooden props made for a particular sketch, such as a painted boat or car façade can transform a routine piece of drama into very effective theatre. Groups may also wish to use video or slide projectors to provide backdrops or even complimentary visual and sound effects.

STREET THEATRE

Generally, it is best to keep props to a minimum in a church setting as you will usually be restricted by the available space. Although space is not usually a problem with street theatre, props should be kept to an absolute minimum for reasons of transport and setting up. Interesting or unusual props can be useful in attracting an audience. Street theatre is a difficult art to master, and one can usually be certain of reaching many in the potential audience, that on the whole, are not familiar with the Gospel.

In street theatre, striking costumes and face paints mark a group of actors, highlighting the difference to others in your surroundings. It is important to establish this distinction and your credentials as a drama group, or you may be mistaken for some one simply acting the fool! The costume also helps to attract an audience. It is quite pointless performing if there is no-one to hear or see the message. Therefore, it is vital to choose a site where there will be plenty of people around. However, trying to present drama at a football stadium on match day, or any venue where there are too many competing distractions, will prove fairly fruitless. You should also have adequate space in which to perform, remembering that a small crowd has the potential to become a fairly large one. Passers by will not thank you for blocking their right of way. Traders will also be aggrieved if access to their shops or stalls is prevented. It can be very helpful to mark out a viewing and performing area with beacons or tape. Be sure to ask permission beforehand and also tell the local police. This will save you the embarrassment of being moved on. Not a very good witness!

Some street workers will perform at the same site on a regular basis. As a result, they will often attract a regular audience as they become a familiar sight to those who use the venue in their normal course of business or leisure. Those who visit the Covent Garden district of London will know how a street performing tradition can develop. The aspiring street drama group must define themselves and their presentation as a piece of theatre, by using costume and props effectively. Well placed signs, posters and symbols can also add to this perception. Sound amplification is very effective and should be used if you have access to outdoor microphones and speakers. It is important however, to realise that actions speak louder than words in street work, therefore, any dialogue should be kept to a minimum. The emphasis should be very much on mime, gesture and over the top acting. Slapstick comedy is an effective tool in this respect, remembering of course, that a clear Gospel message must be inherent in the presentation.

When performing in the street, it is important to make effective use of the time when a crowd has gathered. It is a fact that audiences will quickly disappear if you try to preach a sermon. Whilst a sketch will work in tandem with preaching in church; out on the streets the objective must be for the sketch to have impact with a clear, simple message that can be conveyed from within the drama. The drama will have to be short and fast paced, with few pauses. The message must be simple and repeated in different ways throughout the sketch, in order to register with a passing audience and for it to be remembered.

Finally, street theatre must have a simple message which assumes that the audience has little or no knowledge of scripture. Plain language is essential as religious phrases such as 'saved by the blood' and 'justified by faith' may be totally meaningless to many of the audience. Brave souls who tackle this very rewarding challenge will be taking Biblical teaching back to its roots, emulating the guilds which acted out parables in the Middle Ages.

Workshops

Workshops are a superb way of introducing drama to novices and experienced actors alike. In most churches, workshops are used by youth leaders or drama teachers to introduce people to ways of using drama in order to express themselves. Time spent working together to explore drama can be satisfying and can help participants to understand more about technique, also teaching new insights into familiar stories from Scripture.

Workshops should be challenging and enjoyable. Material that will stretch the imagination of the participants should be interspersed with one or two simple drama games and exercises that help to relax everyone. It is important that everyone participating in the workshops has a clear idea of what is expected of them at all times, as some may lose sight of their objectives and become anxious in case they are getting it wrong.

It is important to start the session with a brief talk about the object of the session. The following example is designed to teach the group how to tackle a well-known Bible story using drama, at the same time gaining a deeper insight into the characters and the situation. This technique can be used for most Bible stories, and in this example, is applied to the very well known parable of the Prodigal Son. Role play will be used to deepen our understanding, providing every participant with the opportunity to discover more about their own designated character, and that of others in the group.

One or two warm up games should be introduced at this point. Choose something simple and familiar and not too physically demanding. Start with something gentle such as 'Feel and guess.' This is a game whereby small everyday objects are placed in numbered fabric bags and sewn closed. Each group member pins a bag onto one arm, and the object of the game is for everyone to feel every bag and guess the contents. This is a simple way of getting everyone to talk to each other, especially if not everyone is acquainted. Follow this game with a few loosening and warm-up exercises and a creative activity such as mirrors - the game of copying partner's actions as a mirror image, described earlier.

The parable (Luke 15:11-32) should now be introduced, read aloud, and then role cards handed to each of the participants. Each role card should briefly describe the character from the story. The number of cards will depend upon the size of the group. Besides the main characters of the father and two sons, use the newfound friends that squandered the prodigal son's money, as additional characters. The father's hired hands, the pig farmer, and even the pigs and the unfortunate fatted calf would all have a perspective on the story and offer good opportunities for creativity. Members should be encouraged to spend a few moments thinking about the characteristics of their role, and could confirm this by describing themselves briefly to a partner. The partner should then ask various questions so that both become familiar with their own character, and the way in which they think. After a few minutes, the partners should swap over, so that the other partner describes their character and is questioned. This first exercise should take place as if the characters are describing themselves before the story begins to unfold.

Now is the time to introduce the storyline. The prodigal son should be persuaded by the leader to look to expand his horizons and ask his father for his inheritance. All the characters, now aware of his intentions, stay in role and split into groups to discuss the possible consequences, including how the son's decision may impact upon them personally. After some time discussing these possibilities, the story should be acted out and this can be done in various ways. Mime could be accompanied by a narration, or a simple script. It is possible to simply read the story, stopping at appropriate points to allow the relevant characters to talk to each other about their present situation. For example, the prodigal son could discuss his feelings with the friends that deserted him after his money ran out. Alternatively, the two sons could discuss their response after the Prodigal Son's return. The fatted calf may also wish to have the opportunity to air its views, offering a fresh perspective on the affair!

Whether you discuss the issues during or after the

narration, it is important for each character to offer their opinion on the development of the story, and its effect upon them. It can be challenging to change the historical setting, moving the timeline, as it is interesting to see how the characters adapt when placed in a more modern setting. Finish off the session with an informal group discussion over refreshments.

Sketches – sourcing and writing

Choosing an appropriate sketch varies from easy to very difficult when trying to find a piece that suits your needs and style. There are dozens of scripts available in books and even more on the Internet on Christian drama sites. A glance at the resources guide at the back of this book will provide you with plenty of starting points and suggestions. There is simply no substitute for the hard work of reading as many script books as you can, unless you have the time, talent, and will to write your own.

Script writing is an immensely rewarding, but sometimes frustrating task. I would encourage everyone to at least attempt to write a drama. You may surprise yourself, and others and discover hidden talents. Writing scripts must be a labour of love. It is usually very hard work, and there are so many good scripts available to you, that if you find you are not enjoying the writing, it is probably better to keep your sanity and to rely upon others to write them for you. If you are determined to write, and prepared for the constructive criticism that is inevitably part of the creative process, then you may find the following guidelines helpful.

First of all, you must determine whom you are writing for? Your audience may be your own local church, a youth group, or for street theatre. The age of your audience determines their attention span, your approach, and how you handle the script and dialogue. A sketch should be succinct, covering the subject adequately without too much embellishment, in order to retain the audience's attention. Most scripts should fit into the framework of two to eight minutes, with the majority between three and five. Your audience will to some extent also determine your subject matter, especially if you are trying to convey a message regarding their particular situation. Be aware that the best scripts are usually written from one's own life experiences or at least drawn from situations with which you are

> *It can be challenging to change the historical setting, moving the timeline, as it is interesting to see how the characters adapt when placed in a more modern setting*

familiar. Writing about areas that you feel deeply about, will often result in a more sensitive piece, full of passion and sensitivity.

Most sketches used in church tend to be written for two or three actors, and are always popular, and perhaps a little easier to write. However many characters that you employ, the essence of most good drama is friction and conflict. This may take the form of gentle disagreement or simply an exchange of slightly opposed views, or may be a violent and aggressive confrontation. Soap operas are so popular for the simple reason that they are overflowing with confrontation, usually about relationships. Conflict need not be restricted to visible or tangible characters, as sometimes tension arises between cultures, or as a result of a clash of ethics or spiritual concerns.

Subtle and humorous confrontation is possibly the most effective format, such as that presented by situation comedy. Very good examples of this type of sketch are the *Eb and Flo* series of sketches. These portray a suburban middle-aged couple who attend their local church. Eb is a well meaning, misguided type of chap who uses his Bible as a safe haven for his lottery ticket, spending the first part of each service correcting the spelling mistakes in the notices. Flo, his long suffering wife, is forever correcting him and guiding him back to the straight and narrow. Characters such as these can provide members of a congregation with scenes similar to their own situations, providing the opportunity to offer a series of drama presentations, where the characters can be seen to develop week by week.

Story lines should be credible to make an impact, as the impossible can seem difficult to comprehend. Consider some films which move way beyond the limits of our imagination. The usual effect is to encourage us to discard the film and treat it as trivial and irrelevant.

The most important part of any sketch is of course the dialogue, which must be presented as it would be spoken. Most people speak to each other in clearly defined sound bytes. We also prefer and use language that is suited to our environment, and this needs to be consistently carried through drama sketches. I have seen so many scripts written for young people, set in a school common room, where the conversation flows quite naturally around homework, the local football team or boy/girl relationships, using contemporary street or teen language. Suddenly, quite out of context, one of the characters quotes a verse from Ecclesiastes or Habakkuk to make a point. This is quite incongruous and has the effect of jarring the senses, immediately putting question marks in the minds of the audience, as the situation is not credible. Teenagers simply don't speak like that.

Finally, we must consider the plot, which should have a clearly defined beginning and ending. The usual method is to set out the nature of the characters and the direction of the plot at the beginning, through description of the background and environment through the dialogue, either implicitly or explicitly. The core of the plot, or contradictory views are expressed and expounded, each character winning and losing points of the argument whilst gradually building tension to a peak. The climax of the play is reached, the crucial points made, and the plot brought to an end with a fairly swift, seamless winding down. This is not always the case of course, and there are variations upon this format, however this framework has proved to be successful. The competent writer will not present an excess of words, may surprise and even sometimes shock audiences, always writing honestly and with integrity. When re-writing, or updating stories from the Bible, it is vital to keep the essence of Scripture intact, holding on to the Biblical truth contained in the original story.

Script writing is a complex process and the first draft is seldom the best. The wise writer will quickly accept re-drafting as a necessary task in the process. It is good practice to give the script to someone that you trust, to offer advice, constructive criticism and sometimes a shoulder to cry on. I gained immense benefit from the help of Michelle Beaumont, a priceless friend who spent hours poring over and editing this book. This is vital to the creative writing process as it is all too easy to miss points or wander away from the focus. An independent eye can quickly put you back on track.

COPYRIGHT

Most of us use sketches that have been written by others. It is important to respect the copyright as defined in each book. Most authors and publishers will outline the copyright conditions and virtually all Christian writers are pleased to offer you their work for worship. It is a matter of courtesy to acknowledge the authorship of others when performing their work, and is also much appreciated.

> 'When re-writing, or updating stories from the Bible, it is vital to keep the essence of Scripture intact, holding on to the Biblical truth contained in the original story'

CREATIVE ARTS IN WORSHIP

Mime covers a very broad canvas that eliminates the spoken word, occasionally uses music and dance, and is linked to both the theatre and the circus. It is a dramatic art form that has been used for centuries, which is finally beginning to have an impact on todays' Church.

Chapter Four
Mime

Silent for a long time!

Many writers have tried to define mime and most have found it difficult to arrive at a full definition in a few words. This is because mime is an attempt to communicate emotions, thought processes and stories by creating illusion, through movement, gesture and facial expression. Mime covers a very broad canvas that eliminates the spoken word, occasionally uses music and dance, and is linked to both the theatre and the circus. It is a dramatic art form that has been used for centuries, which is finally beginning to have an impact on today's Church.

Mime was used thousands of years ago as part of ceremonial ritual, celebrating religious festivals, harvest and battle. Examples of this can still be seen in primitive cultures that survive today. Mime developed into a way of portraying religious and moral themes, reaching its height in Italy in the Commedia dell'arte improvisation theatre. It is from this point, in the 18th century that some of the famous names in mime began to emerge. Classical mime possibly began with an illiterate actor, John Rich, who was compelled to act in silence because of his awkward speech and illiteracy. Working under the stage name of Lun, he transformed the art of mime into a totally silent spectacle that has developed into today's modern form.

French artistes have been very influential in mime. Deburau, Rouffe, Batiste and Decroux introduced characterisations, new illusions and techniques that are still used today. Marcel Marceau is probably the name that most would associate with mime. He is one of the very few who have gained recognition outside of theatrical circles. His techniques are used as a basis for study the world over and all aspiring mimes would do well to gain access to his work through books and video.

Stars from the world of early cinema, such as Laurel and Hardy, Charlie Chaplin, Harpo Marx, and more recently, Jim Carey, may not be instantly associated with mime. However, the gestures, expressions and actions employed by such actors are very good examples of how silent movement can be totally expressive and effectively communicate ideas and feelings.

SILENCE IN CHURCH!

The same accusations of immorality and misplaced use of satire, made by the Establishment against drama, were also aimed at mime. As a result, mime was banned from worship for many years. Drama has recovered to a degree, but mime has not fared so well. Today, mime in worship is making a comeback through such ministries as that of Todd and Marilyn Farley, Steve Murray and Rob Lacey. These artistes use their considerable talents in performing and teaching mime and drama.

Mime is a very visual art form, and visual imagery is vital to our understanding of our own environment and that of God's creation. As worship leaders we have a responsibility to enable our worshipping congregations to express their spirituality through their emotions. It is important that we are able to demonstrate how common emotions, trauma, hopes and dreams, are shared by all. If we can help people to realise that they are not alone in their despair, in their doubts, and their vulnerability, and that they share these experiences with others, then we are helping them to begin to come to terms with those feelings. Mime has a vital role to play in this respect, having the power to assist people in identifying with these shared emotions. Feelings can be expressed in a very moving and vivid way by the experienced mime, who will exaggerate the emotions, placing more emphasis upon them, rather than upon action or movement.

Many people remember more from visual presentations, rather than from isolated, orally given information. We have a responsibility to communicate God's Word through visual means as well as oral, thus reaching those who will not, or are not able to hear. Simple gestures can convey complex ideas, and do not necessarily have to be used in isolation. For example, my wife Suzanne learnt elementary signing at evening classes and is able to accompany several songs that we use in our puppet ministry. Some of the most complimentary and encouraging feedback from those who have seen this ministry in action, relates to this visual sign language. People often tell us that the words of the songs take on a new and deeper dimension as a result of the signing. After all, signing at its very basic level, is a means of communication that could be loosely classed as mime.

The many books that contain the liturgy of our faith testify to the fact that we rely heavily on words in our churches. These traditions have value, but we live in an age of fast moving technology. Communications expertise is now at the cutting edge. The visual image is recognised as the most effective way of promoting and marketing a product. Church leaders need to exploit and develop visual techniques in order to promote and market our own product, the Gospel of Christ. There is certainly a place for the written and spoken word. However I believe that it is absolutely vital that worship leaders present our message using modern visual aids. Congregations will then feel that the church is relevant and dynamic. The evangelist has a vision that souls can be won for Christ through mission. Mime has a role to play in that vision and in that mission. God's Word doesn't change, but our means of communicating it must, so that congregations will be challenged and kept interested.

Most Christians have no problems with the use of

> '*We have a responsibility to communicate God's Word through visual means as well as oral, thus reaching those who will not, or are not able to hear*'

visual symbols. Images such as the Cross, dove, palm leaves, Baptism, praying hands and so forth, are common in our churches, especially on banners. These all help to enhance our understanding of the Christian message. Consider the vivid imagery in the Bible. Most of us who were told Bible stories as children, will remember pictures of Daniel in the lion's den, Jonah and the big fish, Samson straining at the pillars of the temple and Jesus staggering through Jerusalem under the weight of the Cross. These lead me to conclude that mime, with its plethora of visual imagery, is a very effective dramatic tool that is available to worship leaders. When discussing these issues, I often recall the words of an elderly preacher who loved to use drama in worship. He impressed upon me that Jesus would have used thousands of words, teaching and preaching to thousands of people. However, the words of Jesus recorded in the Bible fill only a handful of pages. We are probably influenced more by what He did, than by what He said. His words contain riches that speak to us through the centuries. But it is His actions, not His words that are the key to His message. These are good reasons for using mime and drama to compliment the spoken word in worship.

> *The words of Jesus recorded in the Bible fill only a handful of pages. We are probably influenced more by what He did, than by what He said*

Quiet – there's a mime about!

The principal purpose of any Christian ministry is to promote and communicate the Gospel of Christ. Each creative artist in ministry seeks to do this in a uniquely challenging and entertaining way. This is a problem for some, who feel that entertainment is not appropriate in Church. I disagree. We are encouraged in the Bible to have joy in our hearts, and if a piece of drama, mime or music fills us with joy during the process of teaching about the Kingdom of heaven, then I view that as a positive step. Mime can be very entertaining, but it has many more important aspects to it.

In order to preach our message, we must first seek to attract the attention of our audience. There is little doubt that the expressive mime artiste, especially one with a made-up white face, in a modern traditional costume, achieves this aim very effectively. Mimes are uniquely expressive. A humorous story can be portrayed superbly well by mime, creating laughter with facial expressions alone. Consider for a moment the effect that Tommy Cooper had on an audience, simply by walking on stage.

Some of his audience would fall about laughing helplessly, simply by anticipating his expressions even before he made his entrance! Laughter helps to break down barriers, especially if we are encouraged to laugh at ourselves. This can be a very helpful exercise in worship. We explored earlier how mime can help us, by crystallising our emotions and freeing us to share the experience. This is indeed a very powerful tool, which will often elicit a response from the most reticent in our congregation.

One of the hazards of using some visual, creative arts is that the image becomes too powerful. Focus then becomes centred upon the artist and not the message. For example, the puppets that we use in our own ministry captivate people of all ages. However, some people become so focused upon the puppets, finding them so fascinating, that they simply do not hear or see the message that is being communicated. The same can be said of some well-known, charismatic preachers. Some people in the congregation are so overawed by the preacher's presence that the words spoken become superficial. The mime does not often suffer from this drawback as mime demands intense concentration and participation. There is a tacit understanding between mime and audience that this is so. It is therefore agreed that the audience need to concentrate and use their imagination. Add to this scenario, a mime in make-up and costume and the anonymity is complete. Generally speaking, the attention of the audience will be focused on the movement and expression presented, rather than the mime artiste.

Although much mime-drama is performed to a narrative or to music, mime has its roots in silent expression and there is much to commend moments of quiet in worship. Mime is a very powerful tool and emotional strings will be drawn taut during a performance. Silence in mime is an effective way of calming and preparing people for the next element in an act of worship, albeit preaching, prayer, or simply a time to meditate upon our own condition.

How do we start to use mime?

Whether you perform mime on your own or as part of a troupe, you will need to examine and be clear about your objectives. Besides the principal purpose of spreading the Gospel, you will need to develop your ministry, being constantly aware of the kind of audience you are targeting.

You will need to ask, 'Who they are? Where they will be? and how will you minister to them?' The mime performance will often be a small part of an organised act of worship, usually indoors and to a congregation that is familiar with many Christian themes. There are plenty of opportunities for creativity here, but even more so when you have the opportunity and confidence to perform outside of your home church.

Many churches will welcome drama and mime. However, if this is not the case at your own church, prayerfully approach your minister or church leaders, explaining the benefits that can result from mime in worship. If your mime ministry is not destined to be used in your church, do not despair. If God wants to use your gifts, He will help you to find the right occasion and venue. There are plenty of opportunities where your mime ministry will probably be welcomed, such as schools, holiday clubs, residential homes, hospitals, prisons, youth clubs, mission trips, on the streets and shopping malls.

Working outside of the Church can be tremendously challenging. I have fond memories of time spent in Wellingborough Prison, (as a visitor, I might add!) presenting Gospel magic to a captive, but very responsive audience. The point is, we need to develop material over a period of time, suitable for our congregations. This is particularly relevant in mime, as some Christian themes and doctrines are difficult enough to convey and understand using conventional dialogue and visual aids. Consider how much more difficult it may be for 'un-churched' people to understand the complex concept of atonement, using mime. The general rule is to keep it simple, make it effective, and work in conjunction with the preacher.

In order to communicate the message effectively, the aspiring mime will need to develop good technique, fitness and confidence. Mime can be a difficult art form to master, but repeated practice and study will reward those who seek to use mime in their ministry. You may be someone who has read this chapter out of interest alone, feeling that you do not have the confidence or skills required to offer mime. I would encourage you by briefly sharing with you an experience from within our own ministry team. Daniel, one of the founder members of the team, appeared to be the most unlikely of mime artists, being one of those unfortunate, willing, but awkward sort of chaps that accidents always seem to happen to. However, Daniel is a very capable puppeteer and a vital

> 'In order to communicate the message effectively, the aspiring mime will need to develop good technique, fitness and confidence'

part of the ministry team, as he has always been so very enthusiastic about everything that he does. He offered to help with a mime on a Share Jesus mission. I agreed with misgivings, but was so impressed with his performance that I asked him to present a long and difficult mime at one of the services at our home church. Needless to say, Daniel rose to the occasion and had many of the congregation in tears as he pulled at their heartstrings with a superb piece of mime ministry. Dare to be a Daniel and put your trust in God, secure in the knowledge that He will be there beside you. Go for it!

It is possible to fill volumes with detailed exercises, illusions and body control. Many good books have been written on the subject. (see resources chapter) Whilst this book does not pretend to provide a comprehensive guide to the skills required in order to perform effective mime, there follows a discussion on some of the skills required. You will also find exercises that will help to develop basic technique. One or two ideas for rehearsals are provided, as well as material that can be developed into mime skits for your church. Finally, two full scripts are offered for you to consider using in ministry.

Rehearsals, exercises and performance

Mime can be effective when performed solo or with a troupe. It can enhance worship when performed in silence or when complimented by music, a narration, a Bible reading or story telling. In order to perform mime well, it is important to appreciate how things move and interact with each other. It is particularly important to remember how people move and respond in given situations.

Most experienced actors, comedians and mimes, will have a good appreciation of body language, demonstrated through a conscious effort to observe people going about their normal business. This will reveal a great deal about body language, which may offer surprises, in that different age groups often carry out actions in different ways. For example, an old lady rushing to catch a bus that is already turning the corner into her street, will rarely run, but will attempt to walk quickly, possibly breaking into a slow, but stiff trot. The young child will make a headlong dash, whilst the teenager will often run or trot with slightly less abandon, being more concerned about appearance. The middle-aged businessman may prefer to walk as quickly as he can, but not be seen to be running, hiding his anguish at the possibility of missing the bus by waving his umbrella at it in an authoritative manner. Each type of stereotypical person noted here, demonstrates different degrees of concern at the prospect of missing the bus, and therefore responds in a different way.

Similar characteristics are displayed when eating in a café or restaurant. Those individuals who are in a hurry will look around anxiously for the waitress to appear with their order. When it appears, they will gulp their food, dividing their attention in equal measures between the food and their watch. On the other hand, the two ladies on a leisurely shopping trip will be relaxed as they wait for their meal, anticipating the pleasure to come, and may stop to chat between mouthfuls.

When miming a particular action, we must take into account more than the mechanics of the movement. We must attempt to demonstrate the mental state of the individual whom we are portraying. The timing of the movement and the way that we mime it, will depend very much on what has happened before, what ensues, and how the character feels at that particular time. Body language is very complex, depending not only upon our mood and

'The mime must focus totally on movement and expression, combining both to reflect the attitude'

current environment, but also upon past and future events. Thus, concentration during performance is paramount. The mime must focus totally on movement and expression, combining both to reflect the attitude, feelings, emotion and personality of the character portrayed.

Concentration and full focus on performance cannot be achieved without practice. Structured rehearsal will iron out most of the potential flaws in a performance, allowing time to recognise, understand and enter into any given character or situation. This is a time to get into character and lose inhibitions and self-consciousness. It is important to overcome self-consciousness, as this will quickly spoil the illusions that we try to create. This embarrassment is often caused by having to perform very exaggerated movements and emotions. Remember that it is this intense expression that makes mime so effective.

Attention to detail in rehearsal is important in order to achieve a polished performance. In particular, ways in which we can express ideas and emotions with different parts of our bodies is a worthwhile focus. In order to understand how other people move, it is important to know our own bodies. The following mime exercises are designed to explore different parts of the body and how they relate to one another. It is not suggested that all of these are used in one session.

Warming up exercises and mime games

Simple exercises that loosen the body and stimulate the mind are helpful. After one or two relaxing and toning exercises, such as those described in the drama section, it is worth spending a little time on facial expression. Start with stretching exercises for the eyes, widening and narrowing the pupils, frowning and widening eyebrows. Try wrinkling and twitching the nose, flaring the nostrils and a variety of mouth movements such as pursing lips, kissing, sucking in air and blowing.

Before rehearsals or prolonged exercises, it makes good sense to limber up the body, stretching, rotating and extending each limb, the waist, trunk and neck. There are a variety of warm up exercises that will be helpful. These include mirror type games and interpretation of some of the classic mime characterisations such as *The Robot* and *The Marionette*. These characters are ideal vehicles with which to isolate and separate each part of the body. This is an important discipline in mime, as control over each limb demonstrates recognition that each part of our body has something to say, which can be expressed it in a variety of ways.

The Marionette interpretation is very useful when practised with a partner, as both need to work and interact together. The marionette controller standing on a chair has the opportunity to practice miming the action of applying and releasing tension to the imaginary puppet strings. The marionette mimes the feeling of pressure that is applied to each limb and responds to the controls. This illusion requires great co-ordination between the two participants and is therefore a very useful exercise in timing. Miming simple actions such as dressing or undressing can also prove more difficult than one would imagine. Many mimes have learnt to milk a situation by adding magic properties to their costumes. Each garment appears to float around the room, or animate the part of the body that it touches in some other ethereal manner.

Following the leader's verbal instructions or repeating their actions is a time-honoured exercise which helps to teach a disciplined approach to mime. It is discipline and control that give polish to a performance and helps to create illusion. The audience cannot see an imaginary ball or a brick being held by a mime, but good technique will create an illusion of the object in their minds.

The key to creating this kind of illusion is snap, emphasis and wind-up. The snap is the action of stopping hands when touching an object. Thus, hands that pick up a ball will snap to position when making contact, demonstrating the slight resistance that occurs when objects meet under pressure, even the light weight of a touch. Slightly exaggerating or slowing a movement will often serve to place emphasis upon that action. The wind-up is the brief reverse action employed to provide extra emphasis, especially when performing in a large hall. It precedes the actual movement. For example, when miming the act of pushing a door open, the wind-up would be the slight backward movement of the hands and arms prior to pushing forward. The backward movement draws attention to the hands preparing the audience for the movement proper. The result is more emphasis which is more readily picked up by people seated at the back of a hall or theatre.

It is important to define and clarify shapes and equally important to maintain that definition throughout a scene. Spheres must stay round and be of the same diameter

> 'Control over each limb demonstrates recognition that each part of our body has something to say'

when being carried or held. Cubes must maintain angles, and heavy objects must maintain weight. Exercises such as revolving a ball or handling a cube will develop a sense of familiarity with shapes. Lifting and turning these types of imaginary items whilst varying the position of the hands, will help in the familiarisation process of handling objects. You may feel that this is unnecessary, but I assure you that it really does help. The actual size of an object is defined when the hands are snapped closed around the object. Beginning with arms and hands spread wider and deeper than the object to be picked up, will provide the audience with the correct visual wind-up, preparing their minds to understand the actual size and shape. Whilst imaginary objects may be touched, there is a recognised convention in mime that performers do not actually touch each other, but instead, create the illusion of touch. The mime who hugs another, will surround that person with their arms without actually touching their body.

Every aspiring mime should practise classic illusions such as walking on the spot, climbing a ladder, leaning on a bar, pushing against a wall and feeling their way around the inside of a box. There are several excellent books on mime that describe these techniques, supported by series of photographs to help teach the skills required to perform these basic illusions. These books will prove to be a good investment and are listed in the resources chapter.

It is important to employ basic stagecraft techniques in mime. Staying in a central position for most of the performance is helpful for focus. Any action mimed with your back to the audience will be difficult to convey and understand. Good memory is essential in maintaining real and credible situations. It is therefore important to maintain the same dimensions and space. A box, which has been placed three paces from a desk must be picked up again from the same spot, and not four paces away. Equally, doors must be opened before entering a room, and closed when leaving. Walls and tables, which you have previously leant against, should not be walked through or climbed.

Effective mime attempts to go beyond words and therefore it is good practice to comply with conventions which advocate few props and no spoken words or sounds, other than music or narration. It is for the preacher to provide Biblical exegesis and explanation with words. Mime is not just a dramatic game of charades, or an example of silent preaching. The mime has the task of creating a world within a stage, conveying ideas and

> 'It is important to define and clarify shapes and equally important to maintain that definition throughout a scene'

expressing emotions, taking the audience into areas that are beyond the scope of words and normal language.

SKETCHES, SONGS AND SCRIPTURE INTERPRETATION.

There are several different ways of using your mime skills. The most popular are sketches with a purpose and meaning, miming to a story from scripture or a narration, interpreting a song or a piece of Scripture, and for the more ambitious, spontaneous improvisation.

Song interpretations offer excellent opportunities to perform mime. Enacting a powerful song is a very good way to introduce mime, both to your church and to those who are new to the art. There are dozens of suitable songs, and if you are struggling to find a suitable one, you should find a lot of help at your local Christian bookshop. Most people who work in these establishments have a fairly broad knowledge of available Christian music. There are several suitable albums listed in the resources chapter. Our team can recommend musicians such as Ray Boltz and Carman, who perform dramatic Christian music and song. The work of both of these artists conjures up vivid images from Scripture in a powerful way. Good examples of this are Ray Boltz's *Watch the Lamb*, *Thank You* and *Not Until All Have Been Served*. Carman also offers superb dramatic music, such as the *Raising of Lazarus* and several excellent pieces that portray good against evil.

The mime needs to compliment songs by underlining some of the images and emphasising some of the emotions and feelings. I do not advocate bad or inept performance, and practice must be undertaken to give of one's best, but powerful music can mask imperfections in performance without detracting from the message, enabling novice mimes to begin to perform publicly.

Re-enacting a story or narration from scripture is another excellent way of employing mime. A good performance will illustrate and demonstrate the emotions involved in the story. It is a good idea to update a Bible story sometimes, taking traditional tales into a modern environment. Parables such as the Good Samaritan, Prodigal Son and some of Jesus' descriptions of the Kingdom of Heaven are excellent examples of stories that lend themselves to modern interpretation. Below is a list of Jesus' parables, with Bible references, which will hopefully spark some ideas for improvisation/dramatisation.

THE WISE AND FOOLISH BUILDERS.
  Matthew 7:24-27;Luke 6:47; Luke 6:49
TWO DEBTORS. Luke 7:41-47
THE RICH FOOL. Luke 12:16-21
THE SERVANTS WAITING FOR THEIR LORD.
  Luke 12:35-40
BARREN FIG TREE. Luke 13:6-9
THE SOWER. Matthew 13:3-9; Matthew 13:18-23;
  Mark 4:1-9; Mark 4:14-20; Luke 8:5-8;
  Luke 8:11-15
THE TARES. Matthew 13:24-30; Matthew 13:36-43
SEED GROWING SECRETLY. Mark 4:26-29
MUSTARD SEED. Matthew 13:31-32; Mark 4:30-32;
  Luke 13:18-19
LEAVEN. Matthew 13:33; Luke 13:20-21
HIDDEN TREASURE. Matthew 13:44
PEARL OF GREAT PRICE. Matthew 13:45-46
UNFORGIVING SERVANT. MATTHEW 18:23-35
GOOD SAMARITAN. Luke 10:30-37
FRIEND AT MIDNIGHT. Luke 11:5-8
GOOD SHEPHERD. John 10:1-16
GREAT SUPPER. Luke 14:15-24
LOST SHEEP. Matthew 18:12-14; Luke 15:3-7
LOST PIECE OF MONEY. Luke 15:8-10
THE PRODIGAL SON. Luke 15:11-32
THE UNJUST STEWARD. Luke 16:1-9
RICH MAN AND LAZARUS. Luke 16:19-31
IMPORTUNATE WIDOW. Luke 18:1-8
PHARISEE AND PUBLICAN. Luke 18:9-14
LABORERS IN THE VINEYARD. Matthew 20:1-16
THE POUNDS. Luke 19:11-27
THE TWO SONS. Matthew 21:28-32
WICKED HUSBANDMEN. Matthew 21:33-44;
  Mark 12:1-12; Luke 20:9-18
MARRIAGE OF THE KING'S SON. Matthew 22:1-14
FIG TREE LEAFING. Matthew 24:32; Mark 13:28-29
MAN TAKING A FAR JOURNEY. Mark 13:34-37
TEN VIRGINS. Matthew 25:1-13
TALENTS. Matthew 25:14-30
THE VINE. John 15:1-5

Stephen Fischbacher produced a song called *The Angry Hotel Man* on the album *Just Imagine*. This is a very good example of a familiar story, (no room at the inn in Bethlehem) expressed in song, which can be combined with mime or drama to good effect. The song is also available on cassette, together with a useful resource pack containing suggestions for use with young people or schools. It is possible to perform a solo mime to the song or to break it up into sections and involve lots of young people for mime or drama. Details can be found in the resources chapter.

Using willing members of the congregation to mime different parts of a song or story is a very good way of involving people in creative worship. It is worthwhile producing an acetate of the words used for overhead projection. A brief explanation of some simple actions that would suit the song, allocating lines to each of several willing participants, encouraging them to improvise with their own actions and expressions, offers a particularly effective way of miming to modern worship songs and hymns.

When preparing songs or stories for a performance, it is good practice to read through the words carefully, taking note of the rhythm, speed and timing of the music, or pace of the story. Each emotion found in the story should be considered, as well as the space and the environment that is to be created. Notes should be written against the words and then the script should be walked through, breaking down each line, eliminating any unnecessary movement or expression. The emphasis must be on simple actions that convey the overall meaning, remembering that an audience will also hear the words of the story or the lyrics of the music. It is probably best to record a narration onto tape so that rehearsals and performances can be at a regulated speed of narrative delivery.

Improvisation is an essential part of the creative process in mime, whether it takes the form of spontaneous improvisation or a prepared interpretation. Successful mime can be created from stories and song as we have discovered. However, just a few simple words can be equally inspirational. Two fellow team members and I were challenged on a Share Jesus mission, to produce a short mime illustrating one of the videos used in the Alpha course, entitled *Boring, Untrue and Irrelevant*. After a few minutes thought we came up with a short cameo combining the activities of a train spotter, (boring?) a medium with a crystal ball (untrue) and the crucifixion being witnessed by uninterested passers by. (irrelevant?) The mime underlined the three words in a very dramatic way. There are plenty of other opportunities for this type of creative improvisation, many of which are found in the words of liturgical text.

Prayers, chants, communion and other elements in

> 'Improvisation is an essential part of the creative process in mime'

MIME

worship are good sources for creativity. I can recommend a sketch that you will find in Geoffrey and Judith Stevenson's, *Steps of Faith* published by Kingsway Publications, Eastbourne. The sketch, *The Offering* involves one mime who sits down in a church pew and is repeatedly prompted to put more and more money into a collection bag. After reluctantly putting in all his money, wallet and even his clothes, the mime finally realises what is required and climbs inside the collection bag, giving up his whole life and body to God.

This type of sketch with a purpose is sometimes difficult to find. This may come as a blessing to you, as it may inspire you to write some scripts yourself. If you do not feel inspired to write, or don't know anyone who can, then I recommend that you contact Meriwether Publishing in the USA, by mail or by visiting their website (see resources chapter). This excellent resource for all aspects of theatre, offers some very good mime and drama sketches.

I was made aware of the power of the mime skit in worship when I saw a mime troupe present a sketch demonstrating the conflict between Christ and the Devil, featuring the Devil encouraging and capturing a succession of people broken by drink, drugs and gambling. Jesus wept at the plight of these unfortunate people and invited them to leave the clutches of the Devil and join Him. The Devil, angered by this intervention, challenged Jesus to a tug-of-war, which Jesus won by freezing the Devil's arms onto the rope. He then let go of the rope Himself, and after forcing the Devil to raise it, limbo danced under it, turning and snapping His fingers, forcing the Devil to fall over in a heap. The sketch was a turning point for me, as I witnessed what initially appeared to be a simple but humorous mime, turn into such a powerful piece of teaching.

The following two sketches demonstrate how a skilfully written contemporary sketch can bring a new dimension to Bible stories and themes, making a powerful and effective contribution to worship. Like all good sketches, whilst they carry a valid message in themselves, they serve mainly to prepare the congregation, offering the opportunity to follow up with sound preaching.

These two sketches, entitled *Golf Game* and *Power Source* are copyright Meriwether Publishing Ltd 1986, and have been reproduced in this publication with thanks to, and with the kind permission of the publishers, Meriwether Publishing Ltd., 885 Elkton Drive, Colorado Springs, CO 80907, USA, and author Susie Kelly Toomey.

Parables and familiar stories are not the only source of inspiration for mime to be found in the Bible. For example, the Book of Proverbs contains hundreds of suitable phrases for mime interpretation and *The Golf Game* is based on the following words of wisdom from that Book. 'Like a city whose walls are broken down is a man who lacks self control.' Proverbs 25:28 (NIV)

THE GOLF GAME

A sketch is for two mimes and set on a golf course. Mime 1 (INSTRUCTOR) is teaching Mime 2 (PUPIL) how to hit a golf ball. Both mimes enter, each carrying an imaginary bag of clubs.

INSTRUCTOR lays down his bag, stretches out his arms, flexes his arms and legs pro-style and shows how to address the ball, preparing to hit it.

PUPIL watches INSTRUCTOR intently and imitates all of his actions (although none too gracefully).

INSTRUCTOR then prepares to demonstrate how to actually hit the ball. He selects a club, places a ball on the tee, adjusts his stance, swings and hits the ball. PUPIL and INSTRUCTOR both watch admiringly as the ball sails down the centre of the fairway. INSTRUCTOR is proud of his shot, and the student is very impressed.

PUPIL now steps up and puts his ball on the tee, selects a club, sets himself and swings. Both stare at the ball, stubbornly still on the tee.

INSTRUCTOR slightly adjusts PUPIL'S stance and encourages him to swing again. So begins a series of failed attempts accompanied by a variety of funny antics by PUPIL. On each swing he either swings back too far and falls over, swings too far forward and nearly takes off, swings hard and lets go of the club, and hits the ball only a few yards or backwards. (Use your imagination to create progressively bizarre actions)

Meanwhile INSTRUCTOR, who at first looks on patiently, becomes more and more impatient at each failure, eventually turning into a raving tyrant. The end comes when INSTRUCTOR finally snaps and begins breaking his clubs by smashing them on the ground and one over his knee, walking off in anger.

PUPIL is puzzled by this and after a few moments thought, shrugs his shoulders as if acknowledging that this is normal behaviour and breaks his own club over his knee, before he too exits.

The sketch is ideal preparation for teaching about how self-control should be a characteristic of a Spirit filled Christian. We will fail in this discipline sometimes, but should try to imitate Christ at all times. He provides a perfect example of how to conduct our lives.

The second sketch, *The Power Source* is an example of a mime which illustrates a more abstract concept, that of Jesus being the source of all power. It is based on the words 'All authority in heaven and on earth has been given to me' Matthew 28:18 (NIV).

> 'All authority in heaven and on earth has been given to me'
>
> **Matthew 28:18 NIV**

THE POWER SOURCE

It is a sketch that provides opportunities for five mimes, preferably set on a dimly lit stage. It does require a few simple props: a lantern, a torch, some matches, a candle, a lamp base and a light bulb.

MIME #1 (representing Jesus) enters, holding a lighted lantern. He stands back and off to one side of the stage.

MIME #2 enters, holding an unlighted candle, and is groping through the darkness.

MIME #1 steps forward, holds out his lantern, and beckons MIME #2 to come to him.

MIME #2 looks at the lantern, then at his candle and indicates that he is considering going to join MIME #1.

Suddenly, MIME #3 enters and is very flashy with his torch. His light looks very much more appealing than Jesus' light, so MIME #2 changes his mind, and decides to go to the torch. He accepts the torch from MIME #3 and attempts to light his candle from it, but becomes confused when it will not light, and even more so when he accidentally extinguishes the torch.

MIME #3 takes back the torch and turns the light on again. MIME #2 is startled when the torchlight comes on again, but decides that he cannot trust the torch and moves away from MIME #3, who then exits.

Once again, MIME #1 steps forward and holds out his lantern towards MIME #2.

After taking just one hesitant pace forward, MIME #4 enters, carrying a lamp base with a light bulb. MIME #4 plugs the base into a plug socket (extension lead?) and a bright light comes on.

MIME #2 is impressed and excitedly runs over towards MIME #4 and his bright light and checks it out. He realises how the light works, approaches the extension lead and tries to 'plug in' his candle. (Do not actually push it into the socket of course - just create the illusion) As soon as the candle touches the extension lead, MIME #2 gets an electric shock. After a few humorous contortions, MIME #2 breaks free from the extension lead and quickly gets away from MIME #4. MIME #4 exits.

MIME #5 enters with a box of matches.

MIME #2 watches MIME #5 strike a match and eagerly approaches MIME #5 and taking the matches, tries to light his candle from one, but is frustrated to find that the match goes out. (MIME #5 can turn a little, blowing the match out without the congregation seeing.

MIME #5 exits and MIME #2 is totally dejected.

MIME #1 steps forward again, holding out his lantern to MIME #2.

At first, MIME #2 only looks at the lantern, unsure and not trusting it's power. Shortly, MIME #2 overcomes his reticence and is drawn to MIME #1 and the lantern, discerning something mighty in power. He then falls to his knees and bows his head. He then rises and holds up his candle.

MIME #1 takes the globe off of the lantern and allows MIME #2 to light his candle.

Both turn and exit, with MIME #2 following MIME #1.

This sketch demonstrates that we travel through life constantly looking for a reliable source of power to guide us. Some of us try to draw upon our own energies. Others look to the stars, the occult, fame, money, or a host of other sources, all of which ultimately fail. It is when we recognise our own spiritual poverty that many of us turn to Christ, rejoicing in the power that comes into our lives if we trust in Him
It is tempting to rush into performing a good sketch, when you find one. But, it is vital that everyone involved is thoroughly prepared and that all the expressions and movements are meticulously rehearsed. Make sure that you have one or two people to act as critics. These must be people who are able to make constructive suggestions regarding timing, pace and understanding etc. It is possible to adapt sketches so that fewer mimes can perform them. When changing roles during a mime, the convention is for

the mime to turn away from the audience, remaining motionless for a few moments, before turning and taking on the new character.

Props, lighting and effects

As previously discussed, it is a convention in mime that props should be kept to a minimum, always remembering that we are using this creative art to enhance worship. If the use of props adds to the effectiveness of the mime, do not hesitate to use them. It may be helpful to use props in order to aid novice mimes to create the illusion of handling a particular object. Chairs are sometimes helpful, but do try use props sparingly.

Effects such as smoke machines, back and front projection of images, video and music can all enhance mime presentation. However, do not make the mistake of overwhelming the audience with imagery, or creating too much clutter. Mime is an art form that is dependent upon the focus and attention of the audience. We do not want to inadvertently create unnecessary distractions, no matter how well intentioned.

Well placed lighting can make a big difference to mime. If at all possible, use at least one floodlight or spotlight. Any stage lighting increases the audience's interest and expectations, providing focus.

Wearing make-up or costume in a worship environment may at first sight seem a bit over the top. Some may argue that to do so is inappropriate, but there are sound reasons for their use. Make-up was first worn on stage as a mask and also to highlight actors faces in badly lit theatres. The white face worn by mimes is part of the traditional character, serving to add to the anonymity that leads to better focus, as we discussed earlier. Some mimes enjoy the screen that the make-up gives, resulting in fewer inhibitions, thus giving free rein to their performance.

If you are performing in a large hall or theatre, then it would probably be best to use white face make up in order that your audience can see your expressions from a distance. There are plenty of theatre outfitters that will be able to help you in the selection of the correct pancake make-up or clown white, as well as appropriate brushes. For a five minute mime in church, you may feel more comfortable not using make-up, as you will be able to communicate your message quite adequately without it. However, if you feel more comfortable using make-up, then by all means do so. A brief introduction by the worship leader, explaining your make-up may be helpful, especially for young children who may find the white face a little scary!

There is no set costume for mime. Street clothes will suffice provided that they are fairly loose fitting to allow free flowing movement, but not so loose that the expression in your movement is lost in folds of material. Many mimes wear striped jumpers and black trousers or tights, usually in order to create a character. It is useful to adopt a simple costume when performing regularly, as this will provide you with a recognised special identity and help you to develop your mime character fully. I have found that wearing a neutral colour, which gives a reasonable contrast against the surroundings, is helpful. All black often works well, possibly with the addition of white gloves. Wearing a simple black shirt and trousers or skirt, also allows you to slip back into the congregation unobtrusively when your performance is over. Whatever costume you decide upon, it should not interfere with, or detract from your performance.

Mime which is well prepared, using quality sketches, and presented in a polished manner, is a superb way of expressing worship themes. Your congregations should be blessed by your performance, provided that you practise your art, rehearse and perform mime exercises on a regular basis, and soak each performance in prayer beforehand. Your silence will speak loudly to many!

> 'Whatever costume you decide upon, it should not interfere with, or detract from your performance'

CREATIVE ARTS IN WORSHIP

Dance can be for many, an uplifting experience or spectacle, and a liberating form of expressive worship. The sensual, physical and expressive nature of dance makes it so useful in bringing yet another creative dimension to our worship of Almighty God.

CHAPTER FIVE
DANCE AND MOVEMENT

MOVING TOWARDS THE KINGDOM

Dance and movement have been part of the tradition of worship for thousands of years. In the modern era many have held that dance is not an appropriate activity in Church. Dance has been accused of being too secular, too provocative or too sensual, more like a theatrical performance, and perhaps too challenging. Dance is however, still very popular outside of the Church. It can contain many provocative and sensuous movements. It can be a dramatic performance and has the potential to challenge many. It can also be for many, an uplifting experience or spectacle, and a liberating form of expressive worship. This sensual, physical and expressive nature of dance makes it so useful in bringing yet another creative dimension to our worship of Almighty God.

Mary Jones wrote in her book, *God's People On The Move* that 'Movement becomes dance, where attention is given to the quality of the movement aesthetically – its design, rhythm, variety, meaning and feeling.' Sometimes we find it difficult to understand the magnitude of God and how he interacts with His people. We stand in awe at what He has done for us, and wonder at the gifts with which He continues to bless us. The words of Mary Jones are very helpful, as they conjure up a picture of God's worshipping people focusing on all these characteristics of God. Individual gestures such as cupped hands, symbolising the receiving of God's Spirit poured over us, are very powerful. This can be clearly seen during the singing of some worship songs, when worshippers may show total immersion in God, drawing near to Him by reaching out with their hands, arms and faces.

Those of us who do express worship in this way, have a perfect role model in Paul. 'When he had led them out to the vicinity of Bethany, he lifted up his hands and blessed them.' (Luke 24:50 NIV) Paul encourages us when he says, 'I want men everywhere to lift up holy hands in prayer.' (1 Tim 2:8 NIV) I am not suggesting that these are definitive Scriptural apologetics for dance. They are just two examples of concentrated movement amongst many to be found in the Bible.

Dance has been an accepted part of worship and religious ritual from Old Testament times. There are several examples of processional dance and praise enjoyed by God's people after major events, such as the deliverance from Egypt. David danced with the Israelite nation after the Ark was brought back to Jerusalem, and in the Psalms there are many similar examples of dance in worship. Most references describe situations where God's people use dance as a means of expressing their praise and joy at the blessings that God has bestowed upon them.

Jesus described the father of the Prodigal Son as dancing with joy at his son's return. I like to think that Jesus Himself dances with joy as more and more of His people finally return to Him. Dance may well be one of the tools that worship leaders can use to make that vision possible.

> 'There is a time for everything, and a season for every activity under heaven: ......a time to weep and a time to laugh, a time to mourn and a time to dance'
>
> **Ecc 3:1 & 4 NIV**

Dance in Today's Church

Dance suffered in the 18th and 19th centuries from the same kind of repression from the Church authorities as other creative arts. Worship through movement has seen some revival in today's church, especially in the 'charismatic' and Pentecostal traditions. Churches that do employ innovative and creative worship are attracting new members due to the prominent role of these areas in today's society. Dance and movement are of course only two of several elements that can be used effectively in evangelism, worship, prayer, and teaching. By using the gestures employed in the past, such as folk dance, sacramental ritual, liturgical movement and praise, we are on fairly solid ground. We are simply drawing upon, and developing the dynamic actions from our heritage, using them in a modern worship context. The main problem faced when integrating dance and movement, is not just persuading others that dance and movement are acceptable, but that they are relevant and meaningful to today's worshipping congregations.

We are encouraged to 'Love the Lord your God with all your heart and with all your soul and with all your mind and with all your strength.' (Mark 12:30 NIV) It is but a small step to include our bodies in this word picture as we strive to worship with our whole being. We express ourselves in our everyday lives through facial and bodily action. We are already using gestures and movement in worship, to pray, receive a blessing, and to kneel or bow in homage. It is a logical and natural step to give an additional dimension to our worship through shaping these actions into a more structured form. Thus, we use our actions to focus upon God, giving them to Him as a praise offering.

Dance and movement are nearly always associated with music, although there are occasions when dance can be effective without musical accompaniment. It can sometimes be difficult for people to express personal feelings in a physical way whilst singing worship songs. In the same way that mime can lead to us to deeper understanding, the language of dance enhances and physically interprets themes and moods found in Christian music and liturgy. This can be particularly helpful, as the dancer will share and physically express our emotions, thus liberating our spiritual feelings in a dynamic way.

> 'Movement becomes dance, where attention is given to the quality of the movement aesthetically – its design, rhythm, variety, meaning and feeling'

Movement in the pews

Whether an individual or a group performs a dance, it provides a focus for others. Congregations need not remain mere spectators, as they can be encouraged to participate in simple movements. These can be used to enhance many of the different elements of a service such as prayer, songs of praise, responses and blessings. However, this can seem quite threatening and challenging to some. A sensitive approach must be adopted when introducing dancers, or asking congregations to participate with some movement. It is helpful to provide reminders to the congregation of the movements and gestures that are already used in worship. Examples such as kneeling to pray, or to receive communion may be cited. Some people open palms, or clasp hands when praying or singing. Others may bow in reverence or humility. These are all very simple gestures, providing a starting point from which to explore and develop further movement. We saw earlier how movement becomes dance when attention is paid to the quality of movement. It is this awareness of the significance of a particular movement that is so important when introducing activities of this type to a congregation.

Movement in song

The worship song is probably the best way of introducing movement. A few simple gestures should be introduced at first, in order that the congregation can gain confidence. It is best to select a familiar hymn or chorus and to explain that movements to songs are just a different way of expressing our worship with our minds and our bodies. It is good practice to project the words onto a screen in order to free the hands. If the song is fairly long, encourage the congregation to offer movement just to the chorus or the first and last verse perhaps. Simplicity is the key. Each gesture should be explained and demonstrated, giving the reasons for using that particular movement. The congregation will probably more readily participate if the leader is someone familiar. Our organist is well known to our congregation, and has led them gently and sensitively in simple movements, creating a new awareness of how worship can be physically expressed.

Despite a sensitive and prayerful approach, there may still be some resistance to introducing movement and

> *'Love the Lord your God with all your heart and with all your soul and with all your mind and with all your strength'*
>
> **Mark 12:30 NIV**

DANCE AND MOVEMENT

> *Our organist is well known to our congregation, and has led them gently and sensitively in simple movements*

dance as a form of worship. Some churchgoers still regard any movement as 'charismatic,' and therefore not appropriate for them. It is therefore important not only to invite the congregation to participate, but also to ensure that everyone is aware that there is no pressure to join in. Confirm that God will be glad to accept their worship in song, regardless of whether it is accompanied by dance or movement.

The hymn, *What Shall Our Greeting Be* written by Fred Pratt Green (Hymns and Psalms 806) is about unity and serving the body of Christ. This concept of unity is a good example to use when first introducing movement to a congregation. The penultimate line of each verse invites the congregation to join hands with the words, 'Give me your hand, my friend.' It is logical to suggest that a congregation links hands at this point, demonstrating our unity. However, many people still find this difficult and feel uncomfortable touching one another, so care must be taken before introducing even this simple kind of interaction. One of the best ways of encouraging a congregation to participate is to invite a few confident people to practice beforehand, encouraging them to lead the movements, providing a focus for others. Do not be afraid to suggest this kind of activity as you may be pleasantly surprised by the willingness of some congregations to join together and demonstrate their unity.

The following two songs are fairly well known by many churchgoers. They contain lyrics that worship leaders may wish to choreograph, supported by congregational singing. The movements given are purely suggestions. You may wish to change these if you feel that there are other more appropriate gestures for the lyrics.

The first is a well known older hymn, *Let All The World In Every Corner Sing* by George Herbert (Hymns and Psalms 10). It is reproduced by kind permission of the Methodist Publishing House.

Let all the world in every corner sing
  Circle arms to denote a globe
My God and King!
  Point to the sky extending both arms
The heavens are not too high,
  Arms extended in a Y, palms inwards
His praise may thither fly;
  Turn palms outwards
The earth is not too low,
  Bring arms down to waist, palms down
His praises there may grow.
  Slowly raise arms,
Let all the world in every corner sing:
  Forming a globe once more
My God and King!
  Extending both arms and pointing up

Let all the world in every corner sing
  Circle arms to denote a globe
My God and King!
  Point to the sky
The church with psalms must shout,
  Arms lowered to shoulders
No door can keep them out;
But above all, the heart
  Hands over chest
Must bear the longest part.
Let all the world in every corner sing
  Forming a globe once more
My God and King!
  Extending both arms and pointing up

The song has been chosen because it is well known and fairly short. It contains words that offer praise and worship to God that are fairly simple to choreograph. It is an ideal way to start.

Robert Walmsley wrote, *Come Let Us Sing Of A Wonderful Love*, (Hymns and Psalms 691) over a hundred years ago. The words are timeless and speak of conversion and commitment. It is not good practice to attempt to compliment every word or line of a song with movement. Consequently the suggested gestures in this example have deliberately been kept simple. This is partly because the words are very expressive in themselves. Too much movement could detract the congregation's attention from the message of the song. Reproduced by kind permission of the Methodist Publishing House.

Come, let us sing of a wonderful love,
                Hands across heart
Tender and true;
Out of the heart of the Father above,
                Hands extended in worship
Streaming to me and to you:
                Point outwards and inwards
Wonderful love
                Cross hands over heart
Dwells in the heart of the Father above.

Jesus, the Saviour, this gospel to tell,
                Hands outstretched receiving
Joyfully came;
Came with the helpless and hopeless to dwell,
Sharing their sorrow and shame;
        Cross hands over face
Seeking the lost,
Saving, redeeming at measureless cost.
            Hands to side

Jesus is seeking the wanderers yet;
Why do they roam?
Love only waits to forgive and forget;
            Praying hands
Home, weary wanderer, home!
              'Come' gesture
Wonderful love
Dwells in the heart of the Father above.

Come to my heart, O thou wonderful love,
                Right hand over heart
Come and abide,
                Left hand also over heart
Lifting my life, till it rises above
                Arms raised in worship
Envy and falsehood and pride,
Seeking to be
                Slowly lowered to side
Lowly and humble, a learner of thee.
                Head slightly bowed in humility

A congregation of children and young people may learn movements more quickly than a mature congregation, (although the older generations may surprise you!) so it may be expedient to suggest only using movement to one or two verses. Your knowledge of the nature of the congregation must guide your first steps. Using dance and movement in these simple ways offer many opportunities for expression and creativity. A glossary of suggested movements is provided at the end of this chapter, each movement illustrated with line drawings.

There is a wealth of music and songs written for worship and many of these are suitable for dance and movement. Some movements and songs may be more suited to people staying in, or standing by their seats. Others however, may be more effective when presented in a circle or in a procession, such as the song *Walk by Faith* for example. You will be limited only by your own imagination, creativity and the willingness of the congregation to experiment, although there may be restrictions imposed by the arrangement of the chairs or pews.

INDIVIDUAL MOVEMENT IN PRAYER AND LITURGY

Individual expression as a response to spoken or silent prayer or to a benediction perhaps, can be very helpful. Simple gestures such as bowed heads, cupped hands, hands or arms in a receiving position, or arms raised in worship, can assist individuals to express their feelings in a more dramatic way. These gestures may enhance and crystallise emotions and feelings during quiet times. A laying on of hands during prayers of intercession, or simply joining hands during a blessing or benediction may help some congregational members. These moments of contact in an act of worship will help to develop a sense of unity.

One preacher leading worship in our own church handed out pebbles to each person in the congregation and asked us to grip the pebble hard whilst offering prayers of confession and forgiveness. We were encouraged to slowly release our grip on the stone as we confessed our sins, finishing with open relaxed hands as we heard the words of Grace and forgiveness pronounced by the worship leader. We were encouraged to take the pebble home as a reminder of the stone that was rolled away from Jesus' tomb. It also reminds us that Jesus lives with us today and enables us to receive forgiveness from God. Many found this very helpful as a way of easing tension, symbolising a releasing of thoughts and mental anguish. It certainly demonstrates that movement does not always have to be associated with music.

All those who worship in a Christian gathering may be said to be on a spiritual journey, seeking spiritual truth and guidance. For some, each service attended may be a step of faith on that journey. Encouraging congregations to move out of their seats to a focal point may assist this process. For example, walking to the communion rail and kneeling is a common practice that most will accept willingly, solely because this is the accepted norm as a preparation for receiving the sacrament. It may be helpful to some to be encouraged to move to a focal point in other situations, either to kneel, bow or pause to light a candle. As a local preacher, I have offered opportunities to people to bring their written intercessions, confessions or thanks, to a communion table, cross or a single candle. Not all people feel comfortable doing this however, but many appreciate the opportunity to perform this simple public act of confession, thanks or intercession.

Some congregations are used to carrying objects such as crosses, palm leaves or candles as symbols of events in Scripture. The great Christian festivals provide opportunities for this type of movement. Creative worship leaders may be able to introduce more structured dance movements to these events. These movements may assist people in seeing the event from a new perspective.

For example, Christmas offers opportunities for people to bring gifts to the baby Jesus, or animals and figures to create a manger scene. Harvest involves the bringing of produce. The period of Lent leading to Passion Week involves offering sacrifices and the symbolic use of palm leaves and crosses. Congregations will probably be willing to participate in such services, bringing objects to the front of the church, or taking objects to or from a focal point. Some may be pleased to offer praise in the form of a previously choreographed dance. The possibilities are manifold and creative worship leaders may be able to offer great opportunities to congregations in order for them to develop more creative and expressive worship at these times.

In all the above examples, the emphasis should be on simplicity and clear unambiguous movement, presented in a sensitive manner so that anyone may participate. The worship leader must be sensitive to the fact that some will be unwilling or unable to participate. These people should be made to feel comfortable in this situation. Instructions should be precise, and the congregation made to feel quite at ease and confident in what they are asked to present. Provided that these simple guidelines are followed, dance and movement can be introduced and enjoyed by most congregations. The glossary of movements at the end of the chapter provides many of the gestures that you will find useful, but do experiment, allowing the Holy Spirit to lead the creative process.

STRUCTURED DANCE IN WORSHIP

There are some wonderful dance groups to be seen in worship. Some are very polished in their approach to dance, such as the excellent Springs dance group. The majority however, are not professionally trained, but nonetheless offer superb worship and praise, enjoyed by those who are privileged to see them.

Many of us long to express deep-rooted spiritual emotion, but do not have the means to communicate that emotion as we would like. Watching a well rehearsed, Spirit led dance team can release those feelings in us and allow us to share in the spiritual expression displayed by the dance.

Dance will often enable us to experience worship music in a new way, giving physical expression to the emotions that the piece invokes. A dance may also help congregations focus upon particular lyrics or even Bible passages, as the movement triggers thought processes. Dance may simply offer the opportunity to see other Christians proclaiming their faith and witnessing to the love of God in a graceful, dynamic and vibrant way. All of

'The emphasis should be on simplicity and clear unambiguous movement, presented in a sensitive manner so that anyone may participate'

these are valid reasons for encouraging dance in worship, but there are guidelines to follow.

Firstly, as is the case with all who lead worship, the group should be spiritually prepared, through listening and talking to God in prayer. Dance can then be offered in humble worship, in order to glorify God. The group must be aware of the limitations of the venue and the available space. Dancers should be well rehearsed, and exercise care in transposing the choreography from the rehearsal hall into the confined space of the worship area. Thus, it would be inconceivable to attempt to introduce a twelve-member chorus line into a tiny village chapel worship area. In large worship areas, it may be possible and indeed helpful, to introduce a focal point for the dance group, such as a freestanding cross or banner. This will direct the congregation's vision to a central and meaningful focus.

Dancers should be appropriately dressed for dancing. This means wearing imaginative costumes that are appropriate to the variety of movements that the dance requires. Costumes that are perfectly suited to a discotheque or nightclub dance floor, may well not be appropriate for worship. Dancers should be aware that the nature of some dance costumes might distress or offend some congregation members, as they may be considered provocative. Whilst some dancers may bristle a little at this suggestion, we must always remember that worship leaders are present to assist the congregation. We must always avoid anything that detracts from the objective of the service - that is, meaningful worship. There are plenty of dance costumes that are designed to allow free movement. These combine elegance and charm with the required degree of modesty.

Choreography is the essence of dance and this should reflect the nature, tempo and mood of the music as well as expressing the meaning of the lyrics. The nature of the worship element will be important in choosing the appropriate style of choreography. For example, a dance designed to give meaning to intercessional prayer, may be more dignified and serene than a dance which brings life to a dramatic reading from Scripture, or one which expresses the joy experienced when receiving from Christ.

The choreographer will also need to take account of the nature of the congregation. Residents of a home for the elderly may not appreciate disco style dancing as much as a children's holiday club, although it is important never to take these preconceptions for granted. Not all congregations follow an expected pattern and we must be

> '*Choreography is the essence of dance and this should reflect the nature, tempo and mood of the music as well as expressing the meaning of the lyrics*'

prepared to adapt to their specific needs. Variety is essential if the dance group is ministering to the same congregation on a regular basis. The wise group leader will encourage all team members to participate in choreography brainstorming, so as to ensure plenty of variety in performance.

Although it is healthy for each individual in a congregation to draw whatever value they can from a dance, it is helpful to provide the congregation with a clear idea of the dance group's objective. A dance routine that interprets the message of the lyrics of a worship song will probably be fairly readily understood. However, the meaning of a piece of choreography designed to give life and relevance to an instrumental piece, may not be as readily perceived. It would be helpful in this situation, to offer suggestions to the congregation beforehand, as to what the music and the dance is trying to convey.

It is not essential to interpret each word, or even each line in a Scripture passage or worship song. The words themselves are designed to convey particular meaning. The choreography should be planned so as to reflect the overall mood of the piece, ensuring that the dance flows smoothly. Most dance should be structured in a similar fashion to good drama, insofar as it should have a defined beginning, mid section and ending. The dance should mostly combine body movements from a fixed position, with overall movement of the body that travels from one place to another. Thus, a series of swaying, stretching, bending and shaking gestures should be combined with actions such as walking, running, jumping, sliding and turning etc. This leads to variety and interest. Of course, the advantage of dancing in groups is that the movements of individual members can be co-ordinated and presented in formations and dynamic shapes. The following are just a few examples:

> All the team dance the same steps in unison.
> Mirror images are formed in pairs or larger groups.
> One dancer remains in one position, offering movement and gesture on one spot, whilst others compliment that dancer by moving around that focus.
> The central focus can be on an object such as a cross.
> One dancer could move expressively around and between static groups.

In all these examples, the dance should flow, but should remain disciplined. Formations and shapes should be visible from different angles and levels, to provide and hold interest. Dance should be presented on all levels and through all body heights to levels above normal height, by means of lifting and climbing.

Choreography should not be restricted to musical interpretation, being a relevant approach to other elements of worship such as Scripture reading, Psalms, drama, mime and prayer. An awareness of the available equipment that can enhance dance such as good sound systems, lighting and props should be developed. For example, flags, banners and streamers can add diversity and colour. Simple theatrical ultra-violet light tubes (black light tubes) are inexpensive, and when positioned near the dance area with subdued lighting, can be very effective, especially when fluorescent costumes are worn.

WORKSHOP IDEAS TO DEVELOP

Workshops with keen members of your congregation or dance group will often stimulate the creative process. Participants will experience exciting new choreography and movement, through the use of new and traditional music, poetry and prayer etc. All workshops must be well prepared, ensuring that all the required music and resources are in place. The venue should be safe, warm and uncluttered and the whole event prayerfully and carefully planned to the last detail.

Workshops in dance and movement can take various forms, such as exploring and introducing dance and movement, children's workshops, family movement, or a more in depth exploration of movement in worship for the less inhibited. Whether your group is exploring simple movements in family worship or more advanced choreography, you must prepare the participants for hard work. It is essential that everyone is aware of the objectives of the workshop and prepared mentally and physically, through warm-up exercises. Examples of these exercises have been described in the chapters on drama and mime. If used prior to a dance workshop, more emphasis should be placed on exercises that stretch and tone the body, as sessions often involve hard physical work. Care will need to be taken to ensure that the level of physical effort is appropriate to the age and ability of the participants.

> *Formations and shapes should be visible from different angles and levels, to provide and hold interest*

It is useful to cover some of the non-active elements of the 'dance and movement in worship concept', such as Biblical basis, aspects of worship, the work of the Holy Spirit, prayer and meditation. These factors provide excellent background and a practical springboard for creativity. Worship is by its very nature a spiritual experience. All of our creativity should spring from our own spirituality and the prompting of the Holy Spirit. The workshop group that has explored these important factors will probably offer more creative Spirit filled ideas as a result. However, be sure to provide variety in the workshop and offer light-hearted routines initially, as well as the opportunity to progress to explore deeper spiritual and emotive material.

Choreographing modern worship songs is a popular exercise. Fairly well known contemporary songs such as *Beautiful Saviour, My First Love, My Jesus, My Saviour* and *He Has Risen* offer good opportunities for a group to explore choreography. It is often a good idea to split a larger group and to ask small groups to work on each verse, then bringing all the ideas together.

Country and western music has had a strong influence on Christian music, particularly in the USA. There are plenty of examples of songs that lend themselves to fun routines, such as line dancing and other country style group dancing. These exercises are ideal for family workshops.

Freedom of individual expression is to be encouraged. Many will find time spent expressing ideas and interpreting music very rewarding. A good way to lead into expressive movement is to ask everyone to relax with some appropriate quiet exercises, introducing some soft background music such as pan pipes or flute. Allow some time for the group to feel the mood and then introduce some poetry, prayer or Psalms. The words and music may combine to provide an excellent vehicle for the group to gradually move and interpret with their whole bodies.

Dance improvisation and movement to a Bible passage is a very powerful way for some to express their spirituality. There are forms of writing to be found in the Bible that can assist this process. Try choreographing some dramatic prophetic passages from Isaiah or Daniel. The parables and some of Jesus' words in the Gospels provide stimulating background to dance, or for the more dramatic, the Pentecost story may be powerfully performed. Background music often helps in this type of presentation.

Prayer can be a group or an individual experience, and it is sometimes very helpful to use the words of a prayer to stimulate expression through movement. Using some of the well-known prayers and creeds found in the liturgy of most traditions can be fruitful. The Lord's Prayer is the best known of all prayers and is so often just repeated parrot fashion in our services, without consideration of the content. Offer the opportunity for participants in a dance experience, to interpret the words of the prayer as they are read, allowing everyone sufficient time to reflect and respond to each line. This can be a stimulating and worthwhile exercise.

Group work can take various forms and can provide a comfortable vehicle for beginners to take part in dance. Forming shapes such as circles, squares, processional lines, spirals and other more free shapes, can help participants to cooperate with each other on simple group work, such as interpreting key words in a song or a reading. Smaller groups may work together in threes or fours, choreographing songs whilst always linked physically together, or presenting mirror images.

USING OBJECTS, FLAGS AND STREAMERS

Flags, streamers, ribbons, fabric, ropes and candles are all items that can be used effectively in dance routines. Marie Bensley's *Kingdom Dance* organisation publishes an excellent booklet, *Moving In Praise With Flags*. This offers useful resources for this activity that is becoming very popular at some churches, offering opportunities for all ages to become involved in dance and movement. It is good to see people use flags and streamers in worship, and this kind of individual spontaneous expression is to be encouraged. However, it is worthwhile spending time rehearsing some structured routines with flags and streamers. All too often we miss some of the opportunities offered by these objects in worship, as they are simply waved around randomly by enthusiastic dancers. Each and every method of dance and movement should be used as an opportunity to reach out and to teach God's Word with precision.

Long pieces of coloured fabrics can be linked by dancers in ways that suggest wind, water, rivers, mountains or other land or seascapes. Fabrics can be used

> 'It is sometimes very helpful to use the words of a prayer to stimulate expression through movement'

to portray some of the vivid images of our faith. Several dancers holding two pieces of long fabric could combine to twist and weave a shape of the cross whilst appropriate music is played, or a prayer is read aloud. Similarly, the Pentecost story, or Elijah at the altar of Baal, can be vividly enacted in dance, using several rows or circles of dancers with fabric.

Paper streamers cut into various lengths, can suggest air, wind, fire and gifts of the Spirit. Ropes used to join dancers together can suggest unity or being bonded by sin, slavery or a common faith. You may be surprised or even inspired by the ingenuity of a workshop group when they are offered flags, ribbons and streamers. Offer suggestions by all means, but allow sufficient space for participants to develop their own skills and to use their creativity.

A chapter on dance and movement would not be complete without reference to signing. Those who have learnt signing skills, offer a silent and universal language that interprets the spoken word and song to assist those who have impaired hearing. Signing can also be used very effectively to re-enforce and enhance a song or prayer, as the actions employed provide yet another form of creative expression in worship and teaching of the Gospel. My wife Suzanne, signs very effectively for our ministry team, combining it with puppetry and video. We are constantly encouraged to hear from those who have seen our presentations, that the signing has given extra meaning to worship, speaking to them in a very special and direct way. We have found that a UV black light tube provides a dramatic emphasis and focus whilst signing, especially if white gloves and plain dark clothing are worn.

Whilst I would advocate that some artistic licence might be used, signers should keep to the British Sign Language conventions where possible. You should be aware that Sign language is dynamic and that there are variations through dialects, prevalent in some parts of the country. Also be aware that some resources employ the use of American Sign Language. There are some excellent resources to be found, such as *Religious Signing* by Elaine Costello and *Songs In Sign For Children* by Cath Smith and Elaine McBean. Most community colleges offer classes for those who wish to learn British Sign Language.

Movement vocabulary suggestions

There are so many different ways of expressing ourselves with dance and movement. This chapter can only hint at some of these, offering opportunities for you to go on to develop ideas of your own. The following drawings offer some suggestions for movement interpretation. These are only a starting point, but hopefully will provide a basic framework upon which to build.

Pray for guidance, consider why you are introducing dance and movement, keep the movements simple and have fun whilst you worship!

Permission to use these drawings and some of the suggested interpretations, has been kindly given by the Christian Dance Fellowship of Australia – CDFA Press, and have been reproduced from the book *God's People On The Move* by Mary Jones and members of the Christian Dance Fellowship of Australia.

1. The prayer position with palms out at shoulder height. A gesture of adoration.

2. Cupped hands raised above the head with palms out. A gesture of awe and adoration. Mary Jones suggests the movement advocates preciousness and blessing.

3. The beckoning movement inviting one to draw near.

4. Arm raised with palm out, fingers slightly pointing, offering a blessing.

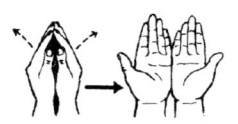

5 & 6. Closed hands to open palms, suggesting an open book or receiving.

7. Head bowed in humility with palms open receiving. With hands clenched this may suggest despair or sorrow.

8. Circling movements. Either continuous to suggest creation, greatness or continuity, or may be in series with arms flung wide quickly at the peak to suggest bursting, opening or discovery.

9. Hands circle out from the heart to open palms signifying offering oneself.

10. Circling hands from a 'V' position, crossing and back to side suggesting receiving and giving out again.

11. Clapping partners hands and moving up and away expresses joy and celebration.

12. Single clap and circle to express personal joy and exultation.

13. Clasped hands suggesting prayer, meditation, healing and wholeness. Conversely, when wrung, can represent despair, sorrow and anguish.

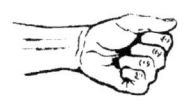

14. Clenched fist for power, strength, might or courage. When beating the chest or sides, can express anguish or frustration. When moving up and down, it suggests confirmation and agreement.

15. Proclaims the Cross.

16. Another sign of the Cross, but also identification and proclamation.

17. The crucified body emphasised by bowed head, cupped hands, slight crouch and bent knees.

18. Crossed hands over the heart expresses repentance, presence of the Holy Spirit and inner awareness. With arms more extended, may suggest love, honesty and integrity.

19. Group forming a crown expressing kingship, sovereignty or Lord of all.

20. Partners forming a crown by joining hands with extended fingers.

21. Individual crown formed by hands with fingers extended.

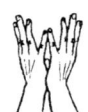

22. Cupped hands signifying receiving or openness.

23. Extended version of receiving and adoration.

24. Even more extended version of receiving and adoration or can express glory above.

25. Cupped hands pushed out from the body, cupped hands at waist height on top of one another and one cupped hand across the chest. All ways of expressing receiving and sometimes offering.

26. Crossed wrists and linked thumbs suggest a dove or Holy Spirit.

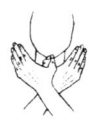

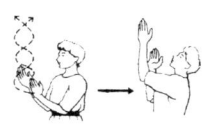

27 & 27a. Fingers pointing up. Hands rotating and crossing with flexible flowing wrists as they move higher and then lower. Suggests fire, wind, ruach or pneuma (Holy Spirit) and turmoil.

28. Open hands and arms from 'V' position rise over the head and are then lowered with elbows bent, finally flowing to receiving position and repeated. Suggests cleansing, peace, flowing water, movement of the Holy Spirit and God moving over the land or people.

29. Cupped hands alternately in an up and over 'bubbling' movement suggesting a fountain or streams of living water, the water of life.

30. Hands together at chest, circling outwards and back in, signifying a gathering in.

31. Joined hands for fellowship, unity, equality and belonging.

32. Joined hands raised to shoulder level suggesting strength and joy in fellowship.

33. Joined hands raised high in praise and glory.

34. One hand on heart. One raised and extended. Expressing love or yearning for God.

35. Lifting hands in offering, praise, raising to life, God's name exalted.

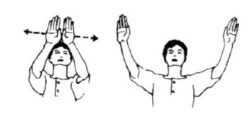

36. Open palms together and then part to reveal the name of Jesus, eternal life, revelation or prophesy.

37. Open heart expressing openness to God or focused on God.

38. Hands raised in prayer, supplication, confession, petition and intercession.

39. Praying with partner. Can also be expressed with each using both hands.

40. Hands pushing down expressing victory, suppression, oppression or dominance.

41. Reaching out from the front to signify giving and receiving as well as reaching out.

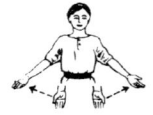

42. Arms reaching out from sides. A more inclusive movement for outreach.

43. Rejection.

44. Singing or shouting out.

45. Starburst - hands clenched and opened quickly with arms raised expressing glory, showered with love or creation.

46. More expressive starburst. Joy, exultation, praise and glory and energy.

DANCE AND MOVEMENT

47. Sway movement side to side.

48. Various positions of praise, awe, wonder, glory and lifting up.

49. Clenched fist of power and victory.

50. Group joining at side – basket hold.

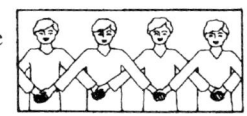

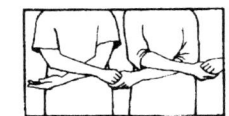

51. Group joining at side – Crossed arms hold.

52. Group joining at side – two-arm shoulder hold. Good for swaying and circle movement.

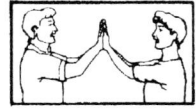

53. Group joining facing – palm to palm

54. Group joining facing – hands joined.

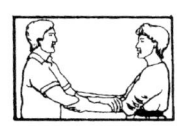

55. Group joining facing – elbow to elbow.

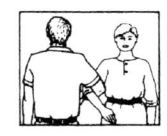

56. Group joining facing – linked elbows.

57. Group joining facing – pivot hold with crossed hands.

CREATIVE ARTS IN WORSHIP

After a few moments, she slowly raised her own puppet that previously had hung limply by her side. I did not say a word to her. For ten incredible minutes, her puppet spoke to my puppet, and discussed much of the hurt, frustration, and brokenness in that child's short life.

Chapter Six
Puppets and ventriloquism

Puppets past and present

Puppets have been used for entertainment and teaching for a very long time. Evidence has been found of puppetry in old paintings and manuscripts from as far as Ancient Greece and Egypt in the West, to China in the East. Traditional stories and legends have been enacted using puppets in many different cultures. These made use of a wide variety of puppet forms. For example, shadow puppets have traditionally been used in the Far East, such as the rod shadow puppets of Java. In Japan, the exponents of Bunraku or Joruri theatre use large puppets and dolls manipulated by puppeteers on stage, who are camouflaged by black clothing.

Puppets were introduced into theatres and market places during the middle Ages, to portray and satirise well-known national figures. Characters such as Punch and Judy, Guignol (France) and Kasperle (Germany) entertained crowds by illustrating traditional tales, domestic life and political satire.

Puppets in the modern age were popularised in the early days of television. British children had the opportunity to watch and enjoy Sooty and Sweep, Muffin the Mule, the Woodentops, Andy Pandy, Bill and Ben: The Flowerpot Men and Basil Brush. Modern puppeteers still use marionettes, shadow puppets, broom and plate puppets, finger and glove puppets. Television shows such as Sesame Street and the Muppet Show transformed puppetry into the effective telecommunication device that it is today. Modern puppet builders now use sophisticated electronics to produce amazing puppets based on animatronics. Such puppets can now be seen in large budget movies such as *Star Wars*.

WHY PUPPETS?

Puppets are fun! This is at the heart of puppetry. People of all ages have enjoyed watching puppets through the centuries. The Muppet Show at its peak, was one of the most popular television programmes of all time. Puppets have universal appeal because they often portray some of the frightening and challenging situations that life offers, but in a non-threatening way. For example, puppeteers can easily portray the results of sin by showing a puppet doing something wrong and getting itself into trouble as a result. Congregations will identify with the problems and consequences suffered, because puppets impersonate people and thus reflect real life. However, because they mimic human behaviour instead of actually performing it, the teaching is one step removed from human experience and therefore less threatening. The teaching and challenge remain, with the pain and reality of the experience redirected, in order to diffuse the hurt.

Over 11 million children regularly watched the Muppet Show, yet only one quarter of that number go to church. It doesn't need a genius to arrive at the conclusion that when entertaining puppetry teaching is combined with effective preaching, the modern worship leader has a very powerful and attractive tool with which to spread the Good News of Christ.

Because of their universal appeal, puppet songs, scripts, and ventriloquist dialogues, offer illustrated teaching that is difficult to match with other forms of preaching. People of all ages will often remember the themes taught by puppetry for a lot longer than teaching by most other means. There is no doubt that children in particular are more likely to listen to a puppet teaching them, than a teacher or preacher! Shy children will often respond and talk to puppets at times when they would not, or could not communicate with adults or other children.

I will never forget an experience at one of our team's puppet workshops, when a young girl opened her heart to a puppet I was holding. The girl was physically disfigured and challenged by severe learning difficulties. These had resulted in a great deal of abuse from her peers, and she had not shown any interest in our workshop at all. I approached her with the only puppet left in the workshop box, a scruffy and dilapidated one-eared misfit that no one else wanted. The little girl's eyes showed just a flicker of interest as I approached her, trying for one last shot at including her in our activities. I sat beside her, turned my face away from her, and left the puppet turned toward her. After a few moments, she slowly raised her own puppet that previously had hung limply by her side. I did not say a word to her. For ten incredible minutes, her puppet spoke to my puppet, and discussed much of the hurt, frustration, and brokenness in that child's short life. It was an amazing experience that may speak to many who are hesitant about using puppets in ministry. That one incident has been instrumental in persuading me that puppetry is a vital tool in our own ministry, and should be considered as an option by all those who have the skills to use it.

> 'For ten incredible minutes, her puppet spoke to my puppet, and discussed much of the hurt, frustration, and brokenness in that child's short life'

WHAT PUPPETS TO USE AND WHO CAN USE THEM?

Anyone with the will to learn and the time required to acquire the necessary skills can perform with puppets. However, puppets should be used as an aid to teaching, not merely as an end in themselves. Puppeteers will need to work closely with others in order to provide the complete teaching package. Some may wish to work alone, using puppets for ventriloquism, or within clown routines. Others may wish to work with one or two puppeteers who interact with them on a live basis. Some may be part of larger teams that can offer more spectacular puppetry, involving choreography for songs, musicals and multi-character drama in large purpose built stages. All these forms are valid and can be used in services, Sunday schools, assemblies, classrooms, shopping precincts, workshops, hospitals, nursing homes, prisons and many other locations. Our own team has offered Christian puppetry in many of these environments and have always been rewarded with a very positive response from those who have seen us.

Most puppeteers use their puppets as part of an organised worship event, such as a church service or assembly, but there is no reason why puppetry should not take a central role. The 'Hands up for God' team have developed puppet ministry to the point whereby the team take responsibility for leading a whole weekend. We begin by offering outreach through workshops or a puppet musical on Saturday, ending with a full length, all-age puppets praise service on Sunday morning. The events are appreciated by young and old, and have been responsible through God's Grace, for leading some to Christ for the first time. This can only be achieved if the whole of your ministry is Christ centred, soaked in prayer, supported by other Christians in your church and carefully and prayerfully planned. Puppet ministry is great fun but requires committed people who have a heart for worship, a love of God and are sensitive to the needs of today's mixed congregations.

Whilst some may offer a worthwhile ministry with shadow puppets or marionettes, by far the most versatile, practical and popular kinds of puppets are the Muppet style characters. This chapter will concentrate solely on this format. Puppets can be acquired from puppetry resource organisations such as our own 'Hands up for God' ministry. You may wish to make your own, employing the talents of someone in your church that can follow one of the excellent puppet patterns that are also available.

The illustration demonstrates the main characteristics of the basic rod-arm puppet. Most are around 24 inches (60 cm) in length and consist of a ¾ inch (2 cm) thick, hollow foam body and head, with a flexible neck and moving mouth. The most practical covering is a fabric with a slight stretch, such as velour, or Antron fleece if you can afford it. Felt can be used, but has too much stretch and will become baggy with regular use. Clothes designed for an 18-month to 2-year old child are ideal for puppets, especially as most are designed as miniature adult clothes with more attractive colours. These can be obtained very cheaply at most charity shops and jumble sales. Rods can be attached to wrists with elastic bands, or screws for some advanced puppets. These are used to manipulate the arms and hands, so that the puppet becomes more expressive and animated. The facial features are added to the basic puppet form to achieve variety in characterisation. Ostrich feathers, fur, cotton wool, plastic or other fabrics can be used for hair, beards, eyes and noses. Rod-arm puppets are operated by the puppeteer's hand entering the puppet from below. This hand operates the moving mouth, which should have elastic straps to keep the fingers and thumb firmly fixed against the mouthparts. The other hand operates the rod/rods which moves the arm/arms.

Full body puppets have legs attached, with a hole in the neck or lower back for the operating hand. These puppets are normally supported over a table or lap, and are usually used by ventriloquists and as friend puppets, which interact with the operator or third parties. They can be used as conventional puppets, but are heavier and therefore more tiring to use unless supported.

Human arm puppets are similar to rod arm puppets, but are normally operated by two puppeteers. One puppeteer positions their arms through a special shirt which gives the illusion of the puppet having real arms, with moving hands and three fingers. (three fingers are traditional in puppets) The other puppeteer performs as close as possible to their partner and has a hand in the puppet's head, providing lip synchronisation. This is a very expressive puppet type that can be operated by one puppeteer. This is achieved by placing one hand in the head and the other through one sleeve of the human arm shirt. The other sleeve is pinned to the side of the puppet to suggest an arm hanging down.

Almost any object can be made into a moving mouth puppet once the basic principle of making the moving mouth is mastered. There are several books available to teach the technique, and patterns available for making clothing to fit this specialist puppet form. Thus it is possible to use puppet dramas and songs that feature speaking or singing trees, flowers, vegetables, animals, walls, musical instruments, hamburgers and light bulbs etc.

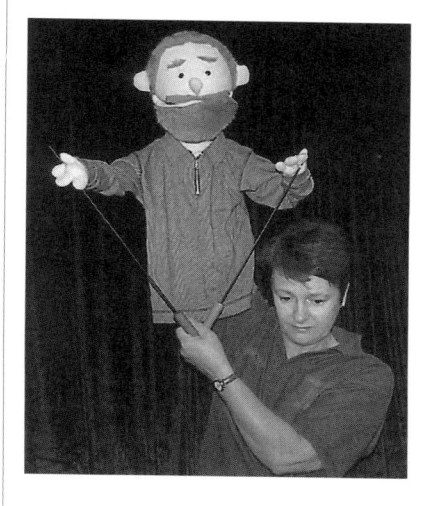

One final thought on puppet types that you may care to reflect upon. Our team was asked to present a puppet workshop to a junior church in London. We ministered to around fifty children aged 6 – 13 years and had a wonderful time with some really talented and enthusiastic children. It was only after the workshop that one of our team pointed out to me that we had presented a workshop to fifty black children, yet we didn't possess a single black puppet. The children were perfectly comfortable with the workshop, enjoyed it immensely and probably not one of them even considered the matter. However, we purchased some black and other coloured puppets immediately after that workshop. It is important to recognise the diversity of people within the Christian Church

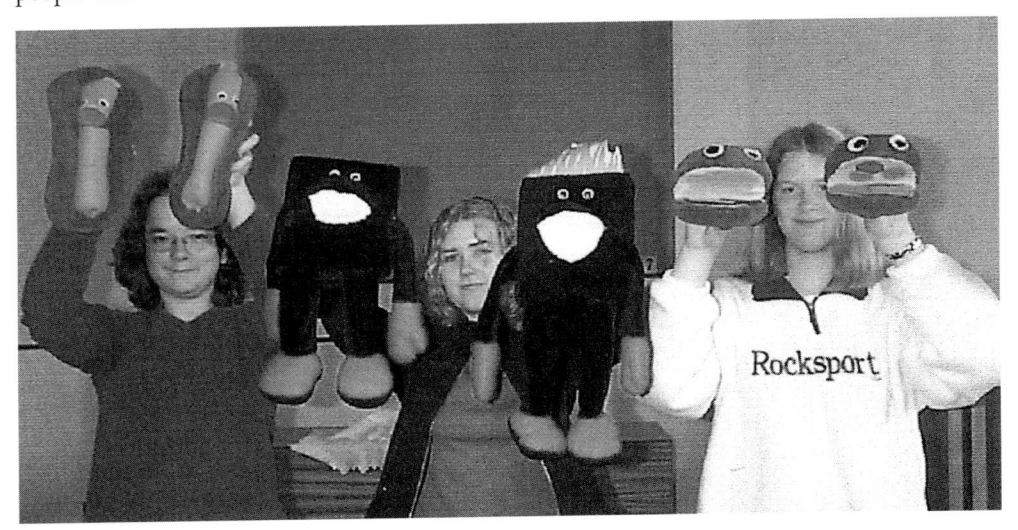

Friend puppets or character actors?

Puppets can be used in many ways. These come down to use either as friend puppets or as story character puppets. The friend puppet is any type of puppet that is used to interact with the audience and will have a personality and character that has been developed by the puppeteer. Thus a ventriloquist puppet, or a character used to introduce Sunday school, or teach a memory verse, is a friend puppet with which the audience can identify as a character in its own right. Friend puppets are neutral, personal and recognise the presence of real people. The story puppet is any puppet that acts out the part of another character in a story or sketch. The puppets are in effect pretending to be other people or objects, in the same way that an actor takes on the character role of the person they are asked to portray. They present different characters as demanded by the nature of the sketch or song.

It is important to differentiate between these two types of puppet roles. It is also necessary to ensure that friend puppets are presented as puppets and not real people. This is because only people have a relationship with God. God's Grace saves only people. Therefore only people should pray, or be capable of a relationship with God and eventually have the opportunity of sharing in the Kingdom of heaven. Friend puppets may be excited about the audience praying or going to heaven, and will be pleased to invite the audience to have a relationship with God, or asking Jesus into their lives They should not suggest or infer that they have that relationship themselves. Allowing friend puppets to pray and to be saved is ultimately confusing and is to be discouraged.

Story character puppets on the other hand, are playing characters in a story and as such may be seen to pray and have a relationship with God, if they are representing people. Thus a puppet may portray almost any character. It is the character that is perceived to pray or to be saved, not the puppet.

The concept of God as a character, or as an entity in a story or drama, is an issue that most puppeteers will need to address at some point in their ministry. Our own team fully recognises the divinity of Christ, and the complete humanity of Jesus whilst establishing His ministry on Earth. We are comfortable using a puppet to play the part of Jesus, but do not use any puppet to portray the more abstract and complex Trinitarian concept of God. We have used a voice-over, combined with a synchronised flashing light or torch, to portray this perception of God. This has been an effective interpretation that has been well received.

WHAT DO PUPPETS DO?

Puppets can't do anything! They are just collections of fur, foam and fabric, and can only be brought to life by the puppeteer's skill. The ventriloquist's puppet is a friend puppet and interacts both with the ventriloquist and with the audience. The ventriloquist may have excellent skills in voice control and pronunciation, showing little sign of lip movement. Whilst this is a highly valued attribute, and may be sought with enthusiasm, it is by no means vital. The essence of good ventriloquism is to be able to present

> 'Puppets can't do anything! They are just collections of fur, foam and fabric, and can only be brought to life by the puppeteer's skill'

the illusion that their puppet is relating a story or dialogue that will hold interest, regardless of whether the ventriloquist is skilled in the basic speech techniques. If the story or teaching is interesting, the audience will rarely even be interested in lip control.

Friend puppets which interact with the audience are popular, and many preachers and teachers use one puppet consistently, which their congregation or class then get to know. Experienced puppeteers learn to use repetitive actions and catch phrases that their congregation come to recognise. The friend puppet gradually develops a character of its own and becomes an established and trusted member of the church family, within the Sunday school classroom, youth club, or an all age congregation.

Story puppets are often used to portray characters in dramas. Congregations are then treated to good drama scripts that deliver Biblical teaching, combined with entertaining skilful puppetry techniques. Preachers quickly learn that puppets can say things to a congregation that a preacher would hesitate to say, yet convey the point without offence.

Puppets that sing songs are very entertaining and are an effective way of presenting Christian themes. Well choreographed puppet songs will remain in the memory of many people, long after a sermon has been forgotten.

CHOOSING THE RIGHT PUPPET

Ventriloquists will probably choose to use a full body puppet. This is not essential, as a standard rod-arm puppet is also appropriate for this purpose. However, the ventriloquist puppet is rarely hidden behind a stage and is usually seated on the ventriloquist's lap or spare arm. It is more lifelike in this situation if the puppet has legs, so a full body puppet is most effective. Some ventriloquists use an alien, animal, or bird puppet. Steve Axtell, a skilled puppet builder from the USA, developed a false arm prop that many ventriloquists use to help create the illusion of their bird puppet perching on their arm.

Puppets used behind a stage will usually be rod-arm puppets rather than the human arm variety. This is because of the greater number of puppeteers required to operate human arm puppets. Rod-arm puppets are easier to use and less expensive to buy and build. Rod-arm puppets can do all the things that human arm puppets can do in terms of body and mouth movement. However, the limited arm and hand manipulation possibilities do produce a slightly less expressive puppet.

Human arm puppets are very expressive, especially when operated by two puppeteers. These make excellent friend puppets, as well as very versatile characters in dramas and puppet songs. They often take the lead role in dramas and songs. They can even be used to perform simple magic tricks and present object lessons.

Object puppets such as hot dogs, trees and flowers, can be very effective. Consider for example, the ways in which a light bulb or candle with a moving mouth, can be used to teach about Jesus as the Light of the world. Each object puppet can deliver a symbolic message of its own.

Puppets without stages – Ventriloquism

When a puppeteer uses a puppet outside of a puppet stage environment, the audience sees two characters – the puppet and the puppeteer. It follows that the puppeteer must create the illusion that the puppet has a life, character and voice of its own. This is achieved by using two different voices and manipulating the puppet in such a way that the audience forgets all about the puppeteer. The ventriloquist can shift the attention of the audience to focus upon the puppet by appropriate body language, eye contact, misdirection and voice projection, drawing their audience's attention back to themselves by speaking in their own voice.

The ventriloquist uses the inability of the human ear to judge precisely the specific directional source of sound. Our eyes combine with our ears to locate the source, so that the skilled ventriloquist can fool the audience's brains into thinking that the voice comes from the puppet. We are further convinced because our eyes see the puppet's mouth moving and not the puppeteer's. We hear the voice and therefore accept the illusion that the puppet is speaking. The illusion is completed when the puppeteer looks at the puppet when it is speaking, and reacts with the appropriate responses and body language, creating an individual persona for the puppet.

Once the puppeteer has developed sufficient confidence in handling the puppet, and has interesting dialogue or a story to relate, that confidence will spill over into the performance. The audience will rarely notice any lip and voice control shortcomings. In ventriloquism, it is important to develop a different character voice for the puppet, which should be used consistently. It is worthwhile stressing that practice leads to perfection. In the early stages, the novice ventriloquist is likely to confuse the audience by mixing up the voice of the character with that of their own, and vice versa.

The ventriloquist can use the puppet in a variety of ways. The puppeteer or the puppet can interact with the congregation, asking questions of specific people. Either the puppet or the puppeteer can respond to the given answers. Mostly, the puppet will be the foil, misunderstanding the teaching and making silly responses. The puppeteer then has the opportunity to correct the puppet, introducing the appropriate teaching or response. Conversely, the questions could come from the congregation, with a similar scenario developed. The puppet gets it wrong and the puppeteer teaches the correct Christian response through appropriate dialogue. Sometimes it is useful to allow the puppet to respond correctly. Children will enjoy the irony of the puppet correcting the adult teacher or preacher.

A story can be told in a similar fashion, using the puppet to either tell the story itself, or to interrupt and question the puppeteer. Many ventriloquists tell a Bible story themselves, using the puppet to ask questions, or make far fetched comments that can be turned around to teach the appropriate response. Skilled and adventurous ventriloquists can even include a song for the puppet to sing, or a Bible verse to recite.

Some puppeteers develop a specific puppet's character so that it appears as a wise friend, dispensing advice and teaching that is readily absorbed by receptive young ears. Using a puppet such as a friendly grandfather or grandmother figure, or even an owl would be very appropriate in this instance. The lovable but naughty, naïve puppet is equally effective, and can provide many opportunities for teaching. More or less any puppet can be used in this role, but often the stereotypical perception of the naughty, freckle faced, cheeky schoolboy is most successful. Other suitable characters include the misbehaving duck and mischievous monkey.

Whichever method is employed, it is important to follow some general guidelines. We have seen how puppets can seem very real to children, who will often react and respond to teaching given through a puppet. It follows that we should be careful to ensure that the puppet is not seen to be using bad language or inappropriate behaviour,

> 'Children will enjoy the irony of the puppet correcting the adult teacher or preacher'

unless the puppeteer or third party corrects it. The puppet in the role of itself should not be Christian, but delight in acknowledging God's love and active role in the world and its affairs.

Children will identify very closely with a ventriloquist's puppet; more so than most stage puppets. Care must be taken in choosing a friendly, rather than a potentially frightening puppet. It is important not to assume that all young children will want to hold and play with a puppet. Some young children are terrified by even a friendly looking grandmother puppet or lovable animal figure. Before you approach a child with a puppet, make sure that the child is not showing signs of anxiety. Most children will eventually welcome being close to a puppet and talking to it, but some, most adamantly will not. Never force the issue!

It is important that the ventriloquist interacts with the puppet as if it is real, in order that the congregation will be equally convinced. Effective ventriloquists will themselves become conscious of two distinct and separate personalities, and some are even surprised at the response of their puppet to their own questioning, as the puppet's response seems out of character!

The voice used by the puppet must be suited to the character, and it is very important to give a name that children will relate to. The illusion of reality will be enhanced if the puppet keeps on the move, maintains eye contact and offers credible believable actions. This is most important when using a human type puppet. It is more acceptable for an animal or alien puppet to perform unlikely or sudden physical actions. For example, it will usually be unacceptable to twist the head of a human type puppet through 360 degrees, but there is no reason why an alien or caricature cheeky animal should not do so.

Children and adults will become bored by long speeches, either from the puppeteer or the puppet. Therefore, good dialogue with puppets should usually be kept short in nature. Whether the piece of dialogue is long or short, good timing is essential. The puppet or congregation must be given time to respond to what is being asked or related. This is especially true of funny lines or jokes. It may seem an obvious thing to say, but the ventriloquist must also react to the puppet! The reaction of the ventriloquist reinforces what the audience is expected to do. So many ventriloquists expect their audience to laugh or respond to their puppet, but fail to do so themselves.

> *The illusion of reality will be enhanced if the puppet keeps on the move, maintains eye contact and offers credible believable actions*

The following sketch is a fine example of a simple, but effective approach to scriptwriting for ventriloquists. The script focuses on the real life fear that children often have of things that go bump in the night. The ventriloquist reassures the puppet, (and therefore the children) and at the same time points to Jesus, who appears as a ghostlike figure. In fact He is very real and able to take command of the situation. The sketch ends with the Good News that Jesus is a reality in all of our lives and always available for us. All of this is encapsulated in a few lines of dialogue. The sketch is entitled *Ghost stories – Jesus in Life's Storms* a puppet sketch for puppet (Sally) and ventriloquist. It is reproduced with thanks to, and with the kind permission of the author, Rachel Moore. Some minor dialogue and spelling changes have been made to suit UK readers. Rachel has several fine scripts for puppet, ventriloquism and drama ministries on her web site, which is detailed in the resources chapter.

GHOST STORIES – JESUS IN LIFE'S STORMS.

VENT: Hey Sally, why are you so quiet today?

SALLY: I'm a little bit scared actually, 'cos I've had a bit of a fright.

VENT: What on earth has made you so frightened?

SALLY: We were telling ghost stories last night…..and I think I saw one!

VENT: Stories like that are scary. I know a story in the Bible about some people who thought that they saw a ghost. They were scared too.

SALLY: No! Not a ghost story in the Bible?

VENT: Well, not quite. Let me tell it to you.

SALLY: I don't know. I think I've had my fill of ghost stories for one day.

VENT: Oh come on Sally. I told you. It's not really a ghost story. Just a bit like one.

SALLY: All right, but you have to stop if I tell you to.

VENT: OK. The disciples were all out on a boat early one morning, long before daybreak. The wind was blowing really hard. All the disciples were straining at the oars. They were rowing like mad but the wind was so strong, that they weren't getting very far at all.

SALLY: Then what happened?

VENT: They looked up and thought that they saw a ghost. The ghost of Jesus walking on the water!

SALLY: Crikey! What did they do?

VENT: They were really scared and they cried out 'HELP!'

SALLY: Aaaghhhhh!

VENT: That's right. Just like that. But then something happened.

SALLY: (shaking nervously) What? What happened?

VENT: Jesus spoke to them and said, 'Take courage! It is I, don't be afraid!'
Then He climbed into the boat and the wind died down, and it was dead calm.

SALLY: Crumbs. It wasn't a ghost then?

VENT: No. They just thought that it was.

SALLY: And He was real. Right there with them. Close enough to snuggle up to?

VENT: Yes, and He spoke to them to comfort and encourage them.

SALLY: Wow! That's a great story.

VENT:	Yes. And it's true. Do you know what that story means for us today?
SALLY:	Don't go out in a boat in bad weather?
VENT:	No, silly. It tells us that Jesus is right there with you, when you are scared.
SALLY:	He's real and He's close isn't He?
VENT:	Yes. He's real, and He's there for us, all through life's storms. Close enough to cuddle up to and to whisper a few words of encouragement in our ear.

Your puppet can welcome worshippers at the door, children to Sunday school, announce birthdays, pick out particular people for mention, lead a song, teach a verse, hold song words, objects, announcements, introduce songs, prayers, tell stories and a hundred and one other things. Be bold when using your puppet and you will be introduced to exciting situations that you may not have expected. The skills of ventriloquism can only be acquired by practice. There are resources available in the form of video and books that provide excellent teaching. Fred Maher's course in ventriloquism is a good starting point. Also recommended are Liz Von Seggen's videos, books and scripts at One Way Street. (See resources chapter)

PUPPETS IN STAGES

Most people will recognise a Punch and Judy booth, and for many this is the limit of their experience of puppet stages. There are however, several types of stages and ways of presenting puppetry effectively. Anything that is used to hide the fact that the puppet is being operated by a puppeteer, may be considered to be a stage. Congregations will be more interested in your puppet if it is well presented in an attractive stage. A Biblical drama can be effectively presented by kneeling behind an upturned tabletop or standing behind a piano. However, sooner or later most puppeteers will want to perform in a real stage.

The nature and size of your ministry will determine what kind of stage is required. It should be lightweight and therefore portable, attractive, practical, sturdy, inexpensive and should pack into a carrying case. This is achievable, as an excellent single tier stage can be made

> 'Be bold when using your puppet and you will be introduced to exciting situations that you may not have expected'

from two camera tripods, one cross bar and a piece of opaque fabric. Our own stage is based on this principle. It is a large three-tier stage with wings at each side. We need 8 tripods, 5 crossbars, 2 sidebars and lots of black velvet curtaining. This was a very expensive but worthwhile purchase. Financial considerations will determine the nature of your stage. The following three examples are of stages that are currently being used effectively by different sized puppet teams.

The wall principle

Any structure that provides an opaque panel for puppeteers to hide behind will provide adequate staging. Attractively painted wooden panels, office screening, or fabrics hung between two supported poles are used by puppeteers as staging. Teams may build wooden blocks and paint them in order to simulate a brick or stone wall, or a wooden fence. The stage should be secure in construction and be at an appropriate height for the puppeteers in order to show the puppets fully.

The enclosed folding stage

This type of stage is a three-sided box, made up of three hinged or taped wooden panels with a fabric top and back, as illustrated. It can be used with or without a one-way viewing screen, made of black net curtain or similar fabric. Used without a screen, the puppeteer sits or kneels on the floor. Used with a screen, the puppeteer may stand

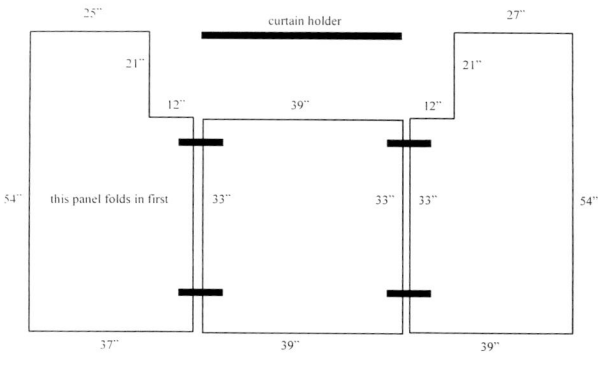

Folding screen stage—flat elevation

up, facing and seeing the audience, but hidden from view. This has the advantage of enabling the puppet to interact on a one to one basis with members of the audience. The puppeteer can react to the response and body language of the congregation. The dimensions of the stage may be varied to provide room for more than one puppeteer. This type of stage will pack flat and may be easily stored. The skilled D.I.Y. enthusiast may be able to build an even more portable version using fabric over wooden or metal poles that fit together into the basic box frame shape. Most D.I.Y shops will stock the required materials.

LARGER SINGLE AND MULTI-TIER STAGES

More puppet teams are becoming established every week and those who hope to present multi-puppet songs and dramas will need a large stage, preferably with two or more tiers, wing panels and a back drop. Space is needed not only to conceal the puppeteers, but also to store puppets and props back-stage ready for use. Two of the most popular stage constructions are the pipe stage and the tripod stage. Both look similar to the pipe stage illustration and are used in the same way. The major differences are the construction materials and the cost.

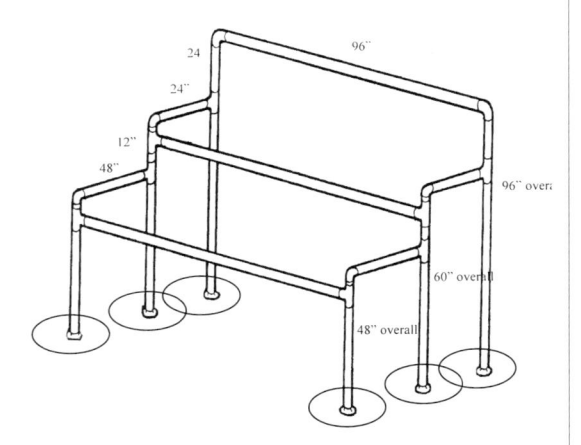

Two-tier pipe stage with backdrop
Adjust lengths and height to suit your puppeteers.

The pipe stage is made from plastic plumbing pipe, which is to be found at most D.I.Y. stores. Our first stage was made from 1.5-inch piping. Larger diameter pipe will be more stable. The choice depends upon your financial resources and requirements. The pipes are cut to size and held together with the plastic joints that are made to compliment the piping. These come in many shapes and combinations, allowing for straight and right angle joints and extensions. The whole construction may be covered with any opaque fabric. The illustration shows a stage that can hold around ten puppeteers. You may lengthen the side panels and cross bars for a larger stage, but it may become fairly unstable if too large. This is a disadvantage of the thinner gauge plastic piping. We commissioned a local steel stockist to cut a metal piping base frame, over which we dropped the front four upright plastic pipes. The metal base combined with wooden prop crossbars provided a very sturdy stage. All joints should be re-enforced with bolts or strong tape.

The photo tripod stage is a very versatile arrangement that can be adapted to suit most puppet teams. It packs into a bag that fits into a small car boot and is easy to erect and dismantle. Jessops, the national camera retailers carry a range of tripods, crossbars and bar joints that are used as studio screens and for mounting cameras and accessories. These can be fairly expensive, but are a worthwhile investment if your team can afford them, especially if you intend to travel to different venues.

All stages of this type require curtains and local market traders are likely to offer suitable fabrics. Velvet and velour are opaque fabrics ideal for staging. Choose sufficiently heavy weight fabric that is opaque enough to hide puppeteers and hangs well. Black is a safe colour to use and will be beneficial if you intend presenting black light puppetry. Ensure that you purchase enough fabric to allow for folds, which give a good appearance and help to prevent any transparency. At least one and a half times the length of each part of the outer stage will be required. Thus, a front panel that is 6 feet in length, will require at least 9 feet in order to be effective. The fabric panels can be held together with pins or tape.

Prop bars are wooden bars approximately 4 inches wide, that are attached to the front of each stage tier. These provide a sturdy base for props such as telephones, flower vases or musical instruments. They are also useful for pinning scripts for the puppeteers to read whilst performing, held in place by hooks attached to the underside of the bar. They can also be rigged with internal lighting such as ultra violet black lights. Be sure to use low power fluorescents that will not become too hot for internal stage use.

Puppetry techniques

There are some very good puppetry technique teaching resources available, including videos, books and cassettes (see resources chapter). This section simply seeks to outline the basic requirements, with suggestions and ideas for team leaders to develop. The basics of rod-arm puppetry manipulation are:

> Height and positioning
> Entrances and exits
> Lip synchronisation
> Eye contact
> Credible action and movement

Height and positioning

No matter how good the script or song, puppet presentation is worthless if the audience can't see the puppets. Good quality puppets should include elastic straps fitted to the moving mouth inside the puppet head, in order to secure the puppeteer's hand. With the hand securely inside these straps, the arms should extend to full length, forming an imaginary straight, vertical line from the top of the puppet's head through the body and puppeteer's arm. The arm should be close to the puppeteer's head, touching the ear.

The belly button of the puppet (if it had one!) should be level with the top of the stage, with the puppet positioned approximately 6 inches from the front of the stage. Novices will find that their arms tire easily, allowing their arm to lean forward. This is a major fault and results in the puppet slowly sinking, as if in quicksand. It is actually more tiring to hold the arm in this forward position than to adopt the correct stance. Practice makes perfect, and a few minutes spent practising each day will pay rich dividends. Try holding a squash ball or small tennis ball in your hand, with the hand in the position that you would hold a puppet's mouth. Squeezing the ball with your thumb for a few minutes with your arm held straight up will quickly strengthen the necessary muscles required for puppetry.

Don't allow puppeteers to lean on the stage as this leads to incorrect puppet height. Stages are not designed to support tired puppeteers and will not carry the extra weight without sagging. It is not professional to fall through the front of the stage! Kneeling pads, chairs or cushioned step-on platforms will help to maintain correct puppet height. These aids will be necessary if you have different height puppeteers in your team.

Entrances and exits

When entering or leaving a room, people don't suddenly appear or disappear like jack-in-the-boxes, and nor should puppets. It will help the puppeteer to think of the puppet as if it is performing on a platform. Practice climbing four stairs to reach the platform, bouncing the puppet slightly as you climb, to suggest climbing and walking. Once on stage, simulate a very short performance by turning the puppet's head both ways, open and close the mouth and then exit. The exit should consist of a 90 or 180-degree turn towards the free arm, followed by climbing four steps down, keeping the puppet straight and bouncing slightly.

Eye contact

Humans usually look at each other when conversing and it is important that puppets do the same. It is equally important that puppets establish and maintain eye contact with the audience. Proper eye contact involves the audience in the drama or song. Stages are usually higher than the audience eye level. Puppeteers must be aware of this difference and ensure that puppet heads are tilted down to the correct angle. Even when they are third parties to a conversation and are not being directly addressed, puppets should be following the dialogue by switching eye contact between the other puppets and the audience. They should not be so animated as to divert attention away from the speaking puppet. Experience will determine where the puppet's attention should be directed. Audiences will quickly tire of a static performance and need to be kept involved with eye contact.

Lip synchronisation

Synchronising the puppet's mouth with dialogue is one of the most difficult techniques to perfect. The puppet's mouth should open with each syllable spoken, but should be kept closed when not speaking. The most common

> 'Audiences will quickly tire of a static performance and need to be kept involved with eye contact'

mistakes are biting words, flipping the lid, and being late with the synchronisation. Closing the mouth on each syllable instead of opening is a common fault known as biting words. This is corrected only by practising and rehearsing in front of others who can point out this type of error.

Flipping the lid involves moving both the lower and upper jaws on each syllable. Humans only move their lower jaw when speaking, thus maintaining eye contact. The puppeteer needs to control the operating hand by holding the palm still, only moving the thumb up and down. This is only accomplished with practice. There are various ways of achieving the correct movement. One way is to cross the second finger over the index finger. The other is to apply pressure on the middle two fingers by slightly squeezing inwards with index and little finger.

Late synchronisation occurs when the puppet's mouth chases the dialogue. The puppet's mouth opens a fraction after the word is actually spoken. This fault can be very distracting to an audience. Team leaders can help to correct this by pinning a copy of the script to the prop bar in front of the puppeteer for them to learn and follow. Memorising and anticipating dialogue is useful, and with regular rehearsal, happens as a matter of course. Open the mouth wide enough to suggest speaking words as a human does, but fully open when shouting or singing. Whilst simulating whispering or speaking softly, it follows that the mouth should only be opened slightly.

CREDIBLE ACTION AND MOVEMENT

Novice puppeteers tend to focus upon the delivery of the dialogue and concentrate on reading the script in front of them, rather than watching their puppet. This is particularly noticeable when performing a new drama. Watching the puppet whilst operating it is important. It will help the puppeteer to spot correctable faults such as keeping an upright position, eye contact and maintaining credible movement. A common fault is to hold the puppet's arm at right angles to the body when using a rod, and puppeteers must be alerted to this obviously unnatural position, which is caused by a lack of concentration.

The experienced puppeteer will maintain an adequate space between all the puppets on stage, manipulating head, arms and body to suggest many actions such as

'Novice puppeteers tend to focus upon the delivery of the dialogue and concentrate on reading the script in front of them, rather than watching their puppet'

yawning, praying, running, crouching, thinking and pointing. All these actions help to create the illusion of life and it is vital that puppets perform only actions that are believable. It helps to create believable and enthusiastic actions by physically moving with the puppet, especially when dancing or presenting puppet songs. For example, puppeteers who present rock guitarists or drummers will transfer feeling to a performance if they are enjoying the music and rocking to the beat themselves. It cannot be over-emphasised that experience only comes after performing; and to perform skilfully requires a great deal of practice. It's a two way process.

Puppets in worship – drama and song

We have seen how puppets can be used in many different ways, and by far the most popular of these are the puppet drama and the puppet song. Both are tremendously effective and require the same basic skills and manipulation techniques. However, dramas usually require less movement. Songs require a greater degree of choreography. However, the two forms can be combined to produce individual musical dramas or longer musicals. This section is designed to provide ideas for aspiring puppeteers and teams of all sizes to develop in both drama and song. There are hundreds of scripts and songs available to you and several suppliers listed in the resources chapter. Different styles of puppetry suit different individuals and you will probably wish to approach the songs and dramas in a different way to our suggestions. Choreography and drama development is good fun and all members of the team should be encouraged to suggest ideas.

Puppet drama takes many forms and there are hundreds of scripts written for two, three or four puppeteers, as well as some very good monologues. The usual rules of drama scripting will apply of course, making sure that the script is appropriate to the congregation and to the general theme of the service or worship event. General guidelines for script writing are discussed at length in the drama chapter.

The first consideration is whether scripts are presented live, with puppeteers speaking the parts, or whether the script is pre-recorded. There are advantages for both forms, but pre-recorded scripts provide the opportunity for the puppeteer to fully concentrate upon operating the puppets. This means they do not have to worry about voice control and reading scripts. Pre-recorded scripts are also consistent, and timing can be perfected by repeated use. However, live voices can interact with an audience and ad-lib when appropriate. Our team always uses pre-recorded scripts except when offering the occasional narrated story or poem.

Scripture interpretation is probably the easiest drama to perform and can be tackled by novice puppeteers. Our first ever performance contained a narration of a poem about the Good Samaritan and involved six puppeteers. Some of our young puppeteers had great fun, going completely over the top when beating up the traveller in the story. Many of Jesus' parables can be presented using modern day puppets and settings. Several scriptwriters have created modern versions of parables such as the Unforgiving Servant, Good Samaritan and Prodigal Son. It is a simple task to adapt and re-write this type of script, as the classic storyline as told by Jesus already exists. The story can be made more relevant to a modern day congregation by applying an up to date setting and contemporary characters. The simulated television interview is an entertaining way of presenting such stories. One of the most successful puppet dramas that we still use is *It's Incredible* which is an interview with Noah as he prepares to build the Ark, whilst being ridiculed by an abusive TV interviewer.

The following sketch, *Joshua, Jericho and God* is based on the story of the breaching of the walls of Jericho, but approached from the perspective of child puppets who have misunderstood the teaching. This is a popular way of approaching Bible stories and has much to commend it. The sketch is reproduced with thanks to, and with the kind permission of the author, Rachel Moore. Some minor dialogue and spelling changes have been made to suit UK readers.

> 'The story can be made more relevant to a modern day congregation by applying an up to date setting and contemporary characters'

JOSHUA, JERICHO AND GOD

Puppets 1 and 2 are marching around blowing trumpets and horns.

P3 Hey! What's all the racket up here?

P1 We're trying to make the walls fall down.

P2 Yeah, like Joshua at the battle of Jericho.

P1 Joshua and the Israelites went out every morning for six days, marching round Jericho and blowing their trumpets

P2 And on the seventh day they marched round seven times blowing their trumpets.

P1 Then Joshua told them to shout really loud.

P2 And the priests blew their trumpets. And the people shouted. And the walls of Jericho came tumbling down.

P3 Well, you seem to know the story well enough, but I think you've kind of missed the point.

P1&2 Point? What point?

P3 Exactly. When you leave out the most important part, the story has no point.

P1&2 I don't understand. What do you mean?

P3 You know that they all shouted, marched and blew trumpets, but they would have looked a bit silly wouldn't they. Do you know why they did those things?

P1 Mmmm. Because that was the way to destroy the wall?

P2 That's right! Because God told them to!

P3 Aah, yes. That's the important part. That's whom you left out of the story. God.

P1&2 Oh!

P3 You see, Joshua didn't make the walls fall down. The people of Israel didn't make the walls fall down. The marching, the blowing and the shouting didn't make the walls fall down.

P1 So what did then?

P3 God did! Because Joshua and the Israelites did what God told them to do. It was God's power that made the walls come down.

P1 So, if we marched and blew our trumpets and shouted all day, the walls wouldn't come down then?

P3 Not unless God wanted them to.

P2 So what's the point of the story then?

P3 If you do what God tells you to, no matter how silly it seems, God can make a real difference to your life. You may think that the problems that you face in life are huge and insurmountable, but God will help you cope and find a way around them.

P1 That's because God knows the answers?

P3 That's right. God knows the answers!

Some stories lend themselves to melodrama and pantomime. 'Daniel in the lion's den,' 'David and Goliath' and 'Jonah and the Whale,' offer opportunities for humour, whilst some of the more poignant stories such as 'The Passion' and 'The raising of Lazarus' offer examples that can be effectively portrayed by puppets, adopting a more serious approach. Converting principal objects to moving mouth puppets can offer effective new perspectives and opinions on old stories. Consider the wall at Jericho complaining about a punk graffiti artist and boasting of the strength of its own construction. Teach congregations about God's love for the marginalized by recording a conversation between a tree and Zaccheus. These techniques can add humour, interest and impact to traditional stories.

Congregations readily identify with puppets because they can see much of themselves in many of the situations that they face. Thus contemporary lifestyle, domestic drama and real life events are a very effective way of illustrating themes with puppets. The following sketch is based upon a children's game and demonstrates how some sketches can be interactive, providing opportunities to stop the action and talk to the congregation. It also introduces teaching opportunities by focusing upon

'Congregations readily identify with puppets because they can see much of themselves in many of the situations that they face'

specific Scripture passages. The sketch is for three puppets in the stage and one adult outside. It is best presented live and is entitled *A Treasure Worth Seeking*. It is reproduced with thanks to, and with the kind permission of the author, Rachel Moore. Some minor dialogue and spelling changes have been made to suit UK readers. Other good scripts can be found on Rachel's web site. (details in resources chapter)

A TREASURE WORTH SEEKING

P1: Ahoy and Avast! And shiver me timbers!

Adult: What are you all doing? And why are you all dressed up like pirates?

P1: Were here for the treasure hunt.

P2: Yeah! I love treasure hunts.

P3: Are we really going to see some treasure?

Adult: Well, there is a treasure hunt here today, but not quite like the one you were expecting.

P1: We don't mind what kind of treasure. We're not picky pirates!

P2: So get on with it. Where's the map?

P3: Yeah! There's always a map.

Adult: There's no map. I will start you off with a clue and then someone will have to follow it up to find the treasures. Find the clues and bring them to me and then we'll see where that leads us.

P1: We'll have to press-gang a search party.

P2: That's right. Get someone else to do the work and then we'll get the treasure.

P3: Let's choose someone from out there.

Puppets point to congregation and encourage some volunteers to step forward to look at the map and one by one, search for clues.

Adult produces the first clue (These are only suggested clues. You may wish to use your own to suit your situation.)

Adult:	The first clue says. 'She's one of the sweetest ladies in our church, drives a red car and teaches in Sunday school. She is a real treasure!'
P1:	Come on you. *(points to a volunteer)* Take the clue and find our treasure! *(Puppets stay on stage, encouraging the volunteers)*

Volunteer approaches the person described and she reads a verse from Scripture: 'Gold there is, and rubies in abundance, but lips that speak knowledge are a rare jewel.' (Proverbs 20:15 NIV)

Congregation member gives the verse and a clue envelope to the volunteer, who returns and gives it to the adult.

P2:	What does it say? What does it say?
Adult:	It's another clue. It says 'Her husband leads the music in our worship services. He's a real treasure.'

Volunteer goes to husband who reads: 'A wife of noble character who can find? She is worth far more than rubies.' (Proverbs 31:10 NIV) He gives volunteer the envelope and it is returned to adult.

P3:	What does it say? Where's the treasure?
Adult:	It's another clue and it says, 'He lives next to the church and teaches us about God's Word. We are blessed to have such a treasure.'

Volunteer goes to congregation member who reads 'But his delight is in the law of the LORD, and on his law he meditates day and night.' (Psalms 1:2 NIV) Volunteer returns to adult with the next clue.

P1:	Where's the treasure? Where's the treasure?
Adult:	Be patient and listen to the next clue. 'It tells of God's love for us, and how to live like Jesus. It's a book full of treasure!'

A Bible (or Bible puppet) should be prominently displayed with two verses marked at Psalm 139:17 and Psalm 119:11. Volunteer brings Bible to adult.

P2:	Here's the treasure!
P1:	Read it out!
P3:	Yeah! Read it out!
Adult:	Let's see what treasures this has inside. *(Reads:)* 'How precious to me are your thoughts, O God! How vast is the sum of them!' (Psalm 139:17 NIV) and 'I have hidden your word in my heart that I might not sin against you.' (Psalm 119:11 NIV)

The Word of God is a very precious thing and this book contains many treasures. You don't need to be a pirate, or need a map to find this treasure. God's treasure is a free gift for all.

The sketch is very simple and can be adapted to suit different passages from Scripture. It is an effective tool with which to introduce specific verses or teaching on the Bible as a code for living. Rachel Moore, suggests introducing a 'Wordless Book' (different coloured felts which suggest the story of salvation - available commercially) and handing out 'Wordless Book' bracelets (also available commercially). The magic prop 'The Flaming Bible' would also be appropriate.

Although some scripts call for several puppets, the majority of puppet sketches are written for two puppeteers. Successful scripts will be of reasonable length, portraying believable and likeable characters, who engage in short, crisp dialogue that contains poignancy and humour. Adapt scripts to suit your own style and rehearse the drama so that each puppeteer is familiar with both the sketch and the actions required to present it effectively. It is a big mistake to allow the dialogue to sell the drama on its own. The puppets will be regarded as actors and must offer a variety of movements and actions that will enhance the dialogue and hold the congregation's interest.

PUPPET SONGS

Many puppet groups start their ministry by showing puppet songs. These are great fun to perform and challenging to choreograph. There are few congregations that will not respond favourably to puppets in colourful costumes singing traditional songs or customised puppet songs. There are a myriad of styles to choose from and many puppet teams present barbershop quartets, rock groups, country and western and rap, as well as some outlandish alien type puppet music groups.

Puppet movements should fit the tempo and style of the music. It is acceptable to adopt incorrect entrances and exits as long as the improper movement is appropriate to the song and all puppets move in unison. Some tunes lend themselves to 'pop corning' for example. This is a movement whereby several puppets bob up and down in time with the beat, repeatedly disappearing from view and re-appearing like a jack-in-the-box.

Rock and roll is a very popular musical genre and appropriately sized guitars, drums, saxophones and other musical instruments can be built or purchased from toy shops. They can be attached to the puppet with elastic bands, pins and Velcro. Larger instruments such as pianos and double basses may be attached to prop bars. Mouth organs may be attached to rods. Puppeteers' imaginations can run wild and produce some incredible ideas. The moving mouth principle can be applied to musical instruments that can be made into puppets with foam and felt and used to sing themselves. Guitars, trumpets and musical note puppets have all been used effectively by puppet teams to sing songs. These are especially entertaining when made from fluorescent material and presented in black light.

Parody songs are well known songs, the lyrics of which have been altered to provide a Christian message. These are a hugely popular and a very effective method of communicating the Gospel. They convey the Christian message using tunes that congregations are familiar with. There are several bands and songwriters producing parody music. The work of musicians such as Mark Bradford and Jim Wideman is widely used on the *Puppets in Concert*

> ❛The moving mouth principle can be applied to musical instruments that can be made into puppets with foam and felt and used to sing themselves❜

PuppetTrax and *Righteous Pop Music* series of CD's and cassettes. The American band Apologetix has produced around one hundred songs that parody popular music from the 50's to modern day.

Chorus line choreography is one of the main elements to work on when presenting puppet songs. Puppeteers should develop a variety of different entrances and exits, using the kind of synchronised movements employed by backing singers. Teams need to be aware of instrumental bridges filling these breaks with movement. Important theme keywords should be seized upon. These may be emphasised with movement and used as a preaching hook after the song. It is important to use all the team when working on choreography, ensuring that lots of different elements are employed in songs to provide variety.

Human arm puppets are effective as lead singers and the addition of a microphone and stand positioned inside the stage for the puppet to hold, will add to the presentation. Volunteers can be encouraged to play blow-up guitars alongside the stage during puppet rock songs. Puppet presentation can be effectively combined with video of Biblical epics. For example, our team uses a video clip from *Jesus The Man* combined with signing, alongside the parody song *His Love Will Go On* adapted from the sound track from the film *Titanic*.

Musical dramas such as those performed by Carman and Ray Boltz are particularly effective. There are several songs by these artists that contain very powerful images from Scripture and church life, which can provide superb opportunities for ministry. Musicals are very popular and there are many written for puppet presentation, based on Christian themes and the Christian calendar. These are usually around 20-40 minutes duration and combine several songs on a theme, linked by short pieces of dialogue.

PUPPET WORKSHOPS AND REHEARSALS

Workshops are a great way of introducing puppetry to novices. They can also serve to teach new skills to more advanced puppeteers. Christian puppetry is such a diverse subject that many different topics can be explored in any given workshop. Work on elements such as basic skills, puppet making, props and effects, choreography and black light. Our own team usually present basic skills workshops for beginners, leading to an act of worship presented by the workshop participants. This basic format, which has been very well received by many different churches, is an effective way to spark interest in puppetry in worship and is outlined below.

First, introduce different types of puppets. Discuss the human arm and the rod arm puppet in detail. Explore the limitations of puppets and the puppeteer's role in bringing them to life, leading into basic manipulation skills, lip synchronisation, position, entrances, exits and credible movement. Show some basic props such as flash cards and object type puppets, before handing out some puppets for group work. Play a five-minute 'puppet aerobics' tape, encouraging the participants to practice the basic skills. There are several puppet aerobics cassettes available. (see resources chapter)

Split into groups and provide each group with an experienced puppeteer to lead. Each group is given a script, cassette tape with one puppet song or drama and a cassette player. If you haven't sufficient experienced puppeteers to lead the groups, simply spend more time on the basic skills session and then appoint team leaders from each group. Provided that you offer some starter ideas for the particular song or drama, you can leave the group to create their own interpretation. Leave each group to learn their song or drama, finally coming together to present an act of worship using the skills just learnt. Each group should present it's own song or drama, guided by more experienced puppeteers. The act of worship should be linked by an experienced worship leader and should include worship songs and prayer as well as puppetry. Encourage participants to invite family and friends to the act of worship, making sure that you explain that the technical skills cannot be learnt in one afternoon. The workshop is designed to stimulate interest. The puppetry may not be perfect, but the worship will still be very much appreciated by God.

Workshops should be presented as a fun event. They will be enjoyed by all ages as long as leaders have an awareness of physical limitations. People with stiff joints will not appreciate being asked to kneel on hard floors for long periods, if at all! Leaders who offer workshops that include people with such limitations, must provide stages that can accommodate them comfortably. We find that we attract many children at workshops and a fair number of adults. We find that we cannot present a workshop effectively with children present under 5-years of age, as they simply do not possess the required stamina or attention span.

Rehearsals

Practicing manipulation skills and stagecraft are of course vital to any puppet team, regardless of how many puppeteers are involved. Experienced puppeteers may be able to learn a puppet drama in just one session, needing only to familiarise themselves with the script in order to present it effectively. Some dramas and songs will require several rehearsal sessions before they can be presented in public. We must always endeavour to offer the best that we can to God. Congregations will not appreciate inadequately rehearsed creative arts, whether puppetry, mime, drama or dance, no matter how well intentioned. We owe it to God, our congregations and ourselves to ensure that all presentations are finely tuned and rehearsed before being used in worship.

Whether the session is designed to develop general skills or to learn a new song or drama, rehearsals should follow the same basic format. Rehearsal time is precious and should be planned with a specific objective in mind. It is best to start regular sessions at the same time and night each week, and to start each session with prayer. All the required puppets, scripts and props should be ready to use. A stage is not always required for rehearsals, as most dramas, and some choreography can be worked out without staging. Even when the staging is used, it is best not to use curtains as the director can more easily spot faults in positioning and technique.

Team members will appreciate some variety and there is little merit in rehearsing the same song over and over again. It is better to break the piece down into separate elements, aiming to get at least one part perfected and then move on to another piece. Puppeteers will be happier and more able to achieve and succeed with small segments of choreography that will build their experience and confidence. Constructive criticism is useful, but should include encouragement of team members at every opportunity. Make sure that every one understands their specific role, and when the piece has been learnt, encourage some members to learn other puppeteers' parts. This will enable others to perform that role if the usual puppeteers are not available to present it themselves.

Listen to the music or script, assign the parts and encourage everyone to suggest alternative interpretation. Then work on the choreography and blocking. Make sure

> *'We owe it to God, our congregations and ourselves to ensure that all presentations are finely tuned and rehearsed before being used in worship'*

that the evening includes some time to let off steam and to have some fun. Begin and end the session with prayer and outline plans for the next rehearsal or presentation. It is important to recognise that rehearsal times are not just for puppet practice. They are also invaluable times of social bonding and fellowship. Fellowship is a vital and integral part of team building.

A common mistake made by some creative arts team leaders is to believe that all team members have nothing else to do with their lives than to be part of a ministry team. This is a major error! Whilst one expects commitment from the team, leaders must remember that ministry is voluntary and that team members are not compelled to be there. Be gentle with everyone and make allowances for individuality. Try to consider and understand each member, meeting each individual where they are, not where you would like them to be.

Props and flashcards

Props can add a great deal to a presentation. Puppets will need to hold telephones to make a call, drink from cups or glasses and play musical instruments. Cups and telephones should be normal size, bearing in mind that audiences will need to be able to readily identify these implements from a distance. Musical instruments can be purchased from toyshops or built to scale from lightweight wood or display board. All props need to be supported and there are several ways of doing this.

Fixed props such as trees, backdrops and windows can be attached to the stage by hooks, Velcro or tape. Small props can be 'held' by puppets, attached to hands by pins or elastic bands or held up to the puppet by rods, such as a telephone, for example. Heavier props such as microphone stands or a dummy computer, can be attached to a wooden prop bar and fixed to the stage uprights by the appropriate clamps or bolts.

Puppet teams can be very inventive and incredible props have been devised using basic materials that can be sourced from any D.I.Y. store. Space ships, cars, trains, garden swings and a fully stocked bar have all been constructed and used effectively in puppet stages. However, by far the most widely used prop is the flash card.

The flash card at its simplest, is a piece of card or display board that carries a key word or image that is used to enhance a song. The card is fixed to wooden rods or

> *'Whilst one expects commitment from the team, leaders must remember that ministry is voluntary and that team members are not compelled to be there'*

battens and presented to stage on the appropriate cue. The lettering or image can be painted or made from coloured adhesive tape. Fluorescent tape or paint on a black background will enable the flash card to be used in black light presentations.

A little ingenuity will produce more interesting flash cards that make a major contribution to a song. For example, our team uses a Bible outline flash card, which has another card superimposed with the word LOVE. This is performed in black light and the song lyrics tell of words which 'leap off of the page,' at which point the flash card operator detaches the word LOVE from the Bible flash card, creating the visual illusion of literally leaping off of the page.

Sound systems

It is important to amplify sound for puppetry. Radio microphone headsets can be used for live presentations, but these are expensive. Only experienced puppeteers should attempt live puppetry. Recorded scripts and songs enable puppeteers to concentrate on puppet manipulation. Good stereo sound, relayed through good quality equipment linked to a loop system is ideal, but beyond the resources of some teams. A decent portable CD, tape player or karaoke machine will be adequate for smaller venues.

There are plenty of pre-recorded scripts available, but most teams prefer to adapt puppet scripts to their own style and record them onto tape or minidisk. Many congregations will have members who have good voices and a gift for drama. This is an ideal opportunity to involve other church members to use those gifts to contribute to and enhance the team performance.

LIGHTING AND SPECIAL EFFECTS

All drama is greatly enhanced by creative lighting and puppetry is no exception. Lighting is not essential of course, but even a small stage will benefit from a spotlight to highlight and focus on the puppet. Lighting creates an atmosphere of expectation and when used effectively can add much to a presentation. More ambitious teams may wish to invest in a full lighting set, with a controller that allows for sequence chasing, lights flashing to the music beat and dimmer effects. Par cans are inexpensive floodlights that can be used with coloured gels to provide different colours for different effects and situations. There are many different types of special lights designed for discotheques that can also enhance puppet songs dynamically. These are quite expensive, but just one of these of exciting effects will prove to be a very worthwhile investment if you can afford one of them.

Black light puppetry is an exciting way of presenting puppets. Most sound and lighting shops will stock ultra-violet black light tubes and holders, in 2, 3 and 4 feet lengths, which can be screwed to a prop bar inside the stage. The ultra-violet light will highlight any fluorescent colours. Used in normal light, the black light will enhance whites and fluorescents. When used in a darkened room, they will produce a stunning effect. For example, moving mouth musical instrument puppets, light bulb puppets, number puppets and flash cards, can be made from fluorescent materials or painted in fluorescent paint. These will appear to be suspended in mid air when presented in black light. A black light tube can be fixed to a tripod or simply laid on the floor to highlight signing. This is particularly effective when the signer wears white gloves.

Special effects such as smoke/fog machines, bubble machines and theatrical confetti cannons may be used sparingly to enhance a presentation. Safety precautions must be taken and care will also be needed to take account of congregations' sensitivities in these matters. Consult the church leadership to establish whether there may be objections to using this type of equipment. It is now possible to purchase non-toxic, non-irritant fluid for smoke and fog machines.

Video used in conjunction with puppets is very

'Lighting creates an atmosphere of expectation and when used effectively can add much to a presentation' effective. Those teams fortunate enough to possess video projectors, have a powerful tool that can be used to project song words, combine dramatic scenes from films with puppetry, and to back project backdrop scenes onto the puppet stage for special effect. Those with modest budgets may use an OHP to project song words or images.

FINANCE

Puppetry can be expensive and teams will often need to organise fundraising events in order to buy puppets, props and equipment. Involve your church congregation from the outset by educating them to fully understand the massive potential that puppets have in evangelism. Adopt-a-puppet schemes are very successful. These take several forms, all involving the encouragement of individuals or groups in contributing towards the purchase of a particular puppet. Newsletters can be produced to inform the sponsor of the ways in which the puppet is used and the effect it has had on those who have seen it used in presentations.

Using puppetry in worship is rapidly growing in popularity. Christian puppetry festivals are now being organised along the same lines as those in the USA, where Christian puppeteers can meet together to exchange ideas, attend workshops and even compete in drama, song and ventriloquism competitions. These festivals make a fantastic contribution to the development of puppetry as a ministry, but there is a real danger that teams can become more focused on puppetry skills than worship or ministry. Puppetry enables people to explore and combine theatre and music in a very special way, providing the opportunity to play with all the innovative toys and special effects that are available to us. Be careful to remember that it is worship that is at the heart of the Church's activity. Puppet ministries need to be very aware of this fact, as there are many in today's church that are all too ready to accuse creative artists of only being entertainers. Approach puppetry prayerfully and carefully, focused on Jesus. In this way you will have at your disposal, a tool that can be used very effectively to reach the lost for Christ.

> *Involve your church congregation from the outset by educating them to fully understand the massive potential that puppets have in evangelism*

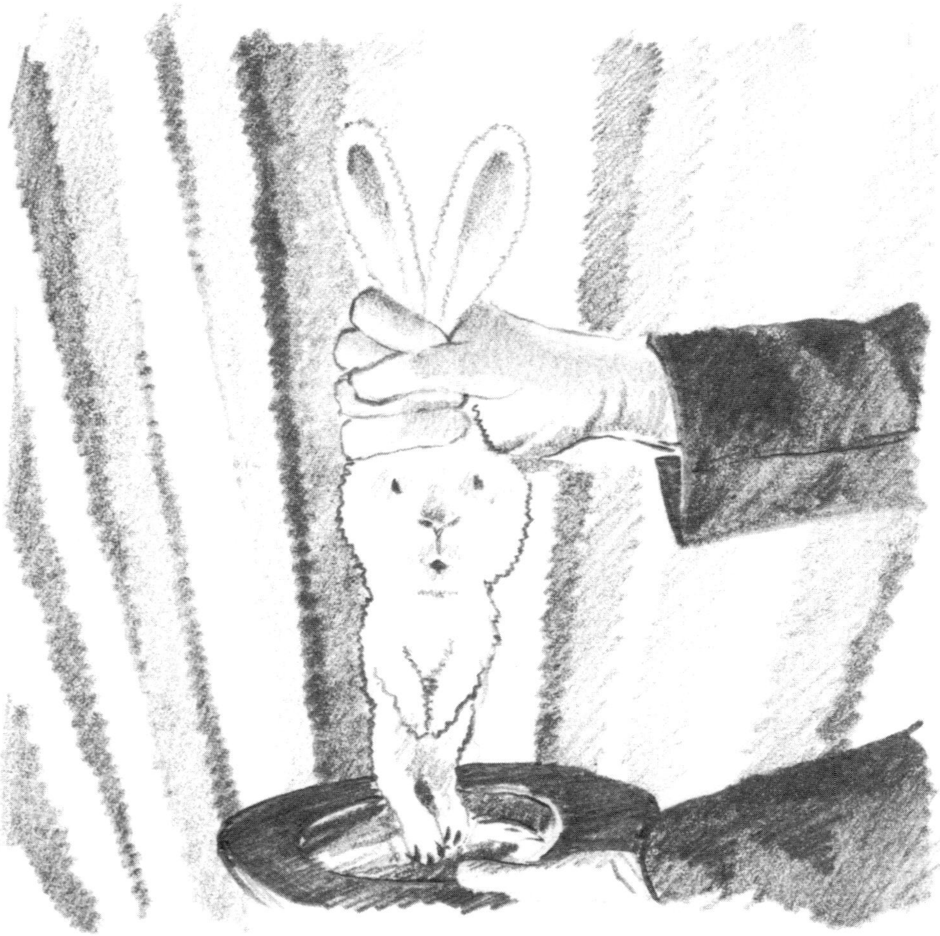

The Gospel magician is able to capture the imagination and grasp the interest of all ages. Having achieved that difficult task, it is then a fairly simple matter to switch their focus onto Jesus and the message of the Gospel.

Chapter Seven
Magic – Gospel Truth through Illusion

Only God does miracles!

Magicians, astrologers and fortunetellers have been woven into the fabric of religion throughout the world for centuries as pagans sought to learn about their origins and their future. Unfortunately, there are many who still seek spiritual truth through cult forms of magic such as astrology, Tarot and mediums, rather than consulting God's Word in the Scriptures.

Mosaic Law expressly forbade magic and the penalty for practicing magic was death. The Jews however consulted oracles, (Judges 18:5-6) and divining cups

(Genesis 44:5) and there are several references to the magicians of Egypt in Exodus. The Jews were ordered not to learn or practice magic, which was called the abomination of the people in the Promised Land. (Leviticus 19:31) Magic mostly disappeared from Jewish culture from that point. The New Testament refers to the Magi in Matthew, but these men were more astrologers than magicians. There are references to magic and sorcery in Revelations and Acts, all of which denounce magic as a wicked practice. There was a mass burning of magic books at Ephesus in Acts 19:18-19.

The Bible reference from Acts at the beginning of this chapter refers to Simon the sorcerer, or Simon Magus, a heretic in the early Church. He is mentioned in several early writings and described as the father of Gnosticism and a corrupter of Christians in Rome. I mention this, simply to place the verse in the right context. This is because Gospel magic is probably the most contentious of all the creative arts discussed in this book. There are many Christians who will not attend a Gospel magic presentation, or would walk out of a service where a Gospel magic illustration is being used. There are many who would not make a stand in this situation, but may not be comfortable with the preacher who uses Gospel magic. Those who hold these views may refer a magician to Leviticus 19:31 NIV, which states, 'Do not turn to mediums or seek out spiritists, for you will be defiled by them. I am the LORD your God.'

I am sensitive to, but saddened by those who do not, or will not understand the difference between satanic practices and Gospel illusions. I would never begin to defend the practice of astrology, the use ouija boards, tarot cards or mediums. Equally, I would challenge any one who seeks to persuade others that they have mysterious, magical or supernatural powers. I much prefer the word illusion to magic, simply because of the misunderstanding of the use of the phrase Gospel magic. The preacher who uses Gospel magic has a superb tool for spreading the Word of God. It is vital that anyone who wishes to use this tool in worship, explains that they are simply presenting object lessons that are puzzles for the eyes. This is achieved by using misdirection, sleight of hand and skills that have been acquired by constant practice. I always begin Gospel magic presentations by telling congregations that they could perform the tricks if they practiced, and that only God does miracles! Those who remain unmoved by these apologetics and still regard

> 'They followed him because he had amazed them for a long time with his magic'
>
> **ACTS 8:11 NIV**

Gospel magic as inappropriate will miss the opportunity of using a valuable tool that does not contradict Scripture in any way.

Why use illusions?

'How did you do that trick, then?' I have presented many Gospel magic effects and there has not been one service, cabaret evening or puppet praise party where Gospel magic has been used, when that question has not been asked by at least one person. Magician entertainers have always fascinated audiences because of the mystery involved. Most people accept that the illusion effect is only brought about by misdirection and sleight of hand. However, the thought still lingers in people's minds that they are seeing something extraordinary. At the very least, most will find magic interesting, and it is this inherent fascination that makes Gospel magic such a powerful tool in worship and Gospel teaching. The Gospel magician is able to capture the imagination and grasp the interest of all ages. Having achieved that difficult task, it is then a fairly simple matter to switch their focus onto Jesus and the message of the Gospel. Combining the illusion effect with a Biblical theme in such a way that it seamlessly leads congregations into a greater understanding is the real magic of the Gospel illusionist.

Gospel magic – the right approach

It would be an arduous task to describe the many effects and techniques that can be used by the Gospel magician and this book does not set out to do that, or reveal a host of magician's secrets. Sorry! It will also not present a long list of tricks and how to do them, although some are described and explained. There are plenty of how to do it books and videos that explain the principles of magic effects and props, and several books on Gospel magic routines. (see resources chapter) It is important to explore some of the techniques that the Gospel magician should employ, and to provide some starter ideas for aspiring Gospel magicians. Therefore this first section is devoted to the principles that a magician should adopt, followed by a discussion on the different types of magic effects, props and equipment. It is hoped that this

> *Do not turn to mediums or seek out spiritists, for you will be defiled by them. I am the LORD your God*
>
> **Leviticus 19:31 NIV**

approach will provide some ideas on presentation that will lead the reader to further explore the skills required to present Gospel illusions.

Share the Gospel message, but keep the illusions' secrets

The above statement is at the heart of Gospel magic and is the mission statement of the Fellowship of Christian Magicians in Europe (FCME), an organisation dedicated to promoting the Gospel by means of illusion. Showing your audience afterwards how a trick was performed is a sure way of destroying the entertainment value and mystery of Gospel magic. I am sure that attendances at football matches would be greatly reduced if we all knew the score beforehand. The same applies to magic. Some magic props and effects are very expensive and most of the inherent value lies in the secret that is behind the effect. By revealing the secret of the trick, the offending magician is depriving others who wish to use that effect in the future. The audience is also robbed of the mystery, with the impact being greatly reduced. Some professional magicians have been robbed of their livelihood by recent television programmes that have featured unprofessional and irresponsible magicians revealing illusion secrets. There are very good reasons for taking care to ensure that when deciding to use Gospel magic in your ministry, secrets will not be revealed by simply telling others or leaving magic props and equipment lying around for inquisitive hands to explore after a presentation.

All creative artists have to examine why they want to use specific creative arts. This is particularly so in the case of the Gospel magician. The magician will be perceived as someone who has extraordinary skills, especially by children. It is imperative that this attention is directed towards God. An explanation that the skills used are gifts from God will greatly assist this process. Creative artists, even Christian ones, will be motivated to some extent by the urge to perform. This is because performing is fun! Most people will find little wrong with that motivation. A creative artist is presenting a show in some respects, and that presentation will be enhanced by adrenalin and a desire to perform. There is a balance to be struck however, and Gospel magicians must want to use illusion skills for

> 'Showing your audience afterwards how a trick was performed is a sure way of destroying the entertainment value and mystery of Gospel magic'

one purpose only. That purpose is to serve the Lord and promote the Gospel of Christ. God will anoint the ministry that is Christ centred and soaked in prayer. Most Christians will agree with these sentiments, and it is important to resist the urge to bolster one's ego with potential acclaim. Douglas Wathen's excellent book, *From tricks to Truth* reminds us of the passage from Scripture which states, 'seek first His kingdom and his righteousness, and all these things will be given to you as well.' (Matt 6:33 NIV)

Tricks only re-enforce preaching

Preachers may approach the sharing of the Gospel in different ways, and all would agree that in order for preaching to be effective, the message has to be remembered by those who hear it. This is the value of Gospel magic. The Gospel illusion provides an excellent memory hook upon which to hang a message. It follows therefore that the Gospel magic preacher must be very careful to use the right words, as those words will also be remembered! Of course there will be those who only remember the trick, but experience shows that these are very much in the minority. The words must be delivered in such a way as to strike home the message, with the trick purely the vehicle for delivery.

For example, I often present an illusion that involves showing a baby bear that changes into a much larger grown up bear. The secular magician would present this trick as an exercise in transformation, emphasising the change in status of the bear, demonstrating how clever the magician is. The magician is expected to do something with the bear, duly performs the trick, accepts the applause and moves on to the next trick in the routine. The Gospel magician however, is using the trick as a means to an end. I tell the Christmas story whilst performing this trick, drawing on people's experiences of the church Nativity play and the enjoyment of hearing the story of the baby in the manger. After explaining that all children are destined to grow into adults, the baby bear is transformed into the adult bear and the congregation are then reminded of the potential often missed by the Church at Christmas time, to proclaim the risen Christ. We have a tendency to leave Jesus as a baby in the manger, rather than presenting Jesus the adult, who is much more challenging. Thus, the message becomes much more important than the trick, serving to capture the audience's attention and re-enforcing the teaching.

Presentation

It is good practice to present a simple trick at the beginning of any Gospel magic that demonstrates the illusory and deceptive nature of magic. I often use an Electric Deck to demonstrate the manipulative skills of the magician. All the cards in an electric deck are joined together by nylon or similar thread, enabling the magician to appear to have amazing card handling skills. After demonstrating these skills for a few moments, I pretend to make a mistake and allow the deck to hang from one hand, suspended in mid-air, revealing how a magician uses special props and deception to fool the audience. This usually allays most fears, but be sure to follow up with a good trick to establish credibility.

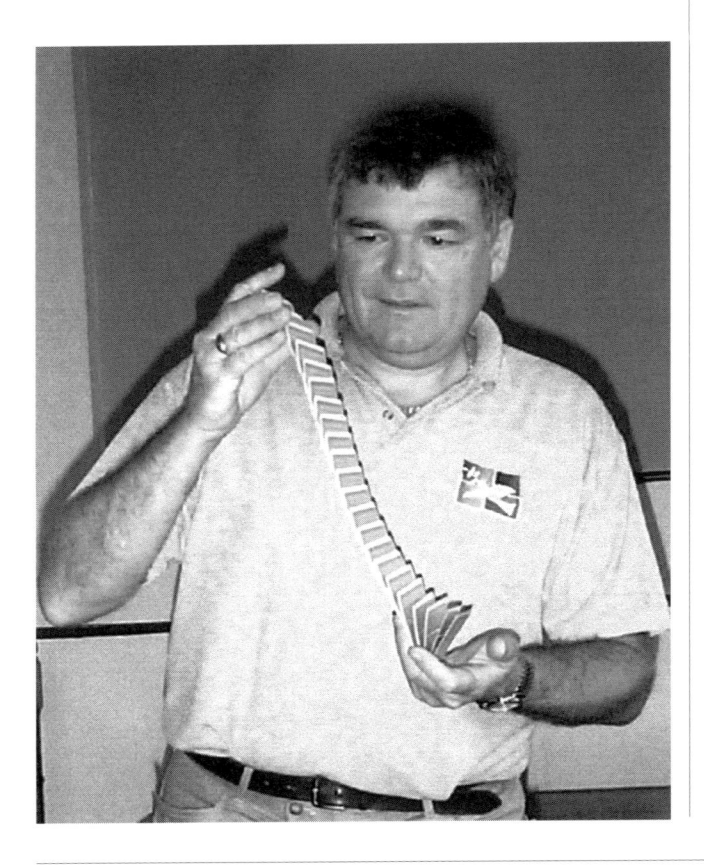

The skilful Gospel magician will combine illusions and preaching so that the two flow closely together. Effective Gospel magicians tell stories whilst performing tricks, allowing the story to unfold in conjunction with the various stages of the trick. Some preachers are masters of this technique and I would recommend aspiring Gospel magicians to watch video footage of Duane Laflin preaching whilst using magic effects. Duane is a superb American preacher who uses a lot of magic with silk handkerchiefs (referred to as silks) to present the Gospel. Whilst miracles appear to happen at his fingertips, the audience are spellbound by his message. This is because the magic and the preaching are so inter-related. It is interesting to note here that very few of the skilled preachers who feature on Gospel magic teaching videos ever use so called magic words or incantations. This is because many of the traditional words used by secular magicians are derived from satanic ritual. Magicians often ask children to offer magic words to cause a trick to work. To avoid comparisons this practice should be avoided as it gives the wrong message to a congregation.

Any approach that is instrumental in persuading the congregation that the magician has special powers should also be discarded. This does not mean that tricks that supposedly rely on mental powers should not be used. Use them by all means, but in such a way that they demonstrate that the effect is achieved by skill and not supernatural powers. Prediction tricks and ESP effects for example, are very good ways of highlighting the deceptive nature of fortune tellers and other so called mystics, whilst presenting the Bible as the source of Truth and full of promises from God that are never proved wrong.

TRICKS ARE ONLY TRICKS

Tricks are deceptions. Magicians should not present them as proof of Biblical teaching or as a demonstration of how Jesus performed particular miracles. God never seeks to deceive. Rather than performing tricks, God actually performs miracles. He doesn't just present the illusion of something happening. Jesus actually did change the water into wine. He didn't simply hide the water and substitute it with wine, hoping that no one would see the deception. He performed a real miracle. The magician can only hope to simulate that miracle by deception in order to emphasise a point. Indeed, it would be useful to perform a similar trick, produce the water, and show that it was simply a deception, then going on to teach about the power of our life changing God.

There has been much discussion in this chapter about deception, as magicians rely on deceiving audiences for effect. However, it is a major mistake to allow that deception to lead to ridicule. Gospel magic should be fun as well as being used to teach. It is not only discourteous, but unacceptable behaviour to belittle members of an audience who volunteer to help. Some well-known magicians on television go too far in this respect, and whilst their technique is to be admired, their interpersonal skills leave a lot to be desired. In the same way that audiences are not entertained by smart-alecs who ridicule them, neither will they accept teaching from such folk.

It is important of course to match a theme or message with the appropriate trick. Most effects will lend themselves to a Gospel routine, although some will not. There are several unused props in my study that testify to this fact! Do try to purchase equipment that will be used. Experience will teach the expensive lesson of waiting for the right prop to come along. The correct way of going about the process of choosing suitable material is to match the message to the trick and not the other way around. This rule is not written in stone however, as occasionally a trick will suggest a theme to the magician. For example, a guillotine type prop prompted me to develop a routine that delivers a very clear message based on trust.

STAGECRAFT

It is of course, vital to be professional in the approach to all forms of preaching. There is no other creative art that will expose a preacher to ridicule more than magic if the routine is not properly rehearsed. Most audiences will encourage a magician to do well as they wish to be entertained. However it is true to say that those who watch a magician work, will be concentrating fiercely, joyfully seizing upon any mistakes. It has been my unfortunate experience to have witnessed this jubilation first hand when I have made an error in one of my performances. Mistakes will happen and you will wish the ground to swallow you up when they occur. The best way forward is to briefly acknowledge the mistake and move on to the next routine. The error will at least serve to prove that the magician is human after all. Unfortunately,

'Gospel magic should be fun as well as being used to teach. It is not only discourteous, but unacceptable behaviour to belittle members of an audience who volunteer to help'

MAGIC

the only way to learn how to deal with this situation is by experience. I pray that you only endure these learning experiences on a few occasions!

Practice and more practice is the only way to avoid these horrors, as only perfection in technique will suffice in magic. The effective magician should be able to perform most tricks blindfolded. Opening night of a stage play is not the time to learn lines. Likewise, a worship event is not the place to rehearse a magic effect and magicians should never attempt to perform a trick unless they are 100% certain that they are fully rehearsed and prepared.

Not only should a magician have learnt the tricks and the routine, but must also be prepared in other ways, as any other preacher should. It is therefore important to use good quality equipment that is clean and tidy. Keep props fully serviced and use only silks without frays and tears. Wooden props should not appear to be in need of a coat of paint. A fancy waistcoat, glitter jacket or other typical magician costume may be appropriate for a Gospel cabaret evening, but may be considered inappropriate when presenting a magic object lesson as part of a church service. Keep all equipment under wraps or out of sight until they are to be used. This is good practice that serves to add to the mystery and anticipation of an illusion. Sloppy performance and inept presentation will sometimes serve to give away secrets, so always approach Gospel magic presentations prayerfully and carefully, so that you too will keep to the adage – share the message and keep the secrets.

TYPES OF MAGIC

There are several ways of presenting Gospel magic. Some are more suited to small groups, whilst others lend themselves to larger audiences and congregations. I distinguish between audiences and congregations, as Gospel magic provides many more opportunities for outreach to non-churched audiences than most forms of preaching, simply because of the fascination that most people have for magic tricks. The trick is to draw the un-churched, through a medium that they have experience of and are intrigued by.

Some secular magicians offer silent routines, whereby the tricks are presented to a musical accompaniment without any patter. It is difficult to visualize a situation where this type of presentation would be appropriate for

> 'Mistakes will happen and you will wish the ground to swallow you up when they occur. The best way forward is to briefly acknowledge the mistake and move on to the next routine'

preaching, but no doubt some may find a way. Most preachers will perform with a single prop, in order to illustrate or introduce a theme, whilst others will present a series of effects linking the tricks to provide a complete teaching programme. This cabaret approach is practical and good fun to perform. It is also an excellent way of reaching out into the community. Our own ministry offers Gospel magic cabaret evenings, encouraging host churches to invite family and friends to a fellowship meal that is accompanied by an hour or so of Gospel magic. The audience will appreciate the magic, and may realise later that they have actually taken part in an entertaining Bible study.

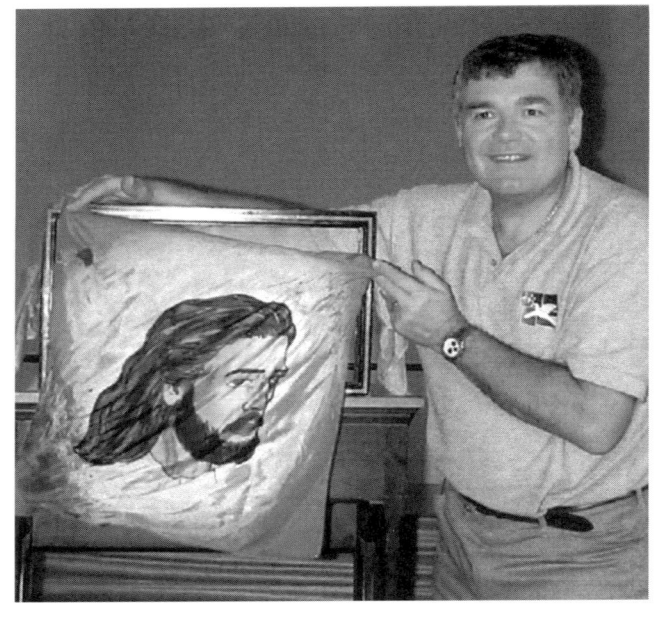

Close-up magic is a very entertaining form of magic. However it has limited value for Gospel magicians because of the numbers of people who can view this type of magic at one time. It is a useful tool to use in situations where the opportunity for one to one contact is made available. I have found it very useful to be able to present close-up magic to youth club members, prison inmates, homeless people at a Christmas shelter and to colleagues and clients at work. Magic has given me the tools and opportunity to preach when other approaches would have been instantly opposed or totally rejected. Two effects come to mind; both use matchboxes as props to illustrate the effectiveness of the close-up approach to magic. Each requires a different magic principle to be employed and the

> *Magic has given me the tools and opportunity to preach when other approaches would have been instantly opposed or totally rejected*

matchbox props are commercially available from magic dealers. You will have to source your own hypodermic needle. (required for the second effect)

The first is based on several verses in the Bible. Romans 6:4 NIV sums up the theme and states 'We were therefore buried with Him through baptism into death in order that, just as Christ was raised from the dead through the glory of Father, we too may live a new life.' The effect uses a matchbox that contains six dice. Each die is shown to have different number showing on its face. The box is then closed with the dice inside showing 1, 2, 3, 4, 5 and 6. A volunteer is invited to use a dice shaker to throw another die onto the top of the matchbox. The die turns up as a 6 and the matchbox is opened to reveal that all the dice inside also now show a 6! Dice are a very useful way to tell others about Jesus. Consider the numbers on dice.

Number 1   There is but one living God.

Number 2   He is revealed to us in the Old and New Testament.

Number 3   We learn of the Three-in-One God, the Trinity; God the Father, God the Son and God the Holy Spirit.

Number 4   All this is told in the 4 gospels.

Number 5   We are the fifth gospel and we have a duty to spread the Good News that Jesus has given us all a new start.

Number 6   In many games, we need a 6 to start. Jesus has thrown a 6 for us to start afresh. This is available to every one of us. We can all be changed.

The second is based on Genesis 1: 27 NIV, which says 'God created man in His own image, in the image of God He created him; male and female He created them.' A matchbox is shown that bears the names of some of the designer label images that our young people recognise, such as Nike, Adidas and Le Coq. Some easily influenced teenagers would no more think of cutting up a sweatshirt or trainers bearing one of these images, than cutting off their own arm. These are images that they hold dear. The matchbox is then pierced with a genuine hypodermic needle, which is seen to go all the way through the matchbox, whilst explaining that some people do not think twice about ruining their own bodies that are made in the image of God. Some abuse their bodies with a variety of chemicals and drugs. Every time they do this, they abuse God. God made us in His image, with a heart of gold. It should be impossible for a Christian to abuse God in this way. If we take Jesus into our hearts He will make us strong like solid gold. At this point the needle is withdrawn and the matchbox opened to reveal a solid block of brass that looks like gold and completely fills the box.

CLASSIC MAGIC PROPS AND HOW TO USE THEM

There are hundreds of different props and pieces of equipment that can be used to produce a magic illusion. It is important to be aware that magic effects that are sold commercially are done so on the basis that a great deal of the value of a trick is in the secret principle behind it. When you buy a trick, you are paying a little for the equipment and a lot for the secret or gimmick that enables the magician to perform it. The magic dealer will be pleased to demonstrate the effect, but it is rare for the dealer to explain the workings of the trick before you agree to purchase. There are many variations on different themes.

These are all contained within a dozen different generic forms. The first of the tricks above is an example of the *Transformation* effect, whereby an object is changed in appearance or changed into something else.

The second trick demonstrated a *Penetration* effect, whereby one solid object appears to penetrate another seemingly solid object.

The *Vanish* effect causes an object to completely disappear. Sometimes the magician causes the object to appear in a different place. This is called a Transposition.

A *Restoration* effect involves destroying or partly destroying something and then restoring it to its original state.

Mentalism creates the deception that the magician is apparently able to read minds and predict future events.

The effect of *Animation* appears to give life to inanimate objects.

Levitation effects give the illusion of objects being suspended in mid-air without visible support.

The magician who produces rabbits from hats or silks from supposedly bare hands, is performing a *Production* effect.

Some magicians perform difficult *Escapes* from locked trunks or straitjackets.

The Gospel magician can cause any one of these effects, but the preacher who performs a series of tricks would do well to use a variety of these in their programme. The following section describes some of the props available. They can be used in a variety of settings such as services, Sunday school, youth events etc, but be sure that the effects and the way that you present them, are appropriate to the audience. Most magicians like to use card tricks, but these are not appropriate to all audiences, especially those predominantly made up of children. Young people are quickly bored by card tricks, especially if standard decks are used that contain the usual hearts, clubs, diamonds and spades, rather than colourful cards that contain interesting images.

I hope that the following routines will provide you with ideas that you can develop to suit your own ministry. Some magicians understandably guard their own ideas, however, I believe that we have a duty to share our ideas with other preachers. I have developed, adapted and applied my own style to many of the ideas and routines used in these effects. Most routines come from ideas discovered many years ago, and I have little doubt that other Gospel magicians have presented some of the effects in a similar fashion.

Ropes hold a particular fascination for many and although I do not share that fascination, I do see the value of performing rope tricks. They require few gimmicks, are portable, versatile and are inexpensive to purchase. There are also many books that demonstrate most of the techniques required to perform rope tricks. (see resources chapter. A simple but useful effect is the Rope Through The Neck illusion, a very old trick that is well documented in most books on general magic. Magicians who present rope magic should use good quality magician's rope, which is available in a variety of colours, and offered with or without the central core. The ends should be taped, sewn or glued; in order to prevent fraying. The rope should be stored in large loops, so as not to develop a memory.

The effect of the Rope Through Neck illusion is designed to deceive the audience into thinking that two ropes, which are tied together behind a volunteer's neck, penetrate the neck without tampering with the rope or hurting the volunteer's neck. The method of performing the trick is described in most magic books. There are several Gospel applications, the best of which expound the concept of being freed from sin. Two more volunteers are required to hold each end of the ropes, representing the forces of evil that bind us in sin. After explaining to the audience how Satan has a grip on our lives, the magician instructs the volunteer to stand still, representing a Christian standing firm in the faith. The two volunteers holding the rope are asked to pull hard, whilst the other volunteer remains still. The ropes then miraculously appear to pull straight through the neck.

There are several commercially made props that are designed to illustrate the theme of control over our lives and the way that Jesus intervenes in difficult situations for us. One of these is the disobedient heart, a device that enables the magician to completely control the descent of a wooden heart, which is threaded onto a vertical rope. The other is the 'Heart Off Rope' prop, which is a more complex, but simple visual illusion involving a heart, surrounded by wooden symbols of society's greed and perceived ways of attaining riches, such as a gold bar, a die, a pill and a skull. Each item is threaded onto the rope. After explaining how each of the four items enslave us and lead to death, the magician encourages volunteers to pull the two ends of the rope, representing Jesus' intervention, and then teaches on the power that Jesus has to set us free from the material things that enslave us.

The Change Bag is a superb utility prop that is used in several different types of effect, all of which depend upon the gimmick that enables the magician to use the bag to transform objects. There are several types of change apparatus that give rise to these effects, such as the Dove Pan. The Change Bag is very appropriate for Gospel magicians however, as it looks and feels very much like a pew collection bag. No Gospel magician should be without this type of prop. Paul Morley, a skilful Gospel magician and evangelist, offers an excellent 'Blendo' effect with small silk national flags. (see resources chapter) Several small flags are shown and the audience asked to decide which nation God loves best. After much discussion, each volunteer places a flag in the bag. The magician then proceeds to show empty hands before picking out all the different flags, but this time all joined together. It is then a simple task to teach how God regards people of all nations as equal, or on the unity of the Body of Christ.

The bag or Dove Pan can be used to change most small objects, especially soft objects such as silks, rope and paper. The Dove Pan can be used to 'cook' ingredients to make cakes. The use of flash paper (special paper that ignites in a spectacular flash) can be used to good effect with this type of apparatus. I use the Change Bag to enhance a prediction effect, whereby several members of the audience are asked to record songs, Bible verses or occupations on a piece of paper, fold it and then place them in the bag. A volunteer is asked to pick out a piece of paper. The message on that paper is shown to match a prediction that has already made by the magician prior to the performance. This type of prediction effect can lead to teaching on Biblical Truth and is a very good lead into the promise given in John 3:16.

The 7th Key is a commercial effect available from magic dealers that can be used with any lockable box. The apparatus is an improved version of Anneman's 7th Key To Baldpate illusion. Six volunteers try to unlock a brass padlock with six different keys. The padlock prevents the opening of a box containing treasures that you may wish to put inside, such as sweets or chocolate money. Each key-holder is designated a role as a Levite, charity worker, businessman or suchlike. Each will find that they cannot unlock the padlocked box. The magician unlocks and re-locks the padlock with the 7th key. The box represents the Kingdom of Heaven containing the gifts of the Kingdom. None of the six keys will open the box at first. Each volunteer is not able to unlock the box because, as the magician will explain later, their character has not tried to enter the Kingdom through Jesus, but by their own good works. The magician's 7th key will open the lock. After doing so, all the other keys are placed on a cross and the volunteers invited to approach Jesus for the key to the Kingdom. As they have now known the love of Jesus, they can of course unlock the padlock and thus secure the benefits of His Kingdom. The effect works well with sweets for children, or perhaps bread and wine for adults inside a crystal box.

'Three Colour Blocks And Silks' is a commercial effect available from Maskell's Magic. The magician shows three wooden blocks that all appear to be white or silver in colour. Three different coloured silks are introduced, together with a wooden rectangular tube. One by one, each block is covered by a coloured silk and passed through the wooden tube. Each block changes to the colour of the silk. Each block is then covered by a silver or white silk and again passed through the tube, whereupon they change back to silver. Each block represents a different person. It is explained that they are without blemish when born and have not as yet taken on a sinful character. The coloured silks are introduced and the colours explained as representing different sinful characteristics, i.e. green = envy, red = anger, yellow = cowardice etc. The silk is put over the block and the whole passed through the tube and reversed. The silk is removed and the block changes to the silk colour. This is repeated for the other two blocks. Each block has taken on the characteristics brought about by maturing and being influenced by the world around us. A white silk is introduced to represent the power of the Holy Spirit. This is placed over each block and passed through the tube again, thus reversing the block to show that it has changed back to white/silver. The Holy Spirit cleanses us of our sinful nature.

'Gods Way Never Fails,' a self working card effect, was the first Gospel trick that I learnt, and was one of the sparks that prompted the foundation of our 'Hands up for God' ministry. Paul Morley showed me the effect some years ago at a conference in the North of England and I am forever grateful to him for starting me off in Gospel magic. Captain Ron Smith, a Salvation Army officer and fellow member of the FCME, also suggested variations on the following Gospel application. The magician shows two packets of cards (preferably jumbo size) each of 10, jack, queen, king and ace. The packets are two different suits, but each packet has cards of the same suit i.e. one packet of hearts, one packet of spades. Each packet is arranged in the same order, 10 through to ace and the two packets placed one on top of the other. The magician 'mixes' the cards by repeatedly cutting the pack, and completing the cut as many times as the audience demands. The top five cards are dealt face down on to a pile. The remaining five cards are placed as a block on the table. The audience is asked which packet they would like the magician to use first.

The important phrase is 'Gods way never fails.' Whichever pile is chosen, the magician proceeds to spell the first word G - O - D- S, placing a card to the bottom of that packet after each letter. He also asks a member of the audience to tell him when to switch packs. Thus the magician may spell two letters, G and O, placing a card for each letter to the bottom of packet (a). Assume now that the magician is now asked to switch packets. He then picks up packet (b) and places the top card to the bottom with each letter until told to switch again. This proceeds until the word GODS is completed. The top card from each pack is then handed face down to a helper.

The process is repeated for each word of the phrase, 'Gods way never fails.' At the end, each volunteer holding a pair of cards is asked to show their cards to the audience who see that each volunteer holds a pair of cards of the same value, i.e. two jacks, two queens etc. Paul's routine was to run through each pair in turn saying that when he was a lad of about ten years old (TENS) he was a bit of a jack-the-lad (JACKS) always getting into trouble. When he was older he was still a bit wild, sometimes chasing the ladies, (QUEENS) but then God came into his life and was King of his heart. (KINGS) God is really ace. (ACES) Thus, Gods way never fails. He redeems our sins, makes up for our shortcomings and generally wins through every time.

The following variations are useful for those who, as yet feel uncomfortable with playing cards, providing two completely different ways of showing that God's way never fails. Blank cards are used with references from the Old Testament written on each of five cards. On another five cards, are written the corresponding verses in the New Testament that fulfil the prediction of the Old Testament verses. The cards are set up in the same order and 'mixed' as before. The cards are worked as above, using the phrase 'Gods way never fails.' At the end the cards are shown to compliment one another. i.e. each pair is the OT prediction and its NT fulfilment.

Another alternative involves ten blank cards, two of which are handed to each of five volunteers They are asked to write their name on one card, and on the other what job they do in the church. e.g. minister or house group leader. (it is useful to know your audience and to choose five volunteers who have different roles in the Church.) The magician collects up the cards with names in one pack, and jobs in the other, both in the same order. The packets are placed on top of each other, 'mixed' and worked as before, using the phrase, 'Gods way never fails.' The magician explains that most of us rebel against God at times, and may at some time have wished to have changed our roles, but God knows how he wants to use us. The paired cards are handed to each volunteer face down after the working of the trick. Each reveals their own name, and of course, their respective roles. Thus, Gods way never fails yet again!

There are classic props such as the Die-Box that can be used for an excellent illustration of the Resurrection. Special dissolving paper enables several tricks and illustrations with water. Gimmicked Bibles burst into flames under the control of the magician. Blank pages in a Bible can be shown to change into pages with black and white drawings and then finally into full colour pages. Those who can afford the props and have the room to store them, enjoy presenting major stage illusions, such as the Zig Zag Lady, Substitution Trunk, or Saw the Lady in Half. These are always well received by audiences and provide great opportunities for preaching.

The Substitution Trunk is a favourite of Gospel magicians as it does offer a superb opportunity to teach on Jesus' intervention, through dying on the Cross for our sins.

How to start to learn magic

There are many, many more effects. Certainly too many to list here, and I pray that some of the ideas discussed here will inspire you to learn some Gospel magic. It is best to begin by purchasing a magic teaching manual and basic utility props. Contact your local Magic Circle, or better still, the FCME. Here you will find like-minded people who will be delighted to help you by teaching you some basic skills.

Most towns support an active Magic Circle, but you will usually be required to interview and audition before becoming a full member. This is not as threatening as it sounds. The local Magic Circle fraternity will want to assess your knowledge and examine your integrity, but you will find these organisations very friendly and helpful. They will support you by pointing you in the right direction in terms of books and videos, assisting you to master a few simple tricks so that you are able to satisfy the Circle of your competence to handle props. I certainly found the Leicester Magic Circle to be very friendly and most helpful in encouraging me to learn a great deal about props, effects, presentation and stagecraft. Most Circles invite prominent magicians to give lectures on all aspects of magic and organise opportunities to perform for charity and competition. Opportunities to present Gospel magic outside of your own church will arise eventually. You may feel as I do, that you should only perform magic when you are able to present the Gospel as well. You should find that local organisations associated with the church will actively seek you out when you have performed competently a few times in your own church.

The Fellowship of Christian Magicians (FCM) is based in the USA. The FCME is the European arm and is made up of Christians who wish to promote the Gospel using magic and its associated skills. The members are very helpful and will provide teaching and lectures that will inspire and encourage you in your ministry. The highlight of the FCME year is the annual 5-day conference. This a superb week of fellowship, worship, lectures, shows and workshops on all aspects of Gospel magic as well as some puppetry and circus skills. Friends made at this gathering are always willing to help and encourage fellow members, and I wholeheartedly recommend any budding Gospel magician to join this network. (see resources chapter)

There are many ways to present Gospel magic and the hundreds of lecture notes and performance videos made by professional magicians will provide a plethora of ways to suit your style. It is helpful to utilise such inspiration and teaching, but remember to allow your own character and individuality to shine through your performance. In this way, congregations will be assured of your sincerity and will more readily embrace your ministry and teaching. Remember however, that whilst we all hope that we can reach out to the lost with our magic skills, these are only part of the jigsaw. Most of your congregations will be anxious to hear the Word of God. Yes, they will hopefully enjoy your magic, but ultimately, Gospel magicians are performing to proclaim the living Christ. Ask someone to pray for you before every presentation, so that you can be confident that your focus remains on the One whom we all strive to serve. Share the Gospel but keep the secrets!

CREATIVE ARTS IN WORSHIP

A skilled clown brings chaos and disorder to our world, engendering sympathy from the audience for his tears, brought about by over emphasised but natural mistakes. The Gospel clown will use comedy to turn that situation into one of joy, just as the Gospel provides hope and comfort to the lost in their time of despair.

Chapter Eight
Clowns, balloons and storytelling

What is a clown?

There are references to fools and jesters from early Egyptian times with some clowns holding positions of great privilege. Kings and queens often had their own personal clown, who would act as confidante and counsellor as well as court entertainer. Clowns have entertained audiences for centuries suffering under various names such as jesters, jokers, buffoons and fools. They may act the fool, but most modern professional clowns are far from foolish. They possess an array of skills, which may include mime, drama, slapstick, magic, puppetry, juggling, balloon sculpting, stilt walking, unicycle riding, storytelling, and above all an ability to make people laugh. There are very few historical references to clowning in worship as this branch of the creative arts is very new to modern day church activity.

Most people's perception of a clown is a character that entertains children in the circus wearing lots of gaudy make-up and strange clothes. This is the stereotyped character that has generally been adopted by contemporary clowns who perform at children's parties, in pantomime or in street theatre. These instantly recognisable characters have evolved over a long period. There are many references to clowns from the Middle Ages onwards. These clowns were talented individuals who juggled, joked and sang for a living. They wore multi-coloured clothing such as pantaloons, oversize jackets, hats and wigs, which were often adorned with bells and tassels. They customarily travelled between towns entertaining on the streets, hoping to earn their living from donations given by the crowds that watched their performances. Clowns were employed as a 'zany' by travelling salesmen in America in the nineteenth century, in order to attract crowds to buy their wares. Their antics and costume were sure to draw a crowd if only through curiosity, and this ability to attract is one of the clown's major strengths in ministry.

Clowns appeared in circus early in the nineteenth century and at this stage it became fashionable for them to wear white face make-up. Tom Belling, an American acrobat transformed the clown's role in circus when he accidentally appeared in the circus ring whilst entertaining colleagues backstage. He was wearing inside-out baggy clothes and a wig worn backwards. The audience fell about laughing and shouted out that he was *'auguste'* a German slang word meaning stupid. The stupid and clumsy Auguste clown evolved as the modern clown, wearing heavy make-up and ill-fitting clothes. This type of clown often appears as a foil to the modern white-face clown who is perceived as highly talented and skilled in music and juggling etc. The 'white-face' typically wears smart well fitting costumes and usually treats the scruffy Auguste with disdain.

CLOWNS IN CHURCH

Most Christians who develop a clown ministry adopt either the Auguste style, comedy whiteface or character clown such as a tramp. It is important for clowns to develop a unique character that will become familiar to congregations. This enables the clown to develop consistency in behaviour, which is particularly important when ministering to a regular audience. Clowns are not well known in churches in the UK, but are becoming very popular in the USA, where several organisations such as 'Holy Fools' exist, offering support, resources and encouragement. (see resources chapter) Many of the skills demonstrated by clowns, such as mime, balloons and magic, can be performed effectively without clown make-up. However, the power of the clown to attract attention, in full costume and make-up, is without question a major asset.

I recall an incident at a church that convinced me that clowns have a role to play in worship. The congregation was waiting expectantly for a guest preacher to appear and begin the service. The preacher had still not appeared three or four minutes after the service was due to start. A figure dressed in full clown costume and make-up appeared at the back of the church and walked slowly to one of the rows of chairs. He squeezed into the middle of the row, sat down next to a smartly dressed couple and asked, 'When will the clown be here?!' The couple were at a loss to know what to say or do. The clown then made his excuses and made his way to the pulpit, read a short psalm as a call to worship and announced that his theme would be, 'No one knows the time or the hour, but the day of the Lord will come like a thief in the night.'

It takes a great deal of nerve to attempt that sort of entrance. The clown was able to carry it off partly because of his costume and make-up. Generally, the clown will use the costume and make-up to attract the attention and focus of the audience, progressing to present a short mime, balloon act or comedy spot, whilst gradually introducing the theme for teaching. Many members of congregations feel an affinity with the Auguste clown in particular, because they can readily identify with the antics of a vulnerable individual who often makes mistakes or becomes a victim of circumstance. Jesus used symbols and stories to illustrate His teaching. Clowns attempt to portray and demonstrate these symbols and stories by using comedy and circus skills.

By acting the fool and contrasting our lack of wisdom with the sometimes perceived 'foolishness' of God, the clown can show in a dramatic way, that in fact God is full of wisdom. He has a perfectly constructed plan for us that will transcend our shortcomings and erroneous perception.

'For the foolishness of God is wiser than man's wisdom, and the weakness of God is stronger than man's strength.' (1Corinthians 1:25 NIV). A skilled clown brings chaos and disorder to our world, engendering sympathy from the audience for his tears, brought about by over emphasised but natural mistakes. The Gospel clown will use comedy to turn that situation into one of joy, just as the Gospel provides hope and comfort to the lost in their time of despair. Laughter and joy are both good therapy and help to create the appropriate atmosphere in which to introduce the Good News.

Some of the skills used by the clown, such as mime, drama, puppets and magic, have already been described in previous chapters. There are particular skills that are especially suited to clowns and appropriate to this form of ministry, which deserve attention in this chapter. These are storytelling, paper tearing and balloon sculpting, three skills that encourage welcome interaction between the clown and the congregation.

There are few people who do not enjoy a good story and the clown is well placed to tell stories, especially to children, who will quickly warm to the friendly clown, who can then take advantage of the relaxed atmosphere to tell a story or parable. There are two main ways of presenting a story. The first is by telling the story directly to the audience using different voices and different effects to add interest. The second method is the illustrated narration. This involves third parties narrating a story illustrated by the clown, using a mixture of mime, drama and slapstick. Both are valid forms of presentation and demand different skills.

STORYTELLING – DIRECT METHOD

It is intended that the storyteller will find help in this section on how to present a story. Hints on where to find such collections of stories to use are provided in the resources chapter. You need look no further than the Bible to find a collection of stories that has been called the greatest ever told. It is difficult to conceive a tale that has more to offer in terms of intrigue, excitement, drama and hope than the story of God's relationship with His people and the intervention of Jesus Christ. The Crucifixion, subsequent Resurrection and anointing of the Holy Spirit, are for Christians, the most exciting stories imaginable.

> 'A skilled clown brings chaos and disorder to our world, engendering sympathy from the audience for his tears, brought about by over emphasised but natural mistakes'

> 'You need look no further than the Bible to find a collection of stories that has been called the greatest ever told'

Christians regard these stories as Truth and the embodiment of God's Word, using them as a blueprint for living and a pointer to our ultimate salvation. There is little doubt that stories taken from the Bible can be presented with great effect, but there are also many secular stories that offer enormous potential for the clown/storyteller. Consider the collection of the *Fables of Aesop* for example, which offer a wealth of short stories with a moral dimension that can be developed for teaching in worship.

In the same way that we identify and sympathise with the personal dilemmas of the clown, we consider the great stories to be those that reflect the human condition and the pitfalls that confront us. Many of these types of stories tell of the rise and fall of heroes and villains, as the good are confronted by evil, temporarily vanquished, and ultimately win the war after losing a battle. Fictional works should not be seen as a barrier to the story teller who uses stories in worship, as fiction often contains great truths about God's Creation and the way that we interact with it and our neighbours. Michael Townsend reminds us in his book on storytelling, (*Story* in the *God's People At Worship* series) that 'To object that there never was a poor little girl called Cinderella who had ugly step-sisters would be to miss the point entirely. In the same way, to insist that there never was a historical sower who went forth to sow, and whose seed fell into four contrasted types of soil, would be to misunderstand the whole point of the story Jesus told in Mark 4:3-9.'

Jesus' parables are good models for the storyteller. He drew stories from everyday situations that His listeners would relate to. His audience were usually simple folk with families who worked the land and lived their lives according to the seasons and festivals. His stories reflected the ups and downs of family life and the ways in which they earned their living, such as farming, and great times of rejoicing such as weddings. The parables contained questions, and mostly relied on the audience finding the meaning for themselves. Whatever stories are told in the worship environment, they should always be related to Scripture. This is fairly simple to achieve as there are collections of stories and anecdotal resources available to preachers that come complete with scripture and thematic indices. Some of these collections are available on CD-Rom enabling fast interactive cross-referencing.

Having chosen an appropriate story, linked with a passage from Scripture, the story teller must address the

> 'The parables contained questions, and mostly relied on the audience finding the meaning for themselves'

question of technique and delivery. The ideal way is to memorise the salient points in the story and relate them in your own words, enhancing delivery through the addition of appropriate voices and effects. This will encourage spontaneity and ensure that the congregation are confident in the clown's familiarity with the story, and therefore it's teaching. Reading stories from a book is perfectly acceptable. Young children in particular may prefer this approach, as they will readily accept that it is a proper story if it comes from a book! Many children will recall happy hours spent listening to family or friends reading them stories from a favourite story book. Our own children learnt favourite stories by heart and corrected every word that Sue and I omitted. Good stories are tremendous aids to Christian preaching, as many will remember stories for years to come, together with the teaching illustrated by them, especially if they are accompanied by visual prompts or gimmicks such as interesting voices and accents.

The right kind of story should be pitched appropriately for the audience's vocabulary and should fit into a 5-10 minute maximum time slot. Whether the story is to be told by a person or a puppet, it is important to maintain eye contact with the audience. An experienced storyteller or preacher will understand that the narrator's eyes should be continually raised from the book to keep the audience focused. It is vital to maintain interest and this can be achieved in a variety of ways. Using character voices to fit the heroes and villains in the story is consistently effective. Adapting the pace and volume of delivery to match the tempo of the story will heighten suspense, enabling the audience to anticipate and absorb plot changes in the story. The clown is expected to use props and these will be very effective in illustrating and emphasising points. Sometimes the prop will not be an important element in the tale, but instead will provide extra interest or comedy. Overhead projector acetates and flip chart easels may be used to re-enforce the storyline will add colour to the spoken word. Employing strategic lighting such as spotlights or candles in a darkened room can create atmosphere and anticipation.

Sound effects are very effective and can be pre-recorded on audio tape or mini-disc and replayed by a third party who is familiar with the timing of the story. It is vital that this method of using effects is well rehearsed beforehand. Alternatively, provide the audience with the appropriate cues and encourage them to offer simple sound effects such as wind, animal sounds, fire and crowd noise. Try splitting the congregation in half, asking one half to take the part of the hero and the other to provide suitable effects for the villain. This may not be appropriate for all stories, but tales such as David and Goliath may benefit. Visual symbols of opposition could be supplied by the clown or the congregation. For example, a Sunday school class could be asked to bring two different colour scarves such as those worn by football supporters!

Storytelling – as a clown skit

The clown skit is similar to the mime sketch, but relies more heavily on the narrative, some dialogue from the clown and the use of comedy. In comparison, a clown skit makes much more of an attempt to interact with the audience and much more use of props. This type of approach is ideally suited to stories from the Bible and the following two scripts are good examples of clown skits that employ this technique.

These two sketches, entitled *God's Beautiful World* and *Work, Work, Work* were written by Mark D. Stucky, and are copyright Piccadilly Books. They have been reproduced in this publication with thanks to, and by kind permission of Mr Bruce Fife, proprietor of the publishers, Piccadilly Books, PO Box 25203, Colorado Springs, CO 80936.

GODS BEAUTIFUL WORLD

This is a sketch for one clown and is about God's creative power as described in the creation story in Genesis. It is designed for all-age worship and requires several props: drum, easel, magic markers (or paint), figures or drawings of stars, sun, moon, fish, birds and animals. A large sheet of black poster board or card should be set in the middle of the performance area on a large easel. Lights should be turned off and a narrator primed to read slowly from a modern translation of Genesis. At the end of each 'day', the narrator should beat a drum.

As the narrator begins, the clown enters, carrying a white poster board, and hovers around the easel, which carries the black poster board.

Day 1 (Gen 1:3-5). The lights are turned on and the clown puts up the white board next to the black board on the easel. These represent night and day. Note that whenever the narrator says, 'God saw that it was good,' the clown does a little jump and claps hands with glee.

Day 2 (Gen 1:6-8). The clown paints clouds and blue water on the white poster.

Day 3 (Gen 1:9-13). The clown paints brown land and green trees on the white poster.

Day 4 (Gen 1:14-19). The clown sticks a smiling moon and stars on the black poster, and a yellow smiling sun on the white poster. At this point the clown becomes excited and sticks a few stars on his/herself.

Day 5 (Gen 1:20-23). The clown sticks figures of fish and birds on the posters.

Day 6 (Gen 1:24-31). The clown makes one or two simple balloon animals or plays with some animal puppets. The clown then goes into the congregation and gets a man and a woman to stand up, hugs them and proudly shows them off to the rest of the congregation. After admiring them, the clown motions to the whole congregation with a sweeping motion, indicating that the Creation process extends to us all. The clown may add some humour at this point by pointing at the man and woman in mock horror and giving them a large paper fig leaf each.

Day 7 (Gen 2:1-3). The clown sits down in a chair to rest and blows a kiss to bless the seventh day, possibly holding up a sign saying, 'Sunday is special.'

The narrator concludes the story by saying, 'This is the story of God creating our beautiful world. Now we see all that God made, and know that it is very, very good.' The clown jumps and claps once more before taking a bow and making an exit.

This is a simple sketch that makes use of several props, some gentle humour, clown skills such as ballooning and puppets, and involves the congregation. This is only a suggestion of course. Please feel free to adapt the sketch to your own style. As is the case with all sketches that you perform, please give due credit to this publication and to the original author for the sketch.

WORK, WORK, WORK

This is a very effective clown sketch that illustrates the themes of work, recreation and the Sabbath. It involves a narrator and just one clown, using various props: construction workers hat, rubbish bag filled with crumpled newspaper, a watch or clock, money, a Bible, juggling balls, (or some other skill if you can't juggle – some acrobatics perhaps) a rubber chicken, slices of bread, a table and a chair. Props such as money and a watch should preferably be exaggerated in size.

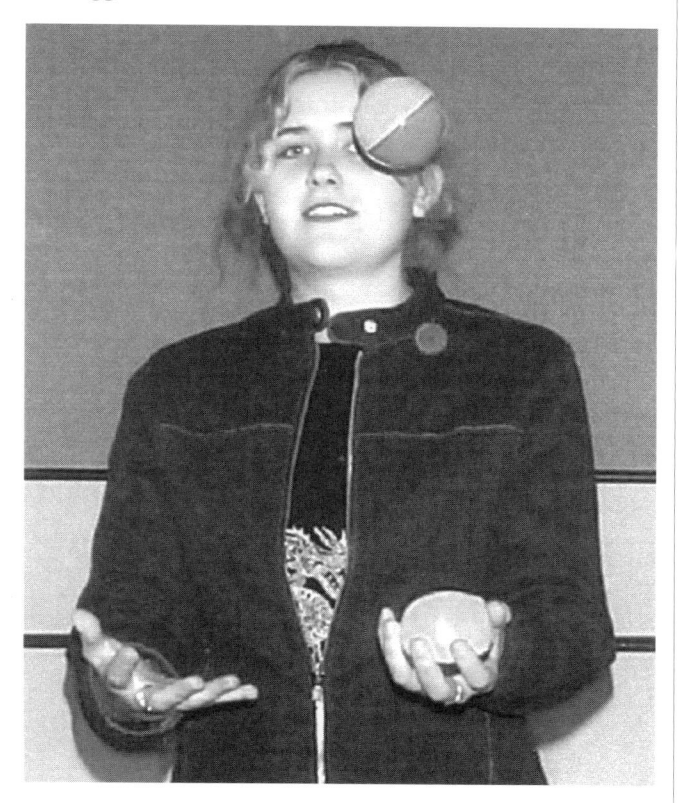

The clown enters, walking hunched over as if carrying an enormous burden, wearing a construction worker's hat and carrying a large dustbin bag stuffed with crumpled newspaper.

Narrator: I once knew a clown who worked very hard. He worked and he worked and he worked and he worked.

Clown walks round rapidly in busy circles.

Narrator: He never had time for his family.

Clown looks at watch or clock, gives a shake of the head and shrugs, throwing away the timepiece.

Narrator: He hardly stopped long enough to eat.

Clown drops the sack, opens it and pulls out a rubber chicken and two slices of bread. The clown makes a sandwich, pretends to take a bite and then throws it away, continuing to walk in circles.

Narrator: He was always tired, but still went to bed very late.

Clown yawns, drops the sack and lies down on the floor asleep.

Narrator: He was tired, but still got up very early.

Clown wakes up to an alarm sound effect, and after yawning, stretching and lots of eye rubbing, gets up, picks up the sack and begins walking in circles again.

Narrator: He was always tired, never got much sleep and went on like this for day after day, week after week. He worked like this so he could earn lots of money.

Clown checks pockets for money.

Narrator: Even though he had plenty of cash, he was always worried that it would run out. – One day his strength ran out because his exhausted body could take no more. He became very ill.

Clown slowly grinds to a halt, drops the bag and falls exhausted onto a table.

Narrator: Whilst he was ill, he had plenty of time to think about things.

Clown looks around the table, sees a Bible, picks it up and begins to read.

Narrator: In the Bible, he read about how God

created the earth in six days and rested on the seventh.

Clown counts on seven fingers.

Narrator: He read the Ten Commandments and was surprised to find that the fourth commandment said to observe the Sabbath day and keep it holy. Only six days should be used for working and one for spending time at rest, dedicated to God. The clown realised that he had been working for seven days a week and not six. He never rested.

Clown shakes head sadly.

Narrator: He never took time to worship God, to be with other people, to rest or to play. Instead, he nearly worked himself to death. Well, he was going to change all that.

Clown nods head in agreement.

Narrator: When he recovered from his illness, he went back to work.

Clown walks in circles but in a relaxed manner, waving happily at people in the congregation.

Narrator: He didn't drive himself nearly so hard and on the seventh day, he rested and relaxed and worshipped God.

Clown stops walking, drops the bag and prays on bended knees.

Narrator: He rested and spent some time with his friends.

Clown sits on chair, then notices the congregation and goes to them, shaking hands with a few.

Narrator: He found time to have a bit of fun.

Clown juggles or plays with a balloon with the audience.

Narrator: He found that as a result he got a lot stronger.

Clown flexes muscles.

Narrator: He still got as much work done as before, but in a shorter time, using less energy. He was a happy clown again.

Clown throws the bag jauntily over one shoulder and exits, waving and blowing kisses to the congregation.

A little imagination and practice will enable the clown to use circus skills to enhance or break up a story such as this, with juggling, tumbling, balloons or magic. These skill spots act as good memory hooks and provide a break to introduce a song or prayer if the story is to be told in small linked sound bytes.

BALLOONS AS AN AID TO PREACHING

Balloon modelling is one of the basic skills expected of the modern clown. Sculpting balloon animals, hats and other objects attracts attention prior to teaching, as well as providing the means to produce appropriate props whilst telling a story. People of all ages watch balloon sculptors with great interest. Children, of course, not only look on with interest, but with great expectation of receiving the balloon as a gift, once it has been completed.

Using balloons can be a rewarding and effective way of teaching and telling stories and is a skill well within the scope of most people. All that is required is a bag of balloons, a balloon pump, (or plenty of puff) and a lively imagination, together with the help of a reference book perhaps. (see resources chapter) You will also need masses of stamina if working with a group of children because if one child is given a balloon, you can rest assured that every other child in the room will also want one. The best ploy is to make up plenty of models beforehand and explain that there are only a limited number of balloons available. It is also useful to have copies of the address of a balloon supplier who can equip those interested with balloons and teaching booklets.

Before reading further, and certainly before presenting your first balloon object lesson, you would do well to commit to memory the following short sentence, 'Never hand out balloons before you have finished your presentation or until the worship event is over.' I once made the mistake of handing out animal balloons whilst telling the Creation story at a holiday club. From the moment the first few children had their balloons, I had lost their attention and my words were lost in the screeching noises made by almost two-dozen balloons being rubbed together. I have never forgotten the lesson of that awful squeaking.

Ralph Dewey is one of the best-known exponents of balloon sculpting in worship and he has produced several booklets on the subject. In his short book, *Dewey's New Balloon Animals,* he notes that balloon modelling is 'a very effective method of communicating Christian thoughts and messages. For example, I write on the back of a Bee balloon, 'bee a Christian.' On the Lion model, I write 'no lion, Jesus loves you'; on the Monkey I write 'don't monkey around, become a Christian.' The simplicity of some balloon modelling is one of it's inherent strengths. Models should be used to attract and enhance, but as seen earlier, our skills are to be used to help others to focus on Jesus in a unique way.

> 'Never hand out balloons before you have finished your presentation or until the worship event is over'

BALLOON BASICS

Most balloon sculptors will recommend Qualitex balloons. The basic requirements are a stock of #260 and #360 pencil balloons supplemented by various specials such as #321 Bee, Hearts and Apples. A balloon pump is a good idea, especially for the beginner, as blowing up balloons requires strong lungs and the correct technique to avoid injury. Whichever method is employed, leave a small nipple at the end of the balloon for expansion when twisting or shaping. Each twist or bend forces air towards the end of the balloon. Twisting the balloon into bubble shapes is the basic technique to be mastered. Always twist in the same direction to avoid unravelling, making sure that your nails are trimmed and that your clothing contains no exposed points.

The bubble twist is the basis for all balloon modelling. Pinching the balloon at the twist point and twisting, forms the bubble. Bubbles can be twisted together to form a lock-twist. I am indebted to Allen R. Cook for the balloon twist illustrations and explanations. These illustrations are copyright Allen R Cook and are reproduced with thanks to, and the kind permission of Allen R. Cook, 409 Prairie Lane, Belton, MO 64012, USA.

The lock twist is used to connect two bubbles together with the addition of a third bubble to form some bodies and faces. Three bubbles are made, the second and third bubbles made the same size. These are twisted and locked together at the base with the third bubble. A basic dog is made from a #360 balloon using three of these twists. The first set makes the ears and nose, the second set forms the neck and front legs with the final set forming the body and rear legs. The remainder of the balloon becomes the tail. There are several variations of the lock twist and various 'tricks of the trade' that combine to make up the balloon sculptors armoury of skills. It would not be possible to do justice to all these variations without dozens of illustrations. It is not the purpose of this book to provide a catalogue of balloon models. Several books and web sites are listed in the resources chapter, providing examples of balloon sculptures and a great deal of teaching on the techniques required to build them.

The balloons that you create will attract an audience, but balloons can also be used as an effective aid to storytelling. The following example, entitled *Airy* is copyright Allen R. Cook and is reproduced with thanks to, and the kind permission of Allen R. Cook, 409 Prairie Lane, Belton, MO 64012, USA. It requires the storyteller to build an alien type balloon creature beforehand, as illustrated. The head may be filled with helium, which can be procured at party and balloon shops. You will also require eight other party balloons, four of which should be filled with helium. The story is based upon (Philippians 4:8-9 NIV) 'Finally, brothers, whatever is true, whatever is noble, whatever is right, whatever is pure, whatever is lovely, whatever is admirable—if anything is excellent or praiseworthy—think about such things. Whatever you have learned or received or heard from me, or seen in me—put it into practice. And the God of peace will be with you.'

'AIRY

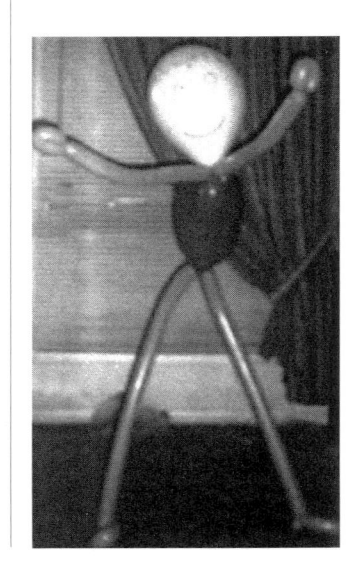

I've brought a friend of mine with me today and his name is Airy. He has been a little down lately and as you can see has a bit of trouble standing up. He has some problems and needs something to occupy his mind. Let's see what we can find. Let's try this – a toy. (attach a party balloon with TOYS written on with a marker, to one of Airy's arms.) Look what happened. That didn't help. He's gone even lower. What next?

Here are a few white lies. These are fibs that Airy has told to cover up when he has been naughty. They are lies though, just the same. Let's tie these on to another arm for him to think about. (attach a party balloon with LIES marked on it.) That didn't help did it. He's even lower than before, weighed down by deceit. Let's find something else. How about a television to take his mind off of the bad things. (attach a party balloon with TV marked on it to Airy's arm.) He's even lower now! Television is fine, but if it takes up too much of your time and energy, it can be destructive. Maybe if he had some money to spend, that would help cheer him up. (attach a fourth party balloon with MONEY marked on it, to his arm.) Money is OK but some people seem to spend all their time and energy trying to make more than they need. It doesn't do them any good in the long run. None of these seem to work because he seems more weighed down than ever. Maybe we should remove all these things and try something else. (remove the four balloons)

After removing the four party balloons, go through a similar routine, but this time using helium filled balloons marked with PRAYER, BIBLE, CHURCH and TELL OTHERS. After attaching the first balloon, PRAYER remark on how Airy is perking up a little. He will begin to look like a new man after reading the BIBLE. Now he is going to CHURCH, he can hardly keep his feet on the ground. He is spending time with other people and learning about God. In fact he is so filled up with the good gifts from God that he wants to take off and tell the Good News to OTHERS. At this point, the helium filled balloons will lift Airy off his feet, so a cotton line should be attached if working outside or in a tall building. Read the passage from Philippians and teach how the Bible encourages us to live a full life, but also instructs us to focus upon things that are true, just, honest and pure. In other words, think about the good things and don't concentrate on all the bad stuff.

Paper tearing and cutting

The final clowning skill that we will discuss is that of paper tearing, which some would include in a 'magic' section. Paper tear object lessons are very effective and are ideal tools for clowns, as there are good opportunities for humour and playacting. Paper tearing is the art of folding and tearing (or cutting) a piece of paper into shapes and images that can be used to help focus people's attention on the teaching of the Gospel. Most paper tricks can be performed with an A4 or preferably an A3 piece of paper. Use a lightweight paper, but preferably not as light as tissue. A clown could use a paper tear whilst telling a story, or use it as an object lesson in itself. Some paper tearers have developed superb, intricate patterns and shapes that enable them to weave long story lines around the images. Others make a simple shape such as a cross or Christian fish sign in order to illustrate the teaching. Whichever you decide upon, you will do well to follow the advice of Ralph Dewey, who advocates pre-folding or marking in pencil the folds that you will be making in the piece of paper, especially for intricate folds and tears.

There are several good resources available for paper tearing, including books and object lessons by Ralph Dewey and Roy Weaver (Decade Ministries). Details can found in the resources chapter. Two paper tear examples are included here for the reader to use, and it is hoped that these will lead you to discover and develop others. The first is a very simple affair that folds and tears into a victory V, a Cross and a Christian fish symbol. This brilliant but simple tear example appears in *Dewey's Gospel Paper Tricks* and is copyright Ralph Dewey. It is reproduced here with thanks to, and with the kind permission of Ralph Dewey, Dewey's Good News Balloons, 1202 Wildwood Drive, Deer Park, Texas 77536, USA.

CLOWNS, BALLOONS AND STORYTELLING

As illustrated, an A4 piece of paper is folded down from the top so that a 2.5'(65mm) flap remains. Fold the 2.5'(65mm) flap back up the sheet. Make a right-angle fold, left over right, and then cut along the dotted line, discarding both sidepieces as indicated in the illustration. Open the remaining shape to form a letter V, explaining that all Christians have victory over death and sin, through Jesus. Open further to reveal a cross and explain that an X marks treasure. This treasure is the gift of eternal life from God through the sacrifice of Jesus. Now open the paper completely to show a Christian fish, explaining that those Christians who become fishers of men as Jesus did will have treasures in heaven. The symbols lend themselves to a wealth of teaching. The example is simply a suggestion that accompanies Ralph Dewey's illustration. You may care to support other teaching with these tear images.

The second tear is a little more complicated, but simple to do nonetheless. The tear example is taken from an excellent booklet entitled *Unfolding the Good News* by Roy Weaver. Roy provides wonderful visual aid resources through 'Decade Ministries' and I am indebted to him for allowing me to reproduce the example here. It is called

Heaven and is copyright Decade Ministries. It is reproduced with thanks to, and with the kind permission of Decade Ministries, Grove House, Limetrees, Chilton, Oxfordshire, OX11 0HY. An A4 sheet of paper is required. The resulting tear pieces can be magnified and shown effectively to a large congregation by laying them on the screen of an OHP. Alternatively, use a larger piece of paper.

The word HEAVEN should be written vertically on an A4 sheet of paper, to about ¾ of the way down the sheet as illustrated in diagram 1. This should be shown to the congregation explaining how someone once went to Sunday school and then drifted away as a teenager, hiding what he had been taught because he was embarrassed.

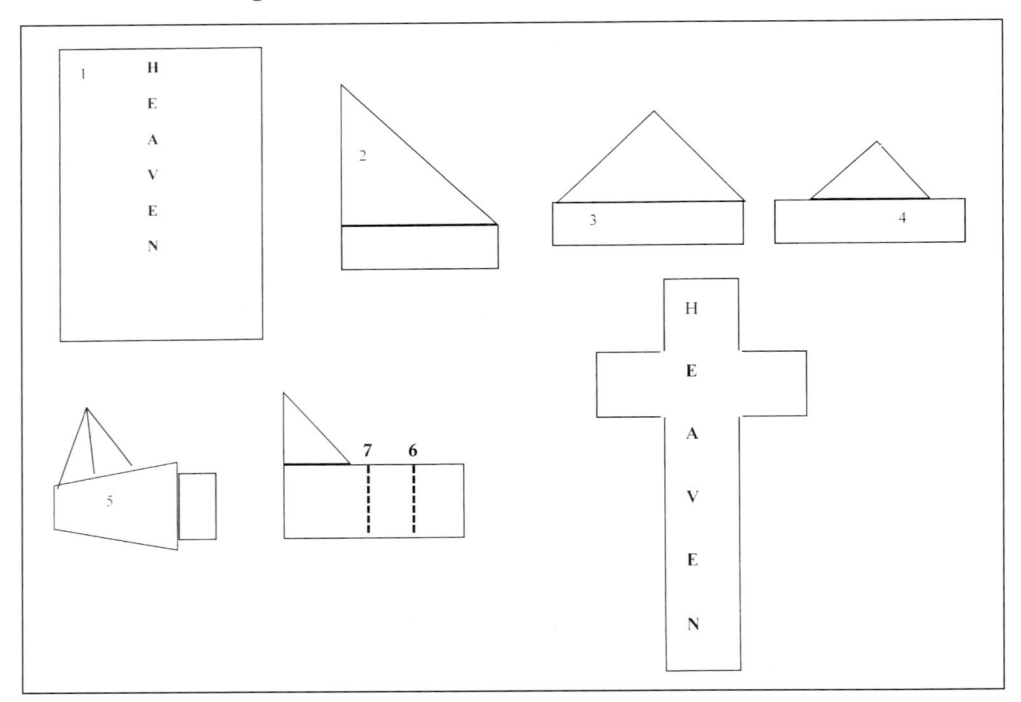

At this point, fold down one corner to meet the opposite edge so that the word HEAVEN is completely hidden from view - Diagram 2.

Time passed and life became more complicated for this person. When questioned about spiritual matters, the person said it was a personal matter and hid his belief even more. Fold down the other corner to match – Diagram 3.

The person grew up and lived by himself in his own house. Fold up the bottom flap to form a house – Diagram 4.

The person was very private and his spiritual life was like a closed book. Fold from side to side, enclosing the house like a book – Diagram 5.

He went through a personal crisis and cut himself off from the Christian community altogether. Cut or tear down the dotted line 6 and place the pieces that you have cut off onto the OHP or display where the audience can see them.

Things got even worse and the person said, 'This is the end, I am having nothing more to do with the Christian faith.' Cut along the dotted line 7, placing the remaining pieces unopened in full view.

Thankfully the person finally looked back upon his life and remembered what he had been taught at Sunday school. Slowly but surely, his life began to open up again. Through God's Grace he saw that Jesus had died in his place and had provided for him a ticket to heaven. Open up the biggest piece of paper and reveal a cross with the word HEAVEN written on it.

Turn on the OHP and begin to open the pieces of paper. You should have two small squares, two straight letter I's, two corners and two letter L's as well as the large cross. Arrange the pieces as illustrated to spell the word HELL – Diagram 8. Explain that the person had come to a point where he described his life as hell, and that was where he was heading, until through faith in Jesus Christ, he began to sort out his life.

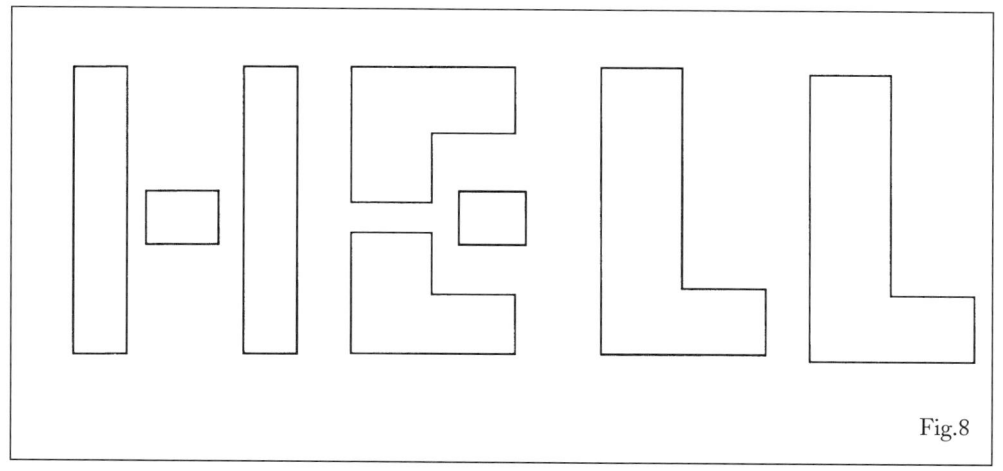

Fig.8

Now re-arrange the pieces to spell the word LIFE – Diagram 9. Use the spare straight piece to underline the word and explain that life became much better and blessings became more abundant.

Fig.9

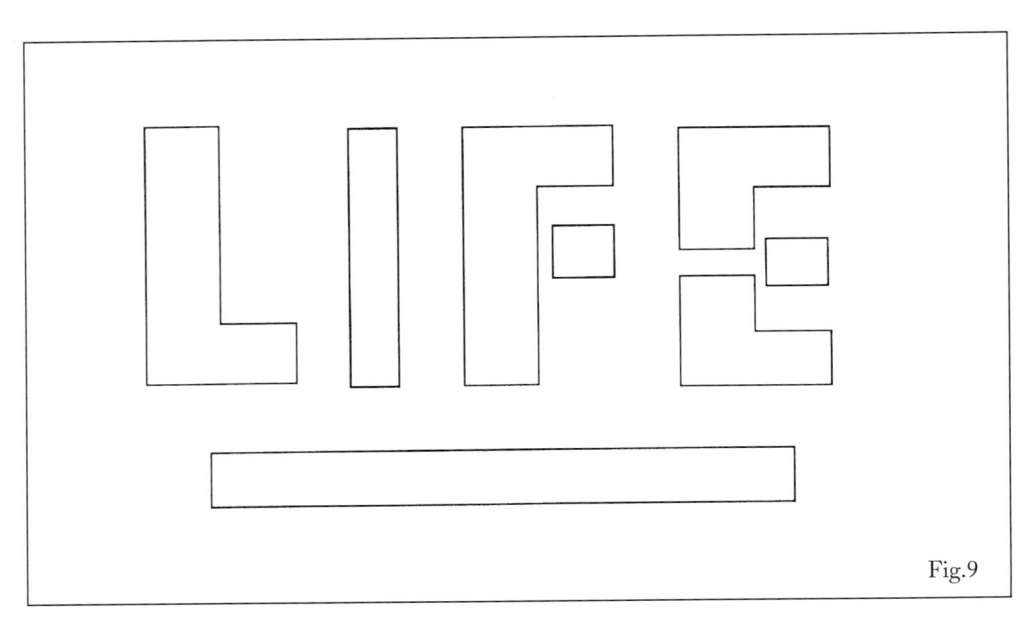

With a little ingenuity you can arrange the pieces to portray the crucifixion scene with the cross in the middle and two robbers either side, one looking at Jesus and one looking away. You may also be able to produce other scenes that can be built from this excellent visual paper tear.

Clowning is an amazingly diverse creative art that can be great fun and very rewarding, but it needs a great deal of confidence to be effective. Like all ministry, we must be prepared to face rejection and apathy. Equally though, we must keep on praying in order to find the strength and courage to soldier on. You never know how you may touch just one person in a special way. I recently saw a group of ten young people in clown costume, from the Baptist church in my hometown of Loughborough. They were a really happy band of youngsters, full of vitality and very enthusiastic in their telling of the 'Parable of the Sower' in the market square. Despite the colour, enthusiasm and dynamic nature of this group, it was clear that they were going to struggle to attract an audience to hear their story. I chatted to them briefly, leaving them to try again on a busy corner of the market place. As I left I sympathised with them as they failed to attract an audience, but my spirits soared when I observed two teenage girls cautiously approach one of the clowns, and after being reassured, sat down beside her and began to listen to the story.

God works in many different ways. I can't be sure, but it may be that this was the only type of ministry that would have attracted those two girls on that sunny afternoon in Loughborough. It may be that this was their first encounter with Scripture. I pray that other Christians find encouragement from that small episode and will find the strength to carry on, when they are in a similar position. In that situation, it may be time to bring on the clowns!

CREATIVE ARTS IN WORSHIP

We live in a changing world. A world in which modern communications through the Internet will change the way we go about our daily lives. God's Word never changes. It is simply the means of communicating it that is so dynamic.

CHAPTER NINE
VISUAL AIDS – SKETCH BOARD AND OBJECT LESSONS

INTRODUCTION

Object lessons using visual aids are one of the most effective and simple methods of teaching Bible interpretation and Christian themes. There are dozens of examples of this kind of teaching in the Bible itself. Consider the symbolism and teaching illustrated by the rainbow in Genesis, wine as the atoning blood in the Gospels, salt in the Gospel of Matthew and the tearing of the veil in the temple, also in Matthew. Scripture references, especially from Matthew, are a delightful example of the way Jesus used objects and stories from everyday life to illustrate His teaching of

God's Word. Jesus used the coin of the day, the Roman denarius, to reveal an important truth to all believers. We all have a double citizenship. We are citizens of heaven yes, but we are also citizens of this world with an obligation to the government authority under which we live.

Had Jesus used this example in a church today, He would be described as presenting an object lesson using a visual aid. Jesus' eagerness to use parables and object lessons strongly suggests that He would be keen to use all the modern communication tools that are available to modern preachers. Devices which reinforce teaching such as overhead projectors, video projectors and sketch boards are invaluable tools that are widely available. Sadly, they are only used by a relatively small number of preachers. Many preachers seem to fear modern devices, feeling that they are inappropriate to worship, or it may be that they are simply unwilling to learn about the new technology and skills needed to use these tremendously useful aids.

Visual aids are not just about new technology. In this chapter we shall also explore how to use household objects to show how God's Word can be clarified for modern congregations. The best way to illustrate the advantages of using such aids is to present practical examples that you can use in your own ministry. The following pages contain a series of object lessons and ideas that use commonly available media. Many of the examples have been developed from teaching that I have gleaned from other worship leaders at churches and conferences or through books. Some are traditional ideas that have been in the public domain for years. Some of the lessons are ones that I have developed from other's original ideas. I am indebted to friends and colleagues who have given permission to reproduce the ideas in this book. I encourage you to use the ideas presented here, but also to take them forward and use them as a basis from which to develop presentations of your own.

SKETCH BOARD

Using a sketch board and easel to illustrate a lesson, (sometimes called a chalk talk) is one of the best-known forms of visual aid teaching employed by preachers. The sketch board is a superb tool for preaching in church and Sunday school as well as an effective method to teach on the streets. One of the most effective preachers I have known is friend and colleague, Paul Morley, an evangelist

> 'Show me the coin used for paying the tax.' They brought him a denarius, and he asked them, 'Whose portrait is this? And whose inscription?' 'Caesar's,' they replied. Then he said to them, 'Give to Caesar what is Caesar's, and to God what is God's.'
>
> **MATTHEW 22:19-21 NIV**

VISUAL AIDS

based in the North of England. Paul is an accomplished Gospel illusionist who offers resources for Gospel magic through his company, Tricks for Truth. He is an expert in sketch board teaching and has a unique style, often employing ladder writing to enhance his presentations. This technique is explained further on in this chapter. Paul lectures on the use of Gospel magic and sketch board evangelism and has produced an excellent booklet on the subject, *Sketch Board Messages For All Occasions*. Some of the material from that booklet is reproduced here and I am grateful to Paul for permission to use it in this publication.

Painting on sketch board attracts attention. It should not be considered as a substitute for good preaching, but merely an aid to that end. As in all things, practice makes perfect and the following guidelines should help to ensure that you keep on the right tracks. Sketch board evangelism is very cost effective and a complete ministry can be set up with a solid easel, a few brushes and powder paints in high-density primary colours and black. Commercial flip charts can be used to paint on, or end rolls from newspaper offices or web-offset printers: most companies are pleased to help. Paints, although often more dramatic and effective, are not obligatory of course and many preachers use wide-nibbed marker pens.

Some preachers feel that they are unable to offer sketch board presentations because they have no drawing skills. This should not be a barrier as faint outlines can be drawn onto the sheet beforehand. These outlines can only be seen from a few feet away so that when you overprint them with marker or paint, the congregation will perceive a picture develop as if from nothing. The source drawing can be traced beforehand or projected using an OHP, onto a larger sheet of paper to be outlined.

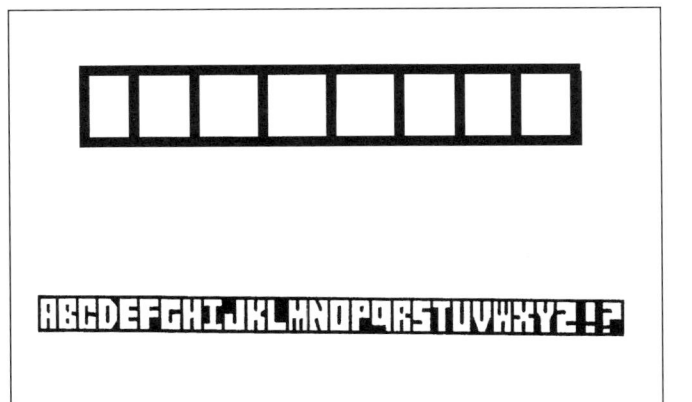

Ladder writing is the art of painting characters in ladder frames, apparently painting the character lines, but in actual fact filling in the spaces to reveal white out lettering. The ladders should contain boxes for letters about the size of an audio-cassette box with separator lines approximately 15mm (1/2 inch) wide. The two illustrations demonstrate the method to be used. The first diagram shows the simple ladder structure. The second is the ladder alphabet. Note the dots, dashes and diagonal lines that form the letters. It is better to use as few brush strokes as possible in order to complete each stage quickly, thus maintaining eye contact with the congregation.

In the same way that simple lettering is presented in different colours on display boards in shops and supermarkets, it is important to use different coloured lettering and illustrations in sketch board work. These give impact and lend interest to the presentation. Words that are negative are best painted blue or black and should appear on the left hand side of the easel. Words that are positive are best in red or black and should appear on the right. It follows that positive images such as the empty tomb, smiling faces and good results, should also appear on the right hand side. This technique adopts the proven techniques of commercial advertising. It is helpful to pre-paint a faint yellow backwash behind the positive wording as this provides ink lift to the ladder writing and thus a more striking effect. As in all things connected with ministry, be professional and use clean materials and fresh paper for each presentation.

GUIDELINES FOR SKETCH BOARD - PREACH WITH CONFIDENCE

Sketch board is an effective ministry in most settings and is especially suited to street evangelism. It is worth noting some of the comments that Paul Morley makes about the technique in this particular environment. The extract is copyright Paul Morley and is reproduced here with kind permission of Paul Morley from his work, *Sketch Board Messages For All Occasions*

Paul writes: 'Nothing has changed over 2000 years. Jesus Christ remains the Way, the Truth and the Life. No one can come to the Father except by Him. Sadly many people today seem to have a lack of confidence in the name, the power and the finished work of Christ. When we go on the streets, we are here to demonstrate His power. We may go in much weakness, fear and trembling, as the Apostle Paul did when he faced the Corinthians, but we can know a strength that comes from the power of God. Many show fear of mentioning Jesus when they go out onto the streets.

What tends to happen is that when a sketch board is used, there is much topical talk and Jesus is left as a last minute tag at the end of the message. The Cross is then hurriedly painted up and followed by a quick 'If you're interested, take a leaflet from me.' This is not preaching, as faith comes by hearing the Gospel Word of God.' The comments often made are, 'If we mention Jesus, God or sin, then people run away.' It is true that some will move away when these are mentioned, as they immediately think that 'this is religion and has nothing to do with me.' However, some do stay and listen to the preaching of God's Word. After all, Jesus is the very reason that we are on the streets with our sketch board in the first place. Like Paul, we must preach Jesus Christ and Him crucified. Don't be afraid to preach the Gospel when you are preaching the Gospel!' The Apostle Paul said to the Church at Rome, 'I am not ashamed of the gospel, because it is the power of God for the salvation of everyone who believes: first for the Jew, then for the Gentile.' (Romans 1:16 NIV)'

It is important to stand to the side of the easel, facing the audience when speaking. If you speak whilst you are painting, with your back to the audience, the impact of your message will be lost, as it will be difficult to hear what is being said. More impact is achieved if the word is written and then spoken, rather than the other way around. As soon as a negative word is painted on the left hand side, immediately point to the fact that there is a positive answer or response to follow on the right. Keep as much eye contact as possible, using body language to interact with the audience. Smile and joyfully proclaim the Word and our faith, but avoid maligning other religions or traditions. The evangelist is there simply to proclaim Truth. Let the Holy Spirit do His work. Try to avoid church language such as 'redeemed,' 'washed in the blood' or even 'born again' as most non-Christians won't have a clue what you are talking about and will be put off by such words. Use simple language and give a clear invitation to respond by taking a leaflet, or inviting to attend a specific function. Be positive in your approach, pick up your paintbrush and win souls for Christ!

SKETCH BOARD MESSAGES TO USE

The following two sketch board messages are copyright Paul Morley and are used with thanks to, and the kind permission Paul Morley, Tricks for Truth, 91 Green Street, Middleton, Manchester.

The first, *Your Future* is about the promises of God. It may be used effectively as a Christian response to counter fortune telling and horoscopes etc as well as presenting a positive and truthful prediction – God's promise of salvation for all those who seek it. The message is recorded here in full, as it may be presented on the streets. You may of course wish to alter the wording and format to suit your own style and setting.

YOUR FUTURE

Good afternoon ladies and gentlemen. Thank you for stopping. As you can see, I am an artist and I am going to paint a word on the board now which may well take you by surprise, because I shall paint it with a red brush and we shall see yellow letters appear. (a yellow wash at the ladder area will have been prepared beforehand.) It's a word that people pay a lot of money to find about. You may even have considered it this morning in your newspaper. It's one of those things that confront us every minute of every hour of every day of our lives. The word is future. (Paint the word FUTURE) I want us to think a little about our futures. I would like you to consider your own future.

People have paid a great deal of money to fortune-tellers, palm readers and crystal ball gazers to try to find out about their future, but I have met few who really believe that stuff. Some people get their palm read. That's crazy, because there is absolutely nothing about your future in your hands. If you are willing to pay good money to have your palm read, then give me a tenner, hold out your hand and I'll slap a bit of red paint on it for you. Then you'll have your palm red! Unfortunately your future may be a puzzle to you, but before you walk away from here, you can know the one who holds all of our futures in His hands. That is possible for you today. I am so glad that I know the One who holds my future in His hands. Sadly, many people don't know that person and for them, their future holds little else but worry. (Paint the word WORRY.)

Maybe you have come out today to do the everyday stuff like shopping or going to work, but you are deeply worried about your future, either short term or long term. You may worry about the bills that have to be paid, decisions that have to be made, or maybe worried about a relationship or family problems. Worry leads to stress and stress is a killer. Our bodies were not made by God to cope with worry because He never intended any of us to be worried. Today there is a place where you can find an answer to worry. (Draw the first line of the Cross) A place where you can know a person who said, 'Don't worry, but trust me.' That person was Jesus.

The great thing about God is that He knows how you're built. The Bible says that we are wonderfully made, but God didn't need to build in a 'cope with worry factor' because He said, 'Cast all your burdens onto me.' As you are stood here today, with all the worries that may be eating you up, just think how good you would feel if you knew that there was somebody who was not only willing to listen to your worries, but will do something about them, because He is the only one who can give that kind of assurance. That's one of the reasons that God sent Jesus down to earth 2000 years ago so that your life needn't be wrecked with worry.

Today, before you walk away from this place, you can know the cure for worry. That cure is the person of Jesus. The sad thing is that many people choose to stay with their worries. If these worries are not dealt with, they will eat you up inside, slowly destroying you. They will make you bitter and angry. Anger and bitterness leads to sin. Worry is often the result of not doing the

> 'God didn't need to build in a 'cope with worry factor' because He said, 'Cast all your burdens onto me''

right thing. As a result we feel guilty and worry about the actual sin and the guilt. We have broken God's laws because we think that we know best. But we don't. The Bible says that this kind of disobedient attitude will result in death and separation from God. God doesn't want us to end up dead and without hope or future. Jesus is able to lead us away from fear, worry, sin and death. He says, 'Come to me.' Maybe you have experienced times when worry has eaten away at you, or you have been racked with guilt over something that you have not been proud of. These are times of great stress and fear. (Paint the word FEAR)

Maybe you have fears that are holding you down and are affecting your potential to lead a fulfilled life. It may be a fear of the dark. It may be fear of loneliness, or a fear of death itself. If that is the case then you are not the person that God wants you to be or leading the carefree life that God has planned for you. Believing in Jesus and what He has done, can work for you because God is interested in your future. God wants you to be with Him in the future, to spend a life free from worry and a life free from fear. Jesus prepared the way for that by making the ultimate sacrifice and paying the price. It was a heavy price to pay. (Paint the other part of the Cross) He was prepared to allow His Son to die instead of you.

The Bible says that Jesus died to give you a hope and a future – what a God! When Jesus died on a Cross, He carried all our worries. He broke all our fears. This means that you and I can walk and live as free individuals, knowing the power of God in our lives. Jesus broke the power of sin, that is, the disobedience barrier that separated us from God, making it possible for us to come to God again. You may say, 'But how can I know God?' Well, the Bible says to turn away from sin, admit your own weakness and realize that you need help. Admit to God that you have done wrong things and said wrong things and ask Him for forgiveness. Even right now, you could say, 'Help me God, forgive me please and set me free.' If that is the cry of your heart, your need, then God will hear your prayer and give you peace. When you know the power of God through Jesus Christ, then you will know peace. (Paint the word PEACE)

What better person to get peace from than the Prince of peace Himself. Jesus is that Prince and you can know His peace. The Bible says that Jesus' peace passes all understanding and keeps your heart and mind safe. It's peace of mind that prevents us from cracking up when we are under pressure, because knowing Jesus doesn't mean the end of all our problems. But it does mean that we can more easily come to terms with them and cope with them in a much more assured way. This is not just theory. Thousands of people every day come to know the power of God and the peace of Jesus. Millions already know that peace and are better, more balanced individuals as a result. Because of Jesus' death on the Cross, you can swap all your fears, anxieties and worry, for His peace and understanding. That is a great comfort to millions of people today and has been for 2,000 years. God's Word contains His promise that has stood the test of time. Furthermore, you can know that if you put your trust in Him today, as so many others will, all over the world, then you will no longer have any fear of dying, as the moment that you die, you will be with Jesus. You will know peace, and as a result you will be secure. (Paint the word SECURE and finish off the hill and path around the Cross.)

You will be secure in His hands, and if you put your life into His hands today, then you will be secure in the knowledge that He will never leave you. He will never let you down. God's security means that you can be comforted and at peace with yourself and with God, no matter what life may throw at you. If you feel that you want to know that kind of peace and security, will you say with me now this simple prayer, right where you are. 'God please forgive me, for the wrong that I have done. I turn to You right now and give You my life. Please be my Lord and Saviour and fill me with Your Holy Spirit, that I might have power for living, Amen.' For those of you who have prayed that prayer with me and are serious about going forward with God, I would ask you to do one last thing. I have here some leaflets that will help you to know more about Jesus. Like God's gift of life and peace, they're free. Please do step forward and take one. God bless you and thank you for listening.

The second message, *'What A Winner'* is another message with an evangelical slant that can be broadly applied in many situations. It was designed for use on a mission crusade on a council estate but can be adapted for use in school assemblies, churches or even for use in prisons.

A broad outline of the message is provided here and readers are encouraged to develop the outline to suit their own style.

WHAT A WINNER

Start with the words WHAT A WINNER already painted on your board.

One of the pet hates of many people is when things get spoiled through bad stewardship, neglect and even deliberate vandalism. This is a problem that prevails throughout the world. Good things, beautiful things are often vandalized by spray paint. Neglect or bad planning ruins beautiful buildings and landscapes. These things start out as good, but before long they often become run down and ruined. They become wasted. (Paint the word WASTED)

There appear to be people in this world that adopt an attitude in life based on the concept that if there is something that is good, but it is not available to them, then they want to smash it or ruin it for other people. This country is full of examples of buildings, land and things of great beauty that have been spoilt and wasted. This country is also full of people whose lives are wasted. There are people who feel that they have accomplished nothing and that life is pointless, as a result of wasted opportunities. Jesus says that the Devil comes to steal, waste and destroy. He's a waster. So often, things that look good to some individuals, end up by eventually wasting their lives. Things such as drugs, greed, violence and pornography, give people a buzz for a while, but it's not long before they totally take over a person's life. Victims begin by believing that these things are good for them, but soon discover that they are dangerous, and sometimes killers, and the knock-on effect means that more lives become wasted. Maybe you feel that things are a waste of time, a waste of energy, a waste of your talent.

If this is the case, you can end up looking and feeling weary. (Paint the word WEARY)

You may feel too tired to go on and feel that you have been battered and bruised enough in life. Well, Jesus said, 'Come to me, all who are weary and heavy laden and I will give you rest.' Maybe you are weary of going nowhere and weary of life itself, feeling that it has no purpose, no meaning and that it is all a waste of time. That's where God comes in. He is interested in you as an individual. He is the Restorer and that is why he sent Jesus down to earth to show that he wants to restore your life back to what He created you for. God demonstrates in Jesus that your life doesn't have to be wasted. You don't have to be weary of living because you are wanted. (Paint the word WANTED)

God wants a relationship with you because he is interested in you. The Cross is a WANTED sign! The Bible tells us that God demonstrates His love by sending Jesus and allowing Him to die for us on a Cross. What He is saying is, 'I love you and look at the lengths that I am prepared to go for you. I will sacrifice my Son so that you can feel wanted and have a life that has real purpose.' Jesus broke the barriers and the power of sin, guilt and death. Jesus won when He died. He didn't lose. People thought that He had lost, but the amazing power of God raised Him back to life after He suffered and died. He paid the price and as you look at your life and wasted opportunities, you can look at Jesus and know that He is a winner and He wants you to be a winner too. (Paint the word WINNER)

To be a real winner in life, is to know Jesus and to put your trust in Him, knowing that the victory goes on even after death. He won. He rose from the dead and you can be part of His victory. That's why the top of the board says, 'What a winner.' Nobody ever fought like Jesus did, and he fought in order to make life special for you. That is why it is really worth your while putting your trust in a winner. Putting your trust in Jesus. You can do that today.

Ladder writing is only one aspect of sketch board ministry. There are different ways that preachers can use this versatile tool and plenty of sketch board lessons that can be employed without the need for drawing skills. The following examples demonstrate this fact. The first is an old favourite and has been in the public domain for many years. It is a simple but effective message, called *The Cross*. It is ideal for presentation on sketch board, however the more adventurous amongst you may wish to use my own

> 'Come to me, all who are weary and heavy laden and I will give you rest'

method. I asked a local steel stockholder to make up a 1.5 metre high cross shape, which was mounted onto a folding wooden easel support. This excellent tool can be used with white flexible magnetic advertising sheet metal or card cut to fit the cross. Whichever method you use, the lesson is effective for all ages and situations. The accompanying illustrations demonstrate how the finished drawing should be laid out. You should start with a blank sheet, adding crosses and the final cross outline as you tell a story. Each cross is drawn as an 'X'. The message is described in outline, which you may well wish to develop and expand.

THE CROSS

This is a story about symbols. There are many different types of symbols, some of which mean different things depending upon what context they are placed in. Take the cross for example. For many of us, the first cross that we experience is the one that we find at the bottom of our first attempts at maths. At first sight we may feel that our teacher has been captivated by our charm and fallen in love with us, providing a symbol of that love, a kiss cross for us to cherish. Sadly, this illusion will be quickly shattered, and we must accept that we have done our sums wrong. The cross indicates that we need to think it through again. (Draw the first 'X' at the top of the sheet)

We will hopefully find in later life however, that a loved one will write to us in endearing tones and end the letter with a loving message and seal it with a kiss. (Draw the second 'X' underneath the first)

Another kind of cross that we sometimes see on some letters or documents, is the cross made by someone who cannot write their own names. The 'X' is the mark they make to represent their signature. (Draw the third 'X' to the left of the second)

Those of us who are eligible, and choose to vote, make an 'X' mark on a voting slip to indicate which candidate or political party that we wish to be elected. (Draw the fourth 'X' to the right of the second)

Many symbols are used on large scale road maps and one of these is an 'X' to indicate a crossroads or major junction. (Draw the fifth 'X' underneath the second)

There are crosses on other maps. Much more exciting maps. Folklore holds that pirates marked an 'X' on maps of exotic desert islands to denote where hidden treasure was buried. (Draw the last 'X' underneath the fifth)

So, we can see that crosses mean different things in different contexts. To Christians, the Cross has a special significance. The crosses that we see here can lead us to an understanding of the meaning of Jesus' death on a Cross at Calvary.

The first 'X' denotes that we have done something wrong. (Circle the first 'X') There is no one in this world that is perfect. We have all done wrong (sinned) in the eyes of God and we need to realize this fact and come before God to ask for forgiveness.

The second 'X' represents love. (Circle the second 'X') Even though we have continually done wrong by disobeying God, He still loves us and wants only the best for us.

The third 'X' is a representation of a person's name, and Jesus gives us a new 'name' and a new life, enabling us to discard all our guilt and shame and start afresh. (Circle the third 'X')

The fourth 'X' is a vote for someone who represents us. We all have the opportunity of new life by voting for Jesus. Choose eternal life and fulfillment by choosing Jesus, just as he chose us to be one with God. (Circle fourth 'X')

The fifth 'X' represents a crossroads. I pray that all of us reach out to the loving arms that beckon us, and take the route to Jesus when we come to a crossroads in our lives. Many Christians come to faith at a low point in their lives, realizing their spiritual poverty and finally turning to God. (Circle the fifth 'X')

The last 'X' represents hidden treasure. The greatest treasure ever given to mankind is hidden only by our own blindness and refusal to acknowledge Jesus as Lord. That treasure is the precious gift of love and eternal life that is offered by our Creator God through the death and Resurrection of his Son, Jesus Christ. (Circle the final 'X')

You don't need to travel to the ends of the earth or to some remote desert island to unearth this treasure. You can have it right now if you only pray this prayer with me ……. Conclude with simple prayer and offer leaflets, an invitation to worship or a teaching event, or further help.

The next message titled *The Gambler* is one that has been used effectively in churches, prisons, schools, and in street evangelism. It is a superb presentation of the Prodigal Son and was devised by David Glover, a skilled evangelist and Gospel magician in the North East of England. The basic story is of course a parable of Jesus, but the idea for this sketch board interpretation originates from David. I am grateful to him for giving permission to reproduce the lesson in this publication. *The Gambler* is copyright David Glover, 30 Garth Twenty, Kilingworth, Newcastle. Start with a 3-D image of a die in the center of your sketch board. Five spots should be showing on the top face and a single spot on the front face. Draw four dice or squares, one at each corner. Draw four spots in the bottom right square, three vertical spots on the top right square, six spots on the top left square and two spots, horizontally in the bottom left square. The squares are completed as shown in the illustration as the story unfolds.

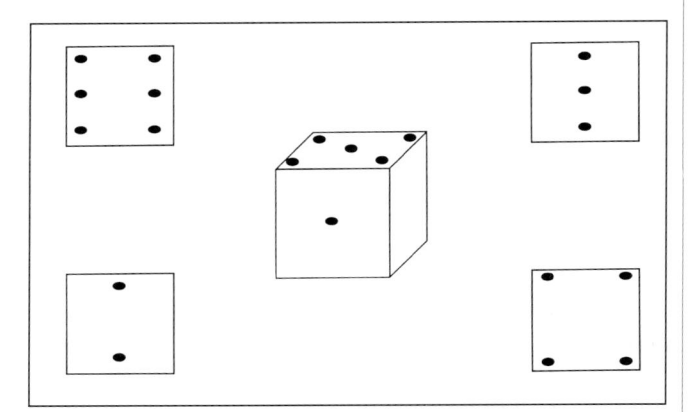

THE GAMBLER

Gambling is considered great fun by millions of people who wager small sums every day on dice, cards, gaming machines, horseracing, greyhounds and other sports as well as bingo and the National Lottery. Whilst a small flutter may be considered harmless by many, there is no doubt that some people are addicted to gambling and they may ruin their own and their families' lives by risking and eventually losing large sums of money.

There are risks attached to many aspects of life and some individuals seem to need to live their lives close to danger in order to seek fulfillment. Our story is about such an individual who lived in his own house on his father's grand estate. His family was rich and he had been indulged and maybe a little spoilt so he had most of the good things in life. He had a fine house, a nice car, a good job and plenty of money to spend. (Draw a cross in the square at the bottom right hand corner to signify windows. Draw a chimney, some smoke and a shining sun to represent a house and contentment. Write the words MOST THINGS underneath)

Our hero had most things that life could offer but he wasn't content with his lot. He had gambled a little and enjoyed the thrill, but one day he took the greatest risk of his life. He sold his house, cashed in all his assets and had a wild time in Las Vegas. Whilst his money lasted he had lots of new friends, but they soon deserted him when his money ran out and he was left with nothing. He was thrown out of his hotel and did not even have enough money to buy a simple meal. He resorted to searching through litter bins, finding and eating food that even pigs would have thought twice about. He had reached rock bottom and had nothing. (Finish off the square at the top left, drawing in details to represent a pig. Write the word NOTHING underneath)

It was at this point that he began to ask questions about his life and the mess that he had made of it. He was at his wits end and began to think of home and the luxuries he had left behind. His life seemed to have no meaning anymore and he longed for someone to comfort him, someone who would make things normal again. He desperately looked for something that made sense in his life once more. Slowly it dawned on him that he had no option but to return home and face the wrath of his father. He was deeply unhappy but at least he had something secure to hang on to. Going home would bring some hope - something that made sense and made him feel content again. (Draw an unhappy mouth in the bottom left square and write the word SOMETHING underneath)

He made his way home to face the music with a heavy heart but was amazed to find that when he arrived at his father's house, looking dirty, disheveled and very sorry for himself, he was greeted with open arms. He began his apologies but his father was so pleased to see him again that he gave a party to celebrate the return of his son to the family home. The son was beside himself with joy. He was home again, made to feel special and appreciative that he had everything in life that he would ever need. (Draw a smile on the top right square and write the word EVERYTHING underneath)

Those who know the parables of Jesus will be familiar with the tale of the Prodigal Son, upon which this story is based. Mankind was given many blessings from heaven that provided us with all that we needed. (Draw an arrow pointing downwards in the centre square, and write the words GOD'S BLESSINGS underneath)

However, we chose to disobey God and went our own way, risking and losing most of what He had given us. God loves us to bits and sent Jesus to us who suffered untold pain and torture before dying on a cross. The world still has its priorities wrong and is too concerned with trivialities. Even the soldiers played dice as the Son of God hung in agony on a cross. (Draw in the crosspiece over the arrow in the centre square)

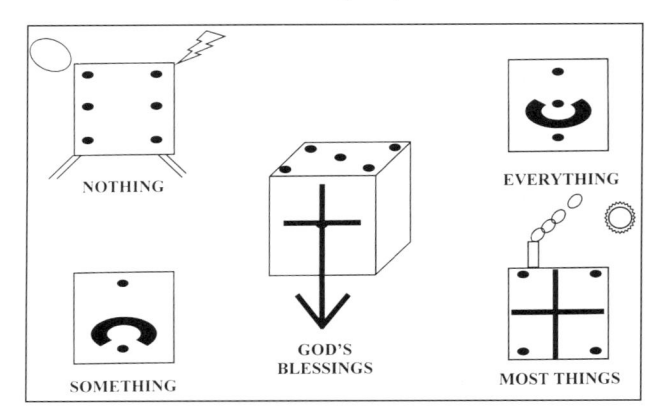

NOTHING

EVERYTHING

SOMETHING

GOD'S BLESSINGS

MOST THINGS

Most Sundays whilst preachers tell of the wonders of God's love and the amazing gift of new life and eternal life with God, many are still more concerned with the trivialities of getting home in time for Sunday lunch. If you have thrown away your opportunities and risked your eternal lives then I encourage you to turn back to God, return home to the One who cares for you, before you find yourself in the same state as our hero. Empty and left with nothing. If you find yourself in that state already, then you should be assured that your Father in heaven is ready to welcome you back home and celebrate your return with a party.

The story has many facets to it and many of the concepts can be used to preach a sermon on their own. This sketch board message combines superbly with any Gospel magic trick that uses dice. The preacher can then use the dice to teach the lesson about Christians being the fifth Gospel described in the Gospel magic chapter.

Sketch board word games

Word games are an excellent way of introducing topics and encouraging people to focus on particular concepts. There are several resources that provide for Biblical word games, which include word-search type games, anagrams and crosswords, and games based on *Pictionary* and *Catchphrase*. These can all be easily presented on a sketch board.

Anagram games can be used for older children and adults, providing a stimulating way of introducing books of the Bible or Biblical characters. The difficulty level must of course be appropriate to the congregation. There are books and computer software available that will work out the anagrams for you. These sorts of games are useful at church family parties and fellowship evenings that are intended to outreach to the wider community. They provide a gentle and non-threatening introduction to Christian concepts and language. You may find the following examples helpful and they may lead you to explore other ways of using word games in Christian teaching. For those of you who like a challenge, try solving them yourselves before looking up the answers at the end of this chapter.

Anagrams of books of the Bible

Meet ten wants
Most talented
Gee! Sins
To my rude one
Rich on saint
A sheep sin
Clue visit

Anagrams of Biblical characters and topics

Handsome agitator	parable
Shoo darn piglet	parable
Slept in Utopia	NT character
Food song	Jesus
The comments tend man	OT topic
Hidden insolent alien	OT story

A few words lend themselves to a whole sermon and such a word is Levi. Mark 2:14 tells of the calling of Levi the tax collector, a story which testifies to the fact that

Jesus came to save the lost and tend to the marginalized and the outcast. Levi was a tax collector. All tax collectors were generally regarded as dishonest and were despised by the Jews. The story of Zaccheus reinforces the same point. The word Levi can be re-arranged to teach on several topics, not least of which, the reason that God sent Jesus to earth in the first place. This play with words can be presented on a sketch board, or better still using four volunteers who each hold a letter of the word. The words are re-arranged to spell a different word in the following order:

LEVI - Tell the story of the calling of Levi by Jesus and refer to the story of Zaccheus, emphasizing that Jesus came to save us all.

EVIL - Briefly explain the fall of mankind in Genesis and how God provided us with a paradise, but we thought we knew better than God and disobeyed Him. This is how sin came into the world.

VILE - Evil breeds from evil and man became more and more disobedient to God. Many times God intervened to save His people Israel but they always turned their faces away from God and ended up in a terrible mess, enslaved by many nations, eventually falling under the oppression of the Roman Empire.

VEIL - God intervened again by sending Jesus to sort us out. Jesus' ministry touched thousands of lives. He healed the sick, performed miracles and taught about the Kingdom of God. He was regarded as a terrorist and crucified. At the moment of His death, the veil in the Holy of Holies in the Temple was physically and symbolically torn in two, thus providing us with access once more to God.

LIVE - By the supernatural power of God, Jesus was resurrected from the dead and now lives in us through His Holy Spirit. We are offered new life through the intervention of God through Jesus. He provides us with the means to come before God to confess our sins, be forgiven by Grace and to live forever in harmony with God.

Overhead Projectors

The overhead projector is a superb tool that is still under utilised by preachers, possibly because many do not know where to obtain the necessary resources to use it effectively. There are several publishers who provide ready made artwork and acetates for OHP work. However it is a fairly easy task to make your own OHP acetates these days by using computer technology. If you do not possess your own computer, there will be someone in your church who has one and would be willing to help you. Desktop publishing, digital cameras, scanners and public domain clipart enable preachers to produce top quality acetates for OHP and these provide superb opportunities for teaching with visual aids. Images such as photographs of the Holy Land, artwork depicting Biblical characters, word puzzles, quizzes, cartoons, newspaper cuttings and contemporary photographs are just some of the images that can be projected onto larger screens. There are also some superb illustrated Bibles available, which are ideal resource material for OHP acetates. Look for items such as *The Graphic Bible* (colour cartoon style Bible) and the innovative *Scroll Bible*, which consists of headlines and stories written in the style of a newspaper. (see resources chapter for details) Be aware of copyright concerns when using other people's artwork though.

Decade Ministries and Children Worldwide – OHP Visuals

I make no apologies for featuring two suppliers in the main body of this book, simply because Roy Weaver's Decade Ministry and David Iliffe's Children Worldwide near Horsham, are two of the best visual aid resources that I have come across. These two organizations offer resources and workshops on the use of visual aids in worship all over the UK. A wide range of superb material designed for OHP use is offered, depicting almost every Biblical theme or concept. For example, there are packs offered around the themes of *Water in the Gospel of John*, *Bible Leftovers*, and *How the Bible Came To Us*.

Most chapters in John have a significant reference to water such as Jesus' baptism, Jesus washing the disciples feet, Jesus healing a man at a pool, and tears in His eyes at certain times of anguish and compassion. This *Water* pack contains visuals of each incident to illustrate John's Gospel in a unique way.

Bible Leftovers is a pack of visuals of leftovers from meals such as the crumbs of the feeding of the five thousand, the remaining wine after the water into wine miracle at the wedding feast at Cana, and leftovers after the Last Supper. Great visuals to illustrate a talk after a faith supper perhaps.

How the Bible Came To Us is a pack of visuals that tells the story of the making of the Bible, from the days of parchment and scribes to the printing press and modern translations. These are but a few of the packs available that comprise superb ready made tools for preachers to use to effectively illustrate teaching.

Decade Ministries offer wallpaper rolls of images to accompany some songs. These are long rolls of wallpaper containing a series of linked cartoons of Christian images to suit secular and Christian songs. These are designed so that the preacher can gradually unroll the images in sequence as the song progresses. There are several available including *If I Were A Butterfly*, *You'll Never Walk Alone* and *The Millennium Prayer* from the musical *Hopes and Dreams*. Our team used 'You'll never walk alone' in a praise party near Liverpool. The response was amazing. Not surprising considering the connection that the song has with Liverpool Football club.

Children Worldwide, near Horsham, offer similar excellent visual aid material, all of which is ideal for conversion to OHP acetates. The wide range of resources available from both these sources should be adaptable to anyone's style of preaching. (see resources chapter for details)

Computers in church!

Some eyebrows are raised when I take a laptop computer to a preaching lectern, but I am confident that Jesus would have used one had it been available to Him. The computer is part of modern day life and many readily identify with its usage and language. There are some superb presentation software tools available, which make home computers excellent aids to illustrating teaching and enhancing worship. Although they are expensive, some churches now have data projectors and video projectors. Computers can be connected to this equipment to project the screen image in the same way as an overhead projector.

> 'Some eyebrows are raised when I take a laptop computer to a preaching lectern, but I am confident that Jesus would have used one had it been available to Him'

VISUAL AIDS

This enables easy song projection for instance. Our team uses Microsoft Powerpoint software to project song words, although Microsoft Word is also a good programme to use if you do not have Powerpoint. It is so convenient to change screens with a single keystroke. Powerpoint was designed as a business presentation tool, but is now widely used for teaching in schools and at many worship events. Visuals such as the ones we have described earlier, can be scanned and input from digital still cameras and video. Bible passages can be projected from Bible software and 3-D photo images of the Holy Land from software designed for use in worship.

There are several Christian software packs available for children that are based on computer type games. One of the best is *Bibleland.Com*, a superb programme that simulates the Internet. This is a virtual World Wide Web environment that most young people will readily and eagerly identify with. It contains web sites of the principal characters in the Bible that are connected by hyperlinks in the same way as the Internet is linked. It is a very useful and fascinating programme that even has e-mail, without having to actually connect to telephone lines or servers. The whole programme is self-contained within a CD. Sunrise Software is probably the largest resource for Christian Computer Software. (See resources chapter)

Video recorders and players are part of the fabric of everyday living and provide excellent resources for enhancing worship. There are stand-alone video presentations available that are designed to teach on specific Christian issues. There are videos of Christian music events, Biblical stories, meditations, cartoon Bible stories for holiday clubs such as *Storykeepers* and a host of others. Video can be effectively combined with many of the creative arts such as music, drama and puppets. There are one or two excellent web sites that offer thematic reference for Biblical themes to be found in both secular and specifically Christian videos. (See resources chapter) It is possible to combine video with computer images by inputting the images into programmes such as Powerpoint using video capture software, if you have the hardware and software to support it. Video can also be combined with computer images using overlay equipment such as the VineGem. This is one way of enabling preachers to overlay graphics with songwords to add poignancy to worship songs.

There are dozens of videos that you will find useful in preaching. Some of the better known ones that our own team has found very effective are clips from *The Mission* for teaching on mission and salvation. *Dead Poets Society* for teaching on seizing opportunities (the poem *Carpe Deum* is a primary theme in the film) and leadership. Use *The Lion King* for a host of teaching opportunities. The whole film is alive with teaching that parallels Biblical concepts, such as guilt, forgiveness, searching within, and returning to the Father. Video presentations as diverse as Adrian Plass and the Alpha course, deal with different issues in different ways. Both are nonetheless effective teaching tools. The great Biblical epic films such as Zefferelli's *Jesus of Nazareth*, *The Passion* and *Jesus the Man* are all good sources of illustration material. Offering clips from these videos, either by themselves or combined with music and other creative arts, provides interesting and refreshing ways of illustrating the Gospel message.

OTHER OBJECTS AND AIDS

Preachers have of course used visual aids since preaching began, using everyday objects to illustrate a particular theme. The following are just a few ideas that you may care to use, or may stimulate your imagination. leading you to use other objects and resources.

CAFOD is a Roman Catholic based charity that provides books and other teaching material. Two excellent examples of these materials are the *Misereor Lenten Veil - Hope for the Marginalised* and the *Misereor Hunger Cloth*. These are two wonderful pieces of artwork that have been the subject of much discussion, providing good tools for preaching. They are both complex paintings made up of different sections, which come with accompanying literature and explanations. These notes can be used and adapted for preaching on the great themes of Creation, the Fall, God's intervention, salvation for all, hope for the lost, environmental issues and a host of other topics. I found it helpful to photograph each part of the paintings or scan them as digital images and project through Powerpoint or OHP. You may wish to use this method or simply use the banner on its own. Both methods are effective. Many paintings and banners offer opportunities for teaching, and a good selection can be sourced from CAFOD and St Paul Multimedia Productions. (See resources chapter for details)

There are some items that have stood the test of time for many preachers. These include teaching the Bible story from a deck of cards, burning prayers written on paper, dissolving written prayers in water using special dissolving paper, (available from Gospel Magic suppliers) Bibles which burst into flame, (an interesting way of illustrating Pentecost or Elijah and the prophets of Baal) and scientific object lessons using different objects and substances. There are usually several good object lessons in such major all age worship resources as Salt or Partners in Learning, which follow the lectionary. I would encourage you to look still further and have listed several resource books and web sites that will help you search for exactly the right material for your style of ministry.

It would be a Herculean task to describe just a small proportion of the object lessons and visual aid lessons that are available and this book does not attempt to do that. Hopefully the ideas given here will prompt you to look further. I will however provide outlines for three object lessons that I have found useful, as they provide teaching on some major Christian issues. They are not definitive sermons by any means, but may inspire you to develop your own ideas.

The first is a lesson on teamwork and families working together, which can be easily adapted to teaching on the Body of Christ and Church unity. It was used at a service at our own church by one of our Circuit local preachers, Alf Moseley. It is of personal interest because my family volunteered to be used in the illustration. It simply involves a family who hold hands in a circle and break the circle at one point so that there is only one pair of hands available to carry out various tasks. Thus if a family of four held hands but broke the circle at mother and daughter, the tasks would have to be carried out with one mother's hand and one daughter's. The tasks are relatively simple and involve opening a bottle of lemonade, opening a packet of maltesers, peeling a banana, turning the pages of a newspaper and others of a similar nature. The results can be quite comical and can readily be used to explore the concept of family and togetherness.

The Trinity is a difficult topic to explain and I have not seen an object lesson that surpasses the Doug Wathen Heart. This is a piece of equipment that I first saw at an international puppetry festival (I-Fest) in Chicago some years ago. It is available commercially from Doug Wathen at One Way Street USA. (See resources chapter) Doug is a Gospel Magician and has produced a remarkable piece of equipment that is not so much a trick as a puzzle. It consists of a wooden heart frame that contains three shaped holes within it. The shapes are a circle, a triangle

> 'The Trinity is a difficult topic to explain and I have not seen an object lesson that surpasses the Doug Wathen Heart'

and a square. Three solid wooden shapes are provided, each of which fills its designated space, but will not fit into the other two spaces. A special wooden shape is provided that is able to do so. It is a simple step from explaining that each shape performs a separate function, but that all three are contained within the three faceted shape. I will leave you to make the connection with the Trinity concept. This fine piece of equipment comes in different sizes and is featured in an excellent Gospel Magic book called *From Tricks to Truth*. (See resources chapter)

The concepts in both of the above illustrations can be developed effectively with the use of Russian Dolls which consist of several different size wooden dolls that are also pull-apart containers that fit inside each other in ever increasing or decreasing sizes, finishing up as one or several dolls in a family.

The final object lesson concerns the greatest story of all, the Passion and resurrection of Jesus - The Easter story. It is told with Easter eggs and is an object lesson that is well known to many in the USA. I am indebted to Brian and Dorrie Beattie who introduced me to the idea some years ago. Brian and Dorrie are two evangelists that I met on the Christpup Christian puppeteers e-mail list on the Internet. It is a simple lesson, but a whole service can be built around it involving many members of the congregation. You will need to obtain eleven hollow plastic eggs that open, similar to a 'Kinder Egg' but made of hinged plastic. A larger twelfth egg is also required. The following items are placed into each of the eleven smaller eggs to represent different parts of the story of Jesus. These are opened by volunteers and the appropriate Bible passage read and expounded as you feel led.

tangled black string	the sinful human condition, Romans 5:12
baby's bootee	Jesus sent by God, John 3:16
piece of bread	the Last Supper, Luke 22: 19-22
piece of rope	Jesus bound and led away, Matthew 27: 1-2
scarlet cloth & thorn	Jesus humiliated and mocked, Matthew 27: 28-30
nails and a cross	Jesus crucified, John 19: 18-19
piece of paper scroll	a sign placed over His cross, John 19: 19-22
piece of sponge	Jesus offered a drink and then died, John 19: 28-30

small toy spear	Jesus' side pierced by soldier's spear, John 19: 33-37
white cloth and small stone	Jesus' burial clothes and the tomb sealed, Mark 15: 46
vial of perfume	they came to anoint His body with spices, Mark 16: 1
empty egg	empty tomb – the Resurrection, Matthew 28: 5-6

You should find willing volunteers to open each egg. The eggs are symbols that will be recognised as representing a traditional Easter, providing a superb opportunity to tell the Gospel story to those who may be attending church for their annual visit.

CREATIVE ARTS AND VISUAL AIDS – THE WAY FORWARD

Creative arts and visual aids are only one way of presenting the Gospel of course. There always has been and always will be a need for well thought out, Biblically based, theologically sound teaching. However, if we do not recognize the need to employ modern communication techniques and re-enforce our teaching with interesting visual imagery and dynamic presentation, then this teaching will be lost to those who are used to modern media, and cannot relate solely to verbal delivery. There are many who yearn for something more than traditional preaching in a service and we do need to be aware that modern communication techniques have led to smaller attention spans. Many people who are asking spiritual questions will not go to a church because they believe that dated teaching, from preachers who are out of touch with their congregations, will bore them.

Creative arts and new technology demand our attention. These new innovations may seem completely alien to some preachers, but once you have experienced how visuals can be brought into worship in such a powerful way, you may begin to appreciate how modern means of communication can enhance worship in ways that were unheard of just a few years ago. We should not be afraid of new technology just because it is not mentioned in the Bible. We live in a changing world. A world in which modern communications through the Internet will change the way we go about our daily lives. God's Word never changes. It is simply the means of communicating it that is so dynamic.

I know of church members who will rebuke a preacher for not using a pulpit from which to preach. This criticism is often not made for practical reasons such as an improved sight line to the preacher, but simply because of tradition. Many church members do find it difficult to cope with change and preachers have a duty to try to meet people where they are, but I find no references to Jesus preaching from a pulpit in Scripture. He preached wherever the people were, who needed to hear God's Word, and he used contemporary stories and situations from life to illustrate His preaching so that people could understand what he was trying to say. Surely we are charged with the same responsibility. That duty is to teach God's Word and His message of salvation in a contemporary and relevant way, in language that people can understand and using every piece of technology that is at our disposal to preach the Gospel effectively. If we ignore the useful tools that are available to us, or dismiss them as irrelevant or even irreverent, as a result of our own ignorance or naivety, then we do our congregations and our calling a great disservice.

ANSWERS TO ANAGRAMS

New Testament
Old Testament
Genesis
Deuteronomy
Corinthians
Ephesians
Leviticus
The good Samaritan
The prodigal son
Pontius Pilate
Son of God
The ten commandments
Daniel in the lions den

I would encourage you to seek other resources. When you find a really good one, please don't keep it to yourself, but share it with others so that they too may build up a rich store of knowledge that may be used to proclaim the wonderful Good News of Jesus Christ, our Lord and Saviour.

Chapter Ten
RESOURCES

The first part of this section is devoted to resources that offer a wide variety of materials, equipment, information and services. Resources specific to each creative art are divided by chapter heading. These contain details of books, publishers, performers, evangelists, resource ministries and web sites, that I have found to be very helpful in the 'Hands up for God' ministry. I would encourage you to seek other resources. When you find a really good one, please don't keep it to yourself, but share it with others so that they too may build up a rich store of knowledge that may be used to proclaim the wonderful Good News of Jesus Christ, our Lord and Saviour.

General Resources

UK Christian Handbook
Definitive reference book of resources - approx 700 pages. ISBN 1 85321 133 8 (Christian Research), Vision Building, 4 Footscray Road, Eltham, London, SE9 2TZ. Tel: 020 8294 1989.
e.mail: admin@christian-research.org.uk

'Hands up for God' Creative Ministries
Incorporates 'Hands up for God' puppet team and 'Gospel Truth through Illusion' Gospel magic ministry, offering creative arts praise weekends and workshops, especially puppetry and Gospel magic. Also suppliers of puppets, patterns, scripts, music and advice on puppetry, Gospel magic and creative arts in worship. 34 Holbourne Close, Barrow-upon-Soar, Leicestershire, LE12 8NE. Tel: 01509 415129.
e.mail: dennis@dldoyle.freeserve.co.uk
www.dldoyle.freeserve.co.uk

Rob Frost Team
Responsible for Share Jesus Mission, Seed Teams, Easter People, Lantern Arts Theatre, event organising and opportunities for mission. Rob Frost Team, The Methodist Church, Tolverne road, Raynes Park, London, SW20 8RA. Tel: 020 8944 5678. www.robfrost.org

Children Worldwide
Resources for children's and youth workers as well as all-age worship material. Puppets, visuals, OHP, teaching, drama, object lessons, flannelgraph etc. Dalesdown, Honeybridge Lane, Dial Post, Horsham, West Sussex, RH13 8NX. Tel: 01403 711032. e.mail: cwide@talk21.com

Alpha
Worldwide mission concept designed to reach out and teach the basics of the Christian faith. Lots of literature and resources to set up and run an Alpha group. Holy Trinity Brompton, Holy Trinity Road, London, SW17 1JA. Tel: 020 7581 8255. www.alpha.org.uk

Christian Resources Exhibition
Regular large events offering a wide range of resources. Esher, Manchester, Birmingham and Glasgow. CRE Ltd, 2 Forge House, Summerleys Road, Princes Risborough, HP27 9DT. Tel: 01844 342894. www.resources.co.uk

RESOURCES

RALPH DEWEY GOOD NEWS
Balloons, object lessons, visuals paper tricks, clowning resources. Many booklets of creative ideas that preachers will find useful. Dewey's Good News Balloons, 1202 Wildwood Drive, Deer Park, Texas 77536. Tel: (001) 281 479 2759.
www.home.flash.net/~balloonz/index.htm

KINGDOM CREATIVE - REV. JIM BAILEY
 (FORMERLY KINGDOM KIDS)
Children's & all age performing arts resources, performances and training. Elim Centre, 45 Rowlands Road, Worthing, BN11 3JN. Tel: 01903 523171.
www.kingdomc.cwcom.net

HARPER COLLINS RELIGIOUS BOOKS
Wide range literature. 77 Fulham Palace Road, Hammersmith, London, W6 8JB. Tel: 020 8741 7070.
www.christian-publishing.com

KINGSWAY
Music, books and other Christian resources. PO Box 75, Eastbourne, BN23 6NW. Tel: 01323 437700.
e.mail: music@kingsway.co.uk

KEVIN MAYHEW
Wide range of literature and music. Buxhall, Stowmarket, Suffolk, IP14 3DJ. Tel: 01449 737978.
www.kevinmayhewltd.com

LION PUBLISHING PLC
Publishers of a wide range literature. Dandy Lane West, Oxford, OX4 5HG. Tel: 01865 747550.
e.mail: custserve@lion-publishing.co.uk

HODDER HEADLINE PLC
Wide range titles and Bibles. 338 Euston Road, London, NW1 3BH. Tel: 020 7873 6000.
e.mail: religious_sales@hodder.co.uk

LANTERN ARTS CENTRE
Part of the Rob Frost organisation. Theatre for the performing arts in worship offering productions, cabaret, workshops and café studio for all ages. Worple Road, Raynes Park, London, SW20 8RA. Tel: 020 8944 5794.
www.gawayn.demon.co/jdc/nc

CHRYSALIS ARTS TRUST
Resourcing churches to present the Gospel through cabaret-style outreach events using the performing arts. 78 The Broadway, Chesham, HP5 1EG. Tel: 01494 581115. e.mail: chrysart@aol.com

PHOENIX PERFORMING ARTS TRUST
Development of training in performing arts from a Christian viewpoint. 26 Manningford Close, Winchester, Hampshire, SO23 7EU. Tel: 01962 8503487. e.mail: swise10@aol.com

MERIWETHER PUBLISHING LTD
Wide range of Christian books on drama, mime, clowning, magic etc. Box 7710 Colorado Springs, Colorado 80933, USA. Tel: (001) (719) 594-4422. e.mail: MerPCDS@aol.com

PICCADILLY BOOKS
Publisher of books on drama, mime and clowning. 4215 Amiable Way, Colorado Springs CO 80917. Tel: (001) 719-550-9887.

SUNRISE SOFTWARE
Large distributors of computer software, clip art, QuickVerse and WordSearch Bible studies, commentaries, book collections, exposition, preaching illustrations and aids, games, song management, prayer guides etc. PO Box 19, Carlisle, CA3 OHP. Tel: 0845 0579 579. e.mail: sales@sunrise-software.com

CAMBRIDGE CHRISTIAN RESOURCE NETWORK
Drama, music and visual aids in evangelism. Thematic video clip reference resource for using in worship. Also have a network of creative Christians available for worship events. 81 Lovell Road, Cambridge, CB4 3BQ. Tel: 01223 423184. Answerphone: 01223 501510. www.ourworld.compuserve.com/Homepages/DesFilby

Cracking The Church Cocoon by Mandy Watsham & Nicki Matthews. (Chrysalis Arts Trust) ISBN 0 7459 3569 9 The Bible Reading Fellowship. Creative evangelism and teaching. 9 full programmes of performing arts presentations for outreach. Song album CD and backing tracks CD also available.

Café Logos by Pete Townsend. ISBN 1 84003 394 0 Kevin Mayhew. Worship material aimed at 11-16 year olds but ideal for all age worship.

Martha's Diner by Pete Townsend. ISBN 1 84003 521 8 Kevin Mayhew. Worship material aimed at 11-16 year olds but ideal for all age worship.

100 Instant Faith Talks by Ian Knox. ISBN 0 85476 646 4 Kingsway. How to share your faith at all types of events.

100 Creative Prayer Ideas For Children by Jan Dyer. ISBN 0 85476 778 9 Kingsway. Tried and tested ideas for creative prayer.

All In The Family by Michael Botting. ISBN 0 85476 546 8 Kingsway. Loads of ideas for family services.

More For All In The Family by Michael Botting. ISBN 0 86065 861 9 Kingsway. Lots more ideas for family services.

Worship Through The Christian Year by Diana Murrie & Hamish Bruce. ISBN 0 7151 4903 2 The National Society – A Christian Voice in Education. All age resources for the 3 year lectionary year A.

The Sermon Slot by Sharon Swain. ISBN 0 281 04696 4 SPCK. Ideas and talks for all age worship.

Getting Through by Rob Lacey. ISBN 1 902134 11 7 Silver Fish Publishing. Resource book for creative communication – stories, drama, mime, poetry.

The Scroll – The Tabloid Bible by Nick Page. ISBN 000 274022 2 Harper Collins. Bible stories presented as newspaper articles. Ideal for OHP.

The Lion Graphic Bible by Jeff Anderson and Mike Maddox. ISBN 0 7459 2708 4 Lion Publishing. The Bible presented in graphic form, illustrated by Jeff Anderson (Judge Dredd, Marvel UK and Fleetway) with fine detail cartoon graphics.

God's Story by Karyn Henly. ISBN 0 85476 818 1 Kingsway. The Bible told as a story, section by section in very readable language. Ideal for all age worship.

The Silent Prophet by Todd Farley. ISBN 1 56043 005 2 Todd Farley. Theology and apologetics on the prophetic ministry of the human body and performing arts.

What Shall We Say To God Today by Helen Albans. ISBN0 7197 0922 9 National Christian Education Council. Prayers to use with young children.

Whispering In God's Ear by Alan Macdonald. ISBN 0 7459 3672 5 Lion Children's Books. Inspired collection of poetry for children and all age worship.

Upside Down by Susan Hardwick. ISBN 1 84003 143 3 Kevin Mayhew. Inspired collection of prayers aimed specifically at teenage girls, but easily adapted for all.

INTERNET RESOURCES

There are thousands of interesting web sites for creative Christians and I would encourage you to experiment with your favourite Internet search engine. The following are just a few of the best that provide thousands of links to other Christian sites. Use the search engines within these sites to navigate to others which are of interest to you.

www.christianbest.com
www.gospel.com
www.gospelcom.net
www.home.att.net/~joybringers/pages/resource.html
www.crossdaily.com
www.oneplace.com
www.mvcs.net/links.htm
www.theotherside.org/resources/arts/links.html
www.omnicast.net/users/ucr/Ministry.htm
www.cybergrace.com/html/resources.html
www.members.aol.com/clinksgold/index.html
www.web.1earth.net/~youth/music.html
www.connect.ab.ca/~kwalden/arts.htm

Music

The following CD collections of contemporary worship include most major recording artists and worship leaders. We have used these successfully in services all over the UK. They are available in most Christian Book and Music shops.

Sing Hallelujah vols 1-6 Kingsway
Classic Songs vols 1-6 Kingsway
Stoneleigh International Live Worship 4 albums in the series. Kingsway
The Source vols 1-5 Kingsway

ALL AGE ACTION SONGS - *Kids Praise Spring Harvest, Kids Songs of Fellowship, Easter People Kid's Praise,* Captain Alan Price, Doug Horley, Dave Cooke and Ishmael to name but a few.

KEVIN MAYHEW
Transposing musical arrangements and other musical publications. Buxhall, Stowmarket, Suffolk, IP14 3DJ. Tel: 01449 737978.   www.kevinmayhewltd.com

ICC - INTERNATIONAL CHRISTIAN COMMUNICATIONS
Contemporary music publishers and distributors. Silverdale Road, Eastbourne, BN20 7AB. Tel: 01323 647880.

ALLIANCE MUSIC
Contemporary Gospel and praise music publishers. Waterside House, Woodley Headland, Peartree Bridge, Milton Keynes, MK6 3BY. Tel: 01908 677074. www.alliancemusic.co.uk

KINGSWAY
Publishers of music, books and other resources. PO Box 75, Eastbourne, BN23 6NW. Tel: 01323 437700. e.mail: music@kingsway.co.uk

CHRISTIAN COPYRIGHT LICENSING (EUROPE) LTD
Copyright agents enabling legal reproduction of Christian music in the UK. 26 Gildridge Road, Eastbourne, BN21 4SA. Tel: 01323 417711. e.mail: webmaster@ccli.com

CHIME
Churches Initiative in Music Education. Provides ecumenical forum for discussion and information about education and training of church musicians. Sarum College, 19, The Close, Salisbury, SP1 2EE. Tel: 01722 424805. www.btinternet.com/~chime

DM MUSIC
Keyboards, sound equipment, installation and training. Specialists for sound equipment in worship. Unit 4, Riverside Estate, Coldharbour Lane, Harpenden, Hertfordshire, AL5 4UN. Tel: 01582 768811. www.dm-music.co.uk

In Tune With Heaven
Church of England Synod report on using music in worship. Published by the Church of England, Church House, Great Smith Street, London, SWIP 3NZ. Tel 020 7898 1000.

DRAMA

MOORLEY'S PRINT & PUBLISHING LTD
Specialists in drama sketches and monologues for worship. 23 Park Road, Ilkeston, Derbyshire, DE7 5DA. Tel: 0115 932 0643. e.mail: 106545.413@compuserve.com

RIDING LIGHTS THEATRE COMPANY LTD
Professional company presenting community theatre. Producers of drama books and scripts. Marketing House, 8 Bootham Terrace, York, YO30 7DH. Tel: 01904 655317. www.users.globalnet.co.uk/~rltc/

STEPHEN DEAL
Humorous scripts and quick sketches for worship. Tried and tested by professionals. 2 Goodson House, Greenlane, Morden, SM4 6SH. Tel: 020 8646 1344. e.mail: stephendeal@deal1.demon.co.uk

ROB LACEY
Dramatist, poet and mime artist offering books, videos and performance for worship. The Administrator, 101 Welham Road, Streatham, London, SW16 6QH. e.mail: roblacey@orangenet.co.uk

RODD & MARCO – THE ACTS DRAMA TRUST
Comedy, drama and music in ministry.
Tel: 01383 824533.   e.mail: marcopalmer@csi.com

FOOTPRINTS TRUST
Educational & community work expressing the Christian faith through storytelling, interactive storymaking, workshops and performances. St. Nicholas Centre, 79, Maid Marian Way, Nottingham, NG1 6AE. Tel: 0115 9586554.

SHOESTRINGS
Apprentice young people expressing the Christian faith through storytelling, interactive storymaking, workshops and performances. Allied to Footprints Trust. St. Nicholas Centre, 79, Maid Marian Way, Nottingham, NG1 6AE. Tel: 0115 9586554.

WILLOW CREEK RESOURCES
Comprehensive drama ministry. Sketches, books, videos and teaching. PO Box 3188, Barrington, Illinois, 60011-3188. Tel: (001) 847 765 0070. www.willowcreek.org

People Like Me - video by Rob Lacey. Video of Rob Lacey performing with discussion starters for youth groups, church groups and personal reflection.

Greatest Skits On Earth by Wayne Rice & Mike Yaconelli. ISBN 0 310 35141 3 Zondervan. Humorous Sketches.

Greatest Skits On Earth vol 2 by Wayne Rice & Mike Yaconelli. ISBN 0 310 35211 8 Zondervan. Humorous Sketches.

The Drama Recipe Book by Alan MacDonald & Steve Stickley. ISBN 1 85424 075 7 Minstrel (Monarch Publications). Sketches and drama tips.

50 Sketches About Jesus by David Burt.
ISBN 0 85476 814 9 Kingsway. Humorous sketches.

Skits That Teach Adults by Colleen Ison.
ISBN 87403 849 5 Standard Publishing. Sketches for adults.

The Big Book Of Bible Skits (104 seriously funny Bible teaching skits) by Tom Boal. ISBN0 8307 1778 1 Gospel Light. Humorous sketches.

Problem Plays by Ann Farquhar-Smith. ISBN 0 7175 0778 5 Hulton Educational Publications. Sketches about life's problems.

Divine Comedies by Riding Lights Theatre Company. ISBN 1 85424 276 8 Monarch Publications. Humorous sketches.

Rolling In The Aisles by Murray Watts. ISBN 0 85476 361 9 Kingsway. Humorous sketches.

Footnotes by Footprints Theatre Company. ISBN 0 340 40579 Kingsway. Workshops and sketches.

Dramatised Bible by Michael Perry. ISBN 0 551 01779 1 Marshall Pickering-Bible Society. NIV Bible translated into drama script.

Dramatised Audio Bible by International Bible Society. NIV New Testament translation in audio form with good characterisation and sound effects.

Drama Ministry by Steve Pederson. ISBN 0 310 21945 0 Zondervan. Drama ministry techniques.

The Best Of The Jeremiah People by Jim Custer & Bob Hoose. ISBN 0 916260 81 X Meriwether Publishing. Humorous sketches taken from Jeremiah People's travelling drama ministry.

Stage Lighting For Theatre Designers by Nigel H Morgan. ISBN 0 435 08685 5 Heinneman. Lighting techniques.

MIME

MIMEISTRY INTERNATIONAL
Resources, workshop and performance ministry by Todd and Marilyn Farley. Mimeistry Europe, The Coach House, Woodhill, Congresbury, North Somerset, BS49 5AF. Tel: 01934 833652. www.mimeistry.org

The Mastery of Mimodrama - video by Todd & Marilyn Farley. Series of in-depth instructional videos on mime technique with accompanying book.

Quiet On The Set Video by Todd & Marilyn Farley. ISBN 1 56043 025 7 Destiny Image. Christian mime performance video.

Mime Ministry by Susie Kelly Toomey. ISBN 0 916260 37 2 Meriwether. Guidebook for teaching and training a Christian mime ministry.

Steps Of Faith by Geoffrey & Judith Stevenson. ISBN 0 86065 275 0 Kingsway. Combined mime and dance instructional book.

The Mime Book by Claude Kipnis. ISBN 0 916260 55 0 Meriwether. Instructional manual on all aspects of mime.

Mime Time by Happy Jack Feder. ISBN 0 916260 73 9 Meriwether. 45 complete mime routines and technique tips.

Morning Mime Time by Debbie Howell. ISBN 1 85205 124 8 Meriwether. One example of many booklets of sketches available from Meriwether Publishing.
Also see *Clown Mimes for Christian Ministry* – Clown Section.

The Angry Hotel Man by Stephen Fischbacher. Innovative Nativity script (no room at the inn) and music tape designed for performance by children. Ideal for mime and drama improvisation. Fischy Music, 11 Royston Terrace, Edinburgh, EH3 5QU. Tel: 0131 552 6556. e.mail: Stephen@fischy.freeserve.co.uk

SIGNING

Religious Signing by Elaine Costello. ISBN 0 553 34244 4 Bantam Books. A superb illustrated dictionary of religious words, concepts and phrases. (linked to American Sign Language, but uses many variations adapted for religious signing)

Communication Link Revised Edition by Cath Smith. ISBN 1 871832 00 4 Beverley School for the deaf. Illustrated dictionary of sign. (based on British Sign Language plus inventions)

Songs In Sign For Children by Elaine McBean. Beverley School for the deaf. Selected songs with sign illustrations.

Signed Hymns from Carberry - video by The Novum Trust. Video collection of eight signed hymns.

Starting Sign - video by Bristol University Centre for Deaf Studies. An introductory sign language course.

Dance

CHRISTIAN DANCE FELLOWSHIP OF BRITAIN
Teaching and training network for dance. 25 Scardale Crescent, Scarborough, Yorkshire, YO12 6LA. Tel: 01723 500031

CHRISTIAN DANCE FELLOWSHIP OF AUSTRALIA
International fellowship providing support, teaching and resources for people involved in dance and movement in worship. Mary Street Drummoyne, PO Box 365, Drummoyne, NSW 1470. Phone/fax + 61 2 9719 2412. e.mail: rodwest@bigpond.com   www.uca.org.au/org/cdfa

DANCE FOR CHRIST
Resources for sacred dance, mime, movement and puppetry. The Farne House, Marygate, Holy Island, Berwick-on-Tweed, TD15 2SJ. Tel: 01289 389247. e.mail: mark@burninglight.co.uk

SPRINGS DANCE COMPANY
Dance performance company. 15 Waldegrave Road, Bromley, Kent, BR1 2JP. Tel: 020 8289 8974. e.mail: springsdc@aol.com

KINGDOM DANCE COMPANY
Resources for sacred dance, movement, banners and flags. Marie Bensley, Sunset Gate, St. Audries, Taunton, Somerset, TA4 4EA. Tel: 01984 633735. www.bensley.clara.co.uk/bod.htm

Moving In Praise With Flags by Marie Bensley. Kingdom Dance. One of a series of booklets on technique and advice on dance, flags and banners in worship.

God's People On The Move by Mary Jones and the Christian Dance Fellowship Of Australia.
ISBN 0592152 2 0 Christian Dance Fellowship of Australia. Definitive reference book on sacred dance and movement technique, with plenty of examples.

Steps Of Faith by Geoffrey & Judith Stevenson.
ISBN 0 86065 275 0 Kingsway. Combined sacred dance and mime instructional book.

The Spirit Moves by Carla De Sola. The Sharing Company. Congregational participation, dances and ideas.

How To Lead People Into Praise & Worship (parts 1 & 2) by Paula Douthett. The Sacred Dance Group. Workshops, dances, technique and ideas.

PUPPETS

'HANDS UP FOR GOD' CREATIVE MINISTRIES
Incorporates 'Hands up for God' puppet team and 'Gospel Truth through Illusion' Gospel magic ministry. Creative arts praise weekends and workshops for outreach, especially puppetry and Gospel magic. Also suppliers of puppets, patterns, scripts, music and advice on puppetry, Gospel magic and creative arts in worship. 34 Holbourne Close, Barrow-upon-Soar, Leicestershire, LE12 8NE. Tel: 01509 415129. e.mail:dennis@dldoyle.freeserve.co.uk
www.dldoyle.freeserve.co.uk

CHILDREN WORLDWIDE
Resources for children's and youth workers as well as all-age worship material. Puppets, scripts and teaching. Dalesdown, Honeybridge Lane, Dial Post, Horsham, West Sussex, RH13 8NX. Tel: 01403 711032.
e.mail: cwide@talk21.com

ONE WAY UK CREATIVE MINISTRIES
Offers training days on puppetry and resources. Tynedale Baptist Church, 2-4 Cressingham Road, Reading, Berkshire, RG2 7JE. Tel 01189 756303.
www.onewayuk.com

ONE WAY STREET (USA)
Puppet resources. 11999 E. Caley Ave, Englewood, Colorado 80111, USA. Tel: (001) 303 790 1188. www.onewaystreet.com

TROY GENIE NIELSEN
International Christian music ministry offering a wealth of music and musicals for drama, puppets and all age worship. www.nilssonmedia.org/intro.html

MAHER STUDIOS
Internationally renowned ventriloquist teaching, puppets and resources. www.maherstudios.com

RACHEL MOORE
Gifted Christian dramatist and puppeteer offering scripts for puppets, drama and ventriloquism from her practical and simple to navigate web site. www.crosswinds.net/~rachan/

See Drama section for list of script resources.

Puppets: Ministry Magic by Dale & Liz VonSeggen. ISBN 0 931529 65 4 Group Books. Advice on setting up and running a puppet ministry.

Puppeteer Training Manual by David and Elaine Cole. ISBN 1 883426 03 0 Children's Outreach. Training sessions on technique, stages and workshops etc.

Handbook Of Christian Puppetry by Grace Harp. ISBN 0 89636 125 X Accent Publications. Teaching techniques of puppetry.

Puppets In Praise by Stuart Holt. ISBN 0-551-02780-0 Marshall Pickering. Puppetry technique, sketches and original ideas.

Perky Puppets With A Purpose by Mary Rose Pearson. ISBN 0 88243 677 5 Gospel Publishing House. Techniques on puppetry, ventriloquism, puppet making and scripts.

Easy To Make Puppets And How To Use Them by Fran Rottman. ISBN 0 8307 1679 3 Gospel Light Publishing House. Technique, patterns and scripts.

Black Light by Marilyn Watkins. One Way Street. A detailed guide to black light puppetry.

52 Quality Puppet Scripts collection published by One Way Street. Sketches throughout the year.

Bird Words From The Word by Susan Anderson. Maher Studios. Ventriloquist sketches for bird puppets.

Practice what you preach with puppets – video by Rob Marsh. Excellent teaching video on puppetry techniques, with accompanying training manual. Available from 'Hands up for God' creative arts ministries

Puppets In Concert – videos vols 1 and 2 by One Way Street. Performance videos of puppetry songs and skits.

One Way Workout – audio cassette tape by One Way Street. Puppet practice tape for lip synch, entrances and exits, etc.

Cousin Albert's Antics - Manipulation audio cassette tape from One Way Street. Stories for training exercises in rehearsal or workshops.

Puppet Aerobics & More Puppet Aerobics audio cassette tapes by Jim Wideman. Teaching puppet techniques for training, rehearsals and workshops.

Developing Character Voices audio cassette tape by Liz VonSeggen. Teaching character voices.

Developing Character Accents audio cassette tape by Liz VonSeggen. Teaching character accents

Fun With Ventriloquism - video by Liz VonSeggen. Step by step teaching on ventriloquism.

Ventriloquism In A Nutshell by Clinton Detweiler Maher Studios. Basic manual for learning ventriloquism.

Outer Space Inner Space – video by One Way Street. Performance video of an innovative puppet musical.

Suggested puppet song CD's and artists:

Puppet Trax series 1-6
Puppets in Concert series 1-10
Righteous Pop Music volumes 1 and 4
You are the Light of the World musical

Albums by Apologetix, (Christian parody) Ray Boltz and Carman provide dramatic rock music suitable for puppetry and mime. Available from their own respective web sites or Internet music stores.

Carman   www.carman.org
Ray Boltz   www.rayboltzmusic.com
Apologetix   www.apologetix.com

All above music resources available from 'Hands up for God' creative ministries.

MAGIC

FELLOWSHIP OF CHRISTIAN MAGICIANS EUROPE
Network of Christian magicians offering resources, newsletter and exchange of ideas. Secretary David Glover, 30 Gareth Twenty, Kilingworth, Newcastle, NE12 0LN. Tel: 0191 268 2829.

GOSPEL TRUTH THROUGH ILLUSION
Christian magic cabaret evening offered by Dennis Doyle (Leicester Magic Circle and FCME) to churches, prisons, youth groups and other organisations interested in reaching out through the performing arts. 34 Holbourne Close, Barrow-upon-Soar, Leicestershire, LE12 8NE. Tel: 01509 415129. e.mail: dennis@dldoyle.freeserve.co.uk www.dldoyle.freeserve.co.uk

PETER MCCAHON - CREATIVE ILLUSIONIST
Presenting the Gospel to all ages through magic, comedy and escapology. Flat 8, 60 Augustine Avenue, South Croydon, CR2 6JJ. Tel: 020 8688 3114. mobile: 07973 135263.

STEVE LEGG
Evangelist and escapologist available for all sorts of church outreach. P O Box 3070, Littlehampton, West Sussex, BN17 5AW. Tel: 01903 779 279 www.breakout.org.uk

RESOURCES

KAYMAR MAGIC COMPANY
Christian magic dealer and evangelist. Ian Vallance, 189a, St Mary's Lane, Upminster, Essex. Tel: 01708 640557.

TRICKS FOR TRUTH -PAUL MORLEY
Christian magic dealer and evangelist. Supplied many of the effects used in 'Gospel Truth Through Illusion' ministry. Paul Morley, 91, Green Street, Middleton, Manchester, M24 2TZ. Tel: 0161 653 6626.

MASKELL'S MAGIC - ERIC MASKELL
Christian magic dealer and evangelist. Tel: 01223 244357.

AMERICAN MAGIC COMPANY
Magic dealer importing quality magic props. 136 Doulton Street, St Helens, Merseyside, WA10 4NZ. Tel: 01744 759653.

DAVENPORTS MAGIC
Magic dealers. 5,6 & 7 Charing Cross Underground Arcade, The Strand, London, WC2N 4HZ. Tel: 0171 836 0408.

QUALITY PROPS
Hand crafted quality magic props and illusions. Supplied many of the effects used in 'Gospel Truth Through Illusion' ministry. 11 Hartridge Walk, Allesley Park, Coventry, CV5 9LF.

LAFLIN'S MAGIC & SILKS
Duane Laflin, international evangelist supplying silks and other magic. Excellent gospel magic video tapes. Gospel Magic with Silk Effects is a superb teaching tape with message. 203 E. Riverside Ave, Box. 3003, Troy, Mt. 59935. Tel: (001) 406 295 7790.

From Tricks To Truth by Douglas L. Wathen. ISBN 1 58302 024 1 One Way Street. Teaching on techniques of Gospel magic with plenty of tricks explained.

Routines For Gospel Conjuring by Paul Morley. Tricks for Truth. 12 magic effects with Gospel routines.

The Amazing Book Of Magic by Jon Tremaine. ISBN 1 85501 400 9 Tiger Books. Step by step illustrated guide to a host of tricks.

Mark Wilson's Greatest Magic Tricks by Mark Wilson. ISBN 1 85605 241 9 Blitz Editions. Illustrated guide to lots of magic effects.

The Amazing Book Of Card Tricks by Jon Tremaine. ISBN 1 85501 399 1 Tiger Books. Step by step illustrated guide to simple but spectacular card tricks.

Self Working Series by Karl Fulves. published by Dover Books. Simple but effective self working tricks set out in a very useful series of books, each devoted to a different branches of magic, which include: card, coins, paper, mental, numbers, table and rope magic. Approx 100 tricks explained in each book.

50 Tricks With A Thumb Tip by Milbourne Christopher. Robbins & Co. Publishers. 50 effects accomplished with this ingenious gimmick, which is a must for all magicians.

Mathematics, Magic & Mystery by Martin Gardner. ISBN 0 486 20335 2 Dover. Diversions and effects arising from mathematical principles.

Abbot's Encyclopaedia Of Rope Tricks For Magicians by Stewart James. ISBN 0 486 23206 9 Dover. The 'Bible' of rope tricks for magicians.

The Royal Road To Card Magic by Jean Hugard & Frederick Braue. ISBN 0 571 06389 6 Faber & Faber. Timeless classic. Step by step teaching to become an accomplished card mechanic.

Easy Basic Card Magic - video by David Jones. published by International Magic. Teaching on basic card techniques.

Basic Coin Magic - video by David Jones. published by International Magic. Teaching on basic coin techniques.

There are hundreds of instructional videos on magic. The dealers listed above will be able to supply a list of available titles. If ordering from overseas, be sure to order in PAL format for the UK.

Clowns and storytelling

PICCADILLY BOOKS
Range of books on drama, mime and clowning in worship. 4215 Amiable Way, Colorado Springs CO 80917. Tel: (001) 719-550-9887.

MERIWETHER PUBLISHING LTD
Range of books on drama, mime, clowning and magic in worship. Box 7710 Colorado Springs, Colorado 80933, USA. Tel: (001) 719 594 4422

VALENTINE INTERNATIONAL CLOWN MINISTRY
Clowning, storytelling and mime for all ages. Evangelism, worship, workshops and performance. 39 Fountain Road, Bridge of Allan, Stirling, FK9 4AU. Tel: 01786 833028. e.mail: johndrane@compuserve.com

FOOTPRINTS TRUST
Educational & community work expressing the Christian faith through storytelling, interactive storymaking, workshops and performances. St. Nicholas Centre, 79, Maid Marian Way, Nottingham, NG1 6AE. Tel: 0115 9586554.

SHOESTRINGS
Apprentice young people expressing the Christian faith through storytelling, interactive storymaking, workshops and performances. Allied to Footprints Trust. St. Nicholas Centre, 79, Maid Marian Way, Nottingham, NG1 6AE. Tel: 0115 9586554.

HOLY FOOLS
Proclaiming the Good News through clowning, circus skills, workshops and performances. 93, Hornes Road, Barkingside, Ilford, IG6 1DQ. Tel: 020 8554 7986.

RALPH DEWEY'S GOOD NEWS BALLOONS
Balloons, object lessons, visuals paper tricks, clowning resources. Many booklets of creative ideas that preachers will find useful. Dewey's Good News Balloons, 1202 Wildwood Drive, Deer Park, Texas 77536. Tel: (001) 281 479 2759.

Clown Mimes for Christian Ministry 1 & 2 by Susie Kelly Toomey. Meriwether. Christian mime skits. One of many booklets in a collection from Meriwether.

The Gospel In Greasepaint by Mark D. Stucky. ISBN 0 941599 30 2 Piccadilly Books. 42 creative Biblical skits for clowns, mimes and other fools for Christ.

Creative Clowning by Bruce Fife, Tony Blanco, Steve Kissell, Bruce Johnson, Ralph Dewey, Hal Diamond, Jack Wiley & Gene Lee. ISBN 1 85729 000 3 Piccadilly Books. Teaches techniques and how to use a host of clowning skills. Discusses all aspects of clowning.

The Clown Ministry Handbook by Janet Litherland. Meriwether. Teaching on clown ministry.

Storytelling from the Bible by Janet Litherland. Meriwether. Making the Scriptures come alive through storytelling.

50 Stories For Special Occasions Throughout The Year by Lynda Neilands. ISBN 0 85476 749 5 Kingsway. Stories for all occasions in worship.

50 Five Minute Stories by Lynda Neilands. ISBN 0 85476 610 3 Kingsway. Short stories for use in worship.

Balloon Magic by Marvin L. Hardy. Pioneer Balloon Company. Fully illustrated book of balloon creations from the makers of Qualitex balloons.

Balloon Ministry by Allen R. Cook. Fully illustrated balloon sculptures and stories for Christian ministry. Allen R. Cook, 409 Prairie Lane, Belton, MO 64012. Tel: (001) 816 331 9131

Visual Aids

Children Worldwide
Resources for children's and youth workers as well as all-age worship material. Puppets, visuals, OHP, teaching, drama, object lessons, flannelgraph etc. Dalesdown, Honeybridge Lane, Dial Post, Horsham, West Sussex, RH13 8NX. Tel: 01403 711032
e.mail: cwide@talk21.com

RALPH DEWEY GOOD NEWS BALLOONS
Balloons, object lessons, visuals paper tricks, sketch board talks, clowning resources. Many booklets of creative ideas that preachers will find useful. Dewey's Good News Balloons, 1202 Wildwood Drive, Deer Park, Texas 77536. Tel: (001) 281 479 2759.

SUNRISE SOFTWARE
Large distributors of Christian computer software, clip art, QuickVerse and WordSearch Bible studies, commentaries, book collections, exposition, preaching illustrations and aids, games, song management, prayer guides etc. PO Box 19, Carlisle, CA3 0HP. Tel: 0845 0579 579. e.mail: sales@sunrise-software.com www.sunrise-software.com

DECADE MINISTRIES,
Masses of visual aids, object lessons, sketch board lessons, wallpaper rolls, paper tears, Bible games and more. A wealth of terrific ideas to use in all types of evangelism. Roy Weaver, Grove House, Limetrees, Chilton. Oxfordshire, OX11 0HY. Tel: 01235 833030. www.decadeministries.co.uk

CAMBRIDGE CHRISTIAN RESOURCE NETWORK
Thematic video clip reference resource for using in worship. Also have a network of creative Christians available for worship events. 81 Lovell Road, Cambridge, CB4 3BQ. Tel: 01223 423184. Answerphone: 01223 501510. www.ccrn.org.uk

CAFOD
Resources for worship and teaching. Includes *Misereor Hunger Cloth* and *Lenten Veil* and other examples of paintings and banners for Bible teaching. CAFOD, Romero Close, Stockwell Road, London, SW9 9TY. Tel: 020 7733 7900. www.cafod.org.uk

ST PAUL'S MULTIMEDIA PRODUCTIONS
Posters and visuals resources for teaching and worship. 199, Kensington High Street, London, W8 6BA. Tel: 020 79379591. e.mail:london@stpaulmultimedia.co.uk

DAVID GLOVER
Evangelist using Gospel magic, sketch board, object lessons and creative arts in worship. 30, Garth Twenty, Kilingworth, Newcastle, NE12 0LN. Tel: 0191 268 2829

Morrison Daylight Projectors
Visual aid equipment for Christians including OHP, video projectors, screens and audio equipment. Unit 8, Becklands Industrial Park, Market Weighton, York, YO43 3GA. Tel: 01430 872729.
e.mail: 101632.674@compuserve.com

Let's Play A Bible Game by Ed Dunlop.
ISBN 1 56608 013 4 Meriwether. Games and puzzles for the OHP in worship.

Over 120 Quizzes For All Occasio by Rachel Green. ISBN0 85421 799 1 Scripture Union. A source of Bible quiz ideas.

Gospel Draw & Tell series by David & Elaine Cole. ISBN1 883426 21 9 Children's Outreach. Series of sketch board ideas for children's worship.

Simple Science Object Talks by Heno Head, Jr.
ISBN 0 7847 0617 4 Standard Publishing. Presenting the Gospel through science object lessons, using household materials.

More Simple Science Object Talks by Heno Head, Jr
ISBN 0 7847 0650 6 Standard Publishing. Presenting the Gospel through science object lessons, using household materials.

Sketch Board Messages For All Occasions by Paul Morley. Tricks for Truth. Teaching and examples of sketch board messages in evangelism. 91, Green Street, Middleton, Manchester, M24 2TZ. Tel: 0161 653 6626.